# BOW JEST
## An account of blessings

# BOW JEST
## An account of blessings

Paul Zetter, CBE

*To Roger with fondest good wishes*

*Paul*

The Pentland Press Limited
Edinburgh · Cambridge · Durham

First published in 1992 by
The Pentland Press Ltd.
5 Hutton Close
South Church
Bishop Auckland
Durham

ISBN  1  85821  007  0

All profits from the sale of this edition of
Bow Jest will be donated to Crown and
Manor Boys Club, Hoxton and Woodberry
Down Boys Club, Manor House

Typeset by Elite Typesetting Techniques, Southampton.
Printed and bound by Antony Rowe Ltd., Chippenham.

# Contents

# List of Illustrations

# Foreword

On the last page of this book the author writes 'I don't believe anyone reading this book will learn much about my character'. He is wrong. You will learn of a man who by his ability, integrity and determination built a multi-million pound Football Pools business and in the doing, together with Littlewoods and Vernons, contributed immeasurably to the Football Association game, the largest spectator sport in our country.

Paul Zetter's life has been dominated first, by the love he received from his parents and by the loving family of his own and second, by his capacity for friendship which he has given with much generosity and loyalty to those he trusts.

Paul's interest in all forms of sport, rugby football, his Monte Carlo Rallies and fishing, is set out with humour and enthusiasm. But above all it is his brilliant and dedicated work as the first Chairman of the Sports Aid Foundation which has crowned his life in sport.

Without Paul Zetter many competitors who have represented the United Kingdom at the Olympic, European and Commonwealth Games would not have been able to go; they won their medals not only by their own outstanding efforts but by the support of the Foundation, the architect of which displayed the same singleness of purpose to win.

This book is the story of a man who has had a happy life and who has brought much happiness to others. No one can ask for, nor do more.

Sir Denis Thatcher, Bt., MBE, TD

# Prologue

I was born in 1923 within the sound of Bow Bells and life has been a bit of a joke ever since, hence the title.

I started writing this book when I had gained the official title of Senior Citizen and nostalgia had become my favourite emotion, although even that isn't what it used to be.

I have done my best to record events as I remember and perceived them and to ensure they accord, as nearly as possible, with the facts. I am aware, of course, that memory is a greater joker than even I, but I think I have largely succeeded.

Writing an autobiography is a bit like singing in your bath: while you may enjoy it, the appeal is clearly limited.

So, to those friendly few who read this, I hope your frowns may be rare and your smiles frequent.

# Chapter 1

# In the Beginning . . .

I was born in Bow on 9 July 1923. My very first memory dates back to 1926 when I was less than three years old. I lived at 133 Grove Road, Bow, E.3. in a large, old, terraced house, which was home for several members of the Zetter and Stodel Families. Stodel was my mother's maiden name and grandmother and grandfather Stodel lived under the same roof. My mother's sister Jane Smith, née Stodel, and her two children Louis and Sadie, temporarily shared our abode. Jane had married an Aussie, Joe Smith, who had served with the Australian armed forces in the 1914–18 war and had spent long enough in England to meet and marry my aunt. Joe was a 'goy' of course, but his alien origin and rugged charm soon established him as a much loved member of the family.

At that time, Joe was still in Australia. He'd been sent back after the war and taken Jane with him. Both her children had been born 'down under'. Jane returned to England with the children in about 1924, leaving Joe behind in Australia to sell his few small possessions prior to rejoining his family in London. That's why they were living with us.

Louis was five years old and my worshipful hero. The day is as bright in my memory as the day I pencil these words on paper. Louis was going to school. Whatever that was, it was going to happen to Louis. I ached for him. I cried for him. I positively did not sleep for him but, as sure as dreadful day followed restless night, Louis crossed Grove Road and set off down Arbery Road into the wilderness.

Our front parlour overlooked the length of that route to infinity and I watched his every step of the way with the absolute certainty that I would

1

never see him again. Three hours later he came home for dinner (lunch!). That was my first conscious memory.

My pre-war years were inevitably a kaleidoscope of memories. My mother's family predominated. All those aunts and uncles, some of them with children, impacted our household with the unerring instinct of homing pigeons. Clearly it was a consequence of 'the old people', Sarah and Jacob Stodel, living there.

Sarah had nine children, six daughters and three sons. All but one son survived to old age. I never knew him – the others were all my very real family. Esther, my mother, married my father Syd in 1919. She had two miscarriages, one before me and one after. I was born during a violent thunderstorm. My mother assured me it wasn't always like that, so I lived to enjoy the full benefit of her abundant love. My father saturated my upbringing with gentle authority. His young life until then had been torn by conflict and tragedy.

At the unbelievable age of eighteen years he had confounded his Jewish associates in the Stepney ghetto by joining the army to fight for his country. A nice Jewish boy from a *gefilte* fish background actually volunteered. There was no doubt about it; he was *mashooga*. His parents grieved at the departure of their youngest son. His sister Rose wailed. His brothers Harry, Hymie and Izzy were deeply embarrassed. But in 1914 Syd Zetter, with a determination that was to stand him in good stead for the rest of his notable life, joined the King's Royal Rifles. Four years and three dreadful wounds later, he had survived the most horrific war ever experienced by mankind.

England was still suffering the effects of that terrible conflict. Those who returned from four years of hell, many appallingly maimed, found a ruined country which was unable to offer them employment.

Over a million young men did not return. The memory of the lost beloved ones was profoundly fresh and solemnly honoured by the whole nation.

A Cenotaph was speedily erected in Whitehall. I clearly remember how my father, with special dignity, always tipped his Homburg hat each time he passed that memorial. Everybody did so. The passing multitude all paid their homage to 'The Glorious Dead'. And each year, on the eleventh hour of the eleventh day of the eleventh month, a two minute silence was observed. This was, of course, the date in November 1918 when the bitter conflict had ended. So we remembered it. On the stroke of eleven, the guns sounded and for two minutes the entire population, where possible, stopped. Trams, buses, cars, horse-drawn vehicles, pedestrians, whatever they were doing, all came to a standstill. As a child I was deeply moved. Tears filled my eyes as I hung my head. I suspect forty million fellow citizens were similarly affected. This noble homage continued right up to the beginning of my war in 1939.

In the late autumn of 1918, while he was still recovering from the last and most serious of his wounds, my father's parents died, both of them within a week of each other, of the 'flu epidemic which ravaged Europe and Great Britain. I never, therefore, met my paternal grandparents.

When Syd married Esther he was taken to the bosom of the Stodel family. The warmth and generosity of their very real affection must have compensated him in no small measure for the loss of his parents. So he moved into the large terraced house and soon became the head of the family . . . including the Stodels. He also became the major breadwinner.

I loved my father all the years of my life. But most of all I loved him during my adolescent years. Everybody respected Syd Zetter. He could always turn an honest living and his honesty was unique in that environment. He was a war hero. Out of all those millions of young men, my own father was the only hero I knew. I loved his tales of the trenches. Never told bitterly, never savagely, but always with enough interest to excite the imagination of a little boy. He taught me so much, did my father, but, perhaps most importantly, he taught me that pride and patriotism were rewarding emotions and a reputation for integrity was the greatest possible personal asset.

My mother was something else. Everybody, but everybody loved Esther. She was simply the most gentle, lovable person imaginable. Her whole being oozed with the milk of human kindness. When she married, communities rejoiced. When she had her first miscarriage, they wept. When I was born, joy was unconfined. She attracted love about her to the same abundant degree that she gave it.

My relationship with her was almost perfect. I can never remember any chastisement. I could do no wrong. I am reminded of the old Jewish joke. The Yiddisher mama was chided for giving her son an Oedipus complex because of her excessive doting. 'Oedipus, schnoedipus,' she responded, 'Who cares so long as he loves his mother?'

My mother's love for me was not, in fact, all-consuming. We were friends, companions. Whereas my father taught me the responsibilities of behaviour which became paramount as I developed, no less important were my mother's contributions. From her I learned humour, humility and above all, respect for my fellow man.

The first seven years passed uneventfully other than the odd incident. I started school at about five, at that selfsame school which had consumed dear Louis a couple of years earlier. He, with his sister Sadie, Aunt Jane and

Uncle Joe from Australia, had long since departed Grove Road. They'd gone to another planet called Chadwell Heath, Essex.

My very early school years quickly established the pattern which pertained for the rest of my academic life. 'Could do better' is the most accurate appraisal, but I do recall one added comment that was keenly latched upon by all interested parties . . . 'may be a late developer.'

My home life was sheer bliss. Happy childhood memories do not necessarily mean a happy childhood, but it was undoubtedly the case with me. I am certainly nostalgic about those years. I had devoted parents, a stable home life and even though we lived among and were lower working class, I don't believe we were poor. At least, not noticeably so compared with the poverty that existed all around us. I have nothing but affection for the recollection of those formative years.

How I loved going to stay with Uncle Joe and Aunt Jane in Chadwell Heath. Real country it was. Fields and streams. Cows and a lively cattle market in the town square in nearby Romford. But the real joy was the company of cousins Louis and Sadie, or more accurately of course, Louis. What a splendid fellow he was. The things he taught me. Cricket, on a scrap of wasteland with an improvised wicket and two bats between about a dozen of us. Fierce competition that put 'The Ashes' into insignificance.

I shall never forget one notable game. The 'Aussies' were batting and we, the 'Pommies', had been successful in dismissing most of them for a meagre run total. Two partners then came together and had begun to make a real stand. One boy especially dominated the square, husbanding the bowling, scoring twos or fours off the first five balls in an over and a single each time off the sixth. The game was clearly slipping away. Every one of us had been given a bowl . . . except me. All to no avail. Nobody could penetrate this pint-size Bradman. Finally, at the end of a particularly frustrating over, in utter desperation, I was given the ball. I was by far the smallest and youngest player on that field and, as I explained to my embarrassed fellow players and amused adversaries, I couldn't bowl overarm. With a resigned nod, my captain told me to get my six balls over as quickly as possible. I stood at my end and, aiming as carefully as I could, lobbed the ball approximately in the right direction. The batsman, with a huge grin on his face, waited in keen anticipation for the ball to reach him. It bounced two or three times on its way and would have missed the leg stump by about two feet. On the last bounce, before reaching the wicket, the ball must have hit a small pebble or something. It reared off in a totally unexpected direction and gently prodded the off stump with just enough momentum to unbalance one bail which fell to the ground. It is the only time in my entire life, before or since, that I became a hero.

Many adventures we had, Louis and I. Putting pennies on railway tracks. Our only motivation was to end up with a flattened penny, not to damage a train, but one wonders if latterday vandalism was born of such innocent beginnings. Hunting sticklebacks, frogs and the rare newt was my most favourite activity. I wonder if that is responsible for my lasting, and expensive, passion for salmon fishing?

Chadwell Heath was memorable for another reason. It was *en route* to Southend. Southend-on-Sea, or paradise, as I knew it. Just one hour along that superb highway, the Southend Arterial Road. It's still there, that road, but allow two hours for the journey today.

Of course my father had a car. He'd always had a car, my father. Well, Syd Zetter would, wouldn't he? There weren't many cars around in those days, which added to the great joy and excitement of motoring. Early Sunday morning down the Mile End Road. Through Stratford Broadway and Ilford. A quick stop at Chadwell Heath to pick up Louis and Sadie and sometimes to exchange the old Stodels for Uncle Joe and Aunt Jane. Then Gallows Corner, of chilling repute, then wonderful Southend.

Dear, dear Southend, where there were days when the sea was below the far horizon and it took a long muddy walk to reach it. I think I liked that best of all. Catching crabs and shrimps in the pools left by the tide. Getting coated in mud and loving it. It was 'good for rheumatism,' my Mother said. 'He doesn't have rheumatism,' my father replied. 'Well, he won't now, will he?' my mother said. So I got muddier and nobody minded.

Beach teas and amusement arcades which I remember as great fun places. They had none of the sinister connotations with which they have now become associated. The Little Wonder was my favourite pinball game. For one penny you had seven chances of getting your ball into a winning pocket. I could never understand the frequency with which I found that single losing one.

Back in Grove Road, playing cards was a favourite pastime. Half a dozen or so sitting around the kitchen table after supper. A typical gathering would be my mother and father, Daddy Dick, as old man Stodel was affectionately known, Tommy Stodel my uncle – a real, rough, illiterate London cockney – and his enormously fat wife Leah, their pretty daughter Julie, who was responsible for my first recognition of sexuality, and finally me. Rummy, with its many variations, was the favoured game. Others included twist, pontoon, put & take and, a bit later, whist which eventually led to solo. These evenings were always good humoured, even though we did play for small stakes. Constant cups of tea were provided by Grandma Stodel, who preferred to be busy rather than to sit and play silly games. We noshed sweets all evening and, sadly, it's a habit that has stuck with me.

On warm summer evenings, of which there seemed to be many, I was sent off to the local dairy, two minutes down the road, with a clean empty bucket and a shilling. I brought back a gallon of the latest sweetmeat, a frozen, creamy substance which was quite delicious. It was the newest thing, from either Italy or America, we were not sure which, and it was sweeping the country. 'It'll never catch on,' Daddy Dick used to say, but 'Walls' and 'Eldorado' didn't agree. They filled the streets with men pedalling large three-wheeled boxes, rather like enormous tea-chests. They were loaded with ice cream as it was called and dry ice to keep this wondrous confection in a suitable condition. 'Walls' was the market leader, with their dark blue tricycles festooned with large white letters urging us to 'Stop me and buy one'. We did!

Christmas was the highlight of the year for our Jewish household. I don't think the preparations for the great occasion started as early as they do today. For instance, I have an entrancing memory of going down Roman Road Market on Christmas Eve to buy the turkey and trimmings for the morrow. The event was a magical one. Throngs of happy people about their delightful purposes. Decorations and streamers linking market stalls, all crammed with the necessary goodies to complement the season. Chocolates and jellies, oranges and tangerines. Toys and games stacked onto barrows groaning under the weight of them. Dead turkeys, mainly unplucked, were in abundance and, I suppose, the reason they were bought at the last minute was because nobody owned a refrigerator, let alone a deep freeze. Blazing kerosene lamps shone down from each stall, illuminating the paraphernalia of Christmas and bringing a fairyland atmosphere to the whole scene.

Present buying was an essential element of the occasion. I usually spent days reconnoitring prior to the final decision day, 24 December. Perfume was the preferred choice . . . it has always made the most desirable gift. A good size bottle (about six inches tall), with a glass stopper and enveloped in a brown hand-worked leather jacket. They were beautiful and many a one I bought for the ladies of my acquaintance. Not bad either for 1s. 11¼d. a go. Change from two bob!

My father always got cigars. Nothing much mattered about them except the size and the box they came in. I loved giving him cigars, but was always a little disconcerted at the way he offered the box around quite so generously.

By Christmas Day the whole family had assembled. That is on my mother's side. Thereafter, for days on end enormous quantities of food and drink were consumed by our Jewish multitude. Parties every night. Games like murder, sergeant major and find the sixpence enlivened the gaiety. The latter game was fairly typical. An innocuous pudding bowl was filled with water and a shiny sixpence thrown into it. A competitor, usually female, was shown the treasure, blindfolded and then told to find it. In the meantime, the bowl was switched for a chamber pot filled with tepid tea. I loved watching that particular game. Especially when the blindfold was removed from the innocent victim.

Music and singing were essential ingredients of those memorable evenings. My mother usually started the ball rolling with her favourite party piece. She would dress for the part by putting on my father's long overcoat and Homburg hat. She carried my grandfather's walking stick and so made her entrance. Everybody knew what to expect and everybody loved it. Her brother Lou was at the piano and Esther started her song. It went like this:

> Mr Finklestein was very rich
> I'd like you all to know
> He made a *barmitzvah* party
> Not very long ago
> *Oi*, I was a dressed
> In all my best
> And didn't I look a sight
> With a diamond pin
> Big as a lulu
> Shining in the night
> *Oi Mazeltov, Mazeltov,*
> Mr Finklestein.

Of course, everybody joined in the last two lines and the laughter and applause set the mood for the whole evening. The more serious business of operatic singing followed. The whole family, it seemed, were famous opera singers. 'The Stepney Polytechnic Amateur Gilbert and Sullivan Society' survived only as a consequence of our family membership.

Many years later (in 1974) I wrote a poem in which I tried to recapture those happy times. Here it is:

### Bethnal Green by Bow

> Oh! such parties that we had
>   those many years ago,
> Such parties, stirring memories
>   of Bethnal Green by Bow.

Enormous family gatherings
  from near, and far and wide,
Delicious female cousins came
  at every Christmastide.
And days and days and nights and nights
  and party games and food,
And sentimental ballads sung
  to cherish that sweet mood.

And roasted chicken, roasting hot,
  potatoes baked with rice,
Cold ham and tongue for supper
  and heated wine with spice;
Port enhanced with lemonade;
  yellow advocaat,
Jelly sweets and fruit and nuts
  Oh! what great times they were.

From Christmas Eve to New Year's Day
  in Bethnal Green by Bow,
Such parties in my father's house
  those many years ago.

Lou Stodel was the Christmas star who sang those 'sentimental ballads' . . .
Uncle Lou. A sweet, good-natured, kindly man – strikingly handsome and
with really quite a pleasant voice. He was almost certainly homosexual,
which is not altogether surprising, having been brought up with six sisters
and he the youngest member of the family. Lou sang lovely songs, not only
Gilbert & Sullivan, but popular Italian and Spanish songs like 'Sorrento'
and 'Aye, Aye, Aye'. Lou was so cosmopolitan with his wide circle of
intellectual friends and his foreign holidays. To my certain memory Lou, in
those years, went to Belgium, France, Switzerland, Italy and Spain. Indeed,
he was in San Sebastian at the outbreak of the Spanish Civil War. That was,
of course, in 1936 when I was thirteen years old. Oh, what blood-curdling
tales he told of the twenty-odd hours he spent getting out of revolution-torn
Spain, across the border, into France.

   During the early thirties Lou Stodel left home. He had become friendly
with a toff . . . Frank Heard. Actually, Frank was a butler! A west country
man, from an impoverished genteel background, who found his way into
domestic service. Domestic service was the main employer of labour and

fortunate was the individual who found a good position with a wealthy family. Frank buttled for the Maccatas, an extremely wealthy Jewish banking family living in fashionable Bayswater. I have no idea how Lou and he established their friendship. They had so little in common except, I suppose, the most important aspect of their lives. Anyway, they set up home together in a tiny flat in Quex Road, Brixton. I don't think it was posh, but it was certainly a bit up-market from Bethnal Green. Lou gave up his cloying, family environment and left a distraught mother. Frank gave up the Maccatas and they both joined my father who had just started his Football Pools business.

Lou's departure brought about some significant changes at home. It was as if my father had lost a rival as head of the house. Mind you, I don't think Lou had ever posed a threat but, from then on, my father assumed his rightful leadership. Syd was consulted on everything. Repairs, decorations, should we install the new 'electric' and get rid of the smelly gas? We did. We also installed the first telephone for miles around. It wasn't used much, but it was great to have one.

We, Dad and I, did the garden. Together we cleared the rubbish and laid out some beds, with old bricks to outline the borders. We spread hoggin, a sand and gravel mix, on the paths and planted a promise of great colour potential. We relied on blue lobelia, white alyssum, antirrhinum, tobacco plants and a few rose bushes. What a show they made and how proud we were. The best garden on our street and I had helped create it. Lovely it was, but it was still my play garden and that's how I used it. I even continued to ride my tricycle round and round those little hoggin pathways, notwithstanding the terrible ruts it caused. I loved the open air life to which our garden had introduced me. Somehow, to feel the magic of nature in the middle of the East End slums of the early thirties was incongruous, but even more pleasing for so being. To see things grow and know that I had played a part in their growing was immensely rewarding. The only bad memory I have of that time was being made to collect fertiliser. This onerous task consisted of following one of the many horse-drawn vehicles that were still on the road. Armed with a small shovel and a large bucket, I quickly learned the skills required to identify the right horse at the right time and so to return home triumphantly with a full load. Many a fight I got into and many more I avoided on those particular treasure hunts. Whole gangs of kids, all similarly equipped with their collecting gear, would compete for the same pungent deposits. Being small, quick and agile, I was between those cartwheels and out again with my bucket teeming. Our roses were the best for miles around.

It was about this time my father collared old Tommy Stodel, Lou's older brother and the dark sheep of the family. We wanted a bathroom installed. There was an outhouse just a couple of yards from the back door which would do nicely. Actually, I think it was my mother who inspired the thought. She used to have her weekly washdown by climbing into the boiler in the outhouse. One day the fire beneath flared up and she evacuated in a hurry. Anyway, she wanted a proper bath and Tommy was an artisan, wasn't he? As a matter of fact, he was a self-taught, inefficient, bone-idle electrician, so that qualified him. We all mucked in. The plumbing went easily. Daddy Dick knew someone who had a real bath to sell. A bit pitted, but you could paint it and 'What do you expect for three quid?' The boiler was a bit of a problem. They were expensive and you needed a gas supply installed by the Gas Company at a prodigious fee. Well, we found an old but serviceable boiler down the Roman Road. Then we simply neglected to pay the gas bill. During the twenty-four hour period we were shut off, Tommy hacksawed his way through the existing lead pipe and welded an extension running to our new boiler. The gas was turned on again the next day, after we'd paid the bill, and the boiler worked a treat. I was the first one to use our new luxury. It was a bit 'parky' crossing the backyard in the winter, but it was a joy for all that. Many a happy hour I spent soaking in that bath.

Going to the cinema was, undoubtedly, another important aspect of my life during the thirties. That's probably true of most people of that time. The silver screen filled our lives and enlivened our minds as nothing had ever done before. Hollywood was producing superb 'talking pictures' and the entrepreneurs were quick to realise the tremendous profit potential of this new entertainment. Fantastic Picture Palaces mushroomed all over the country, and veritable palaces they were. Plush seating, velvet curtains, glamorous lighting and stucco-splendid edifices arose amidst our slum dwellings. They weren't all quite so plush, of course. Crummy little 'flea houses' and poorly renovated theatres vied with each other to attract an audience. And what treats we had. *The Jazz Singer, Gone with the Wind, All Quiet on the Western Front, For Whom the Bell Tolls, Lost Horizon*: films that have become classics in their own right. And the stars who created them and were created by them! Stars whose magical performances became available for the first time ever to millions of people through the celluloid miracle. Charlie Chaplin, Al Jolson, Clark Gable, Spencer Tracy, Katherine Hepburn, Bette Davis, Barbara Stanwyck, Greta Garbo and more and more. I honestly think I could name a hundred of them* and every one a household name. It's hardly surprising, I suppose. I went to the 'flix' at least six times a week during my early teenage years. Not every day, maybe, but often twice in one day and occasionally, even three times. Well, there were cinemas everywhere and for sixpence you could get a good seat. On Saturday morning matinees, when the family wanted you out of the way, you could go to the local flea-pit for just one penny and see the latest Buck Rogers serial. We thought sex and violence were used fairly extensively and films began to be categorised to avoid youngsters viewing improper or unacceptable scenes. So category 'U' was for Universal showing, 'A' was for Adults (who could, nevertheless, take in juveniles) and then 'X' which, I suppose, meant 'explicit' and 'H' for 'horrific'. You were supposed to be over sixteen to get into those, but we all managed to see most of them. I suspect the very worst 'X' or 'H' wouldn't even required a 'PG' ('Parental Guidance') today.

*I have just done it . . . easily!

| | | |
|---|---|---|
| Ronald Reagan | Freddie Bartholomew | Henry Fonda |
| Jack Oakie | Adolphe Menjou | Franchot Tone |
| Cary Grant | Janet Gaynor | William Powell |
| Slim Sumerville | Walter Pidgeon | Gary Cooper |
| Judy Garland | Edward G. Robinson | Noah Beery |
| Mickey Rooney | Greer Garson | Esther Williams |
| Rudolph Valentino | Betty Grable | Conrad Veidt |
| Harold Lloyd | Lana Turner | Bela Lugosi |
| Johnny Weismuller | C. Aubrey-Smith | Bebe Daniels |
| Leslie Howard | Gregory Peck | Sydney Greenstreet |
| Dorothy Lamour | Robert Taylor | Deanna Durbin |
| Merle Oberon | Walter Huston | Nelson Eddy |
| Ingrid Bergman | Eddie Cantor | Peter Lorre |
| Carole Lombard | Humphrey Bogart | Andy Devine |
| Buck Rogers | Bing Crosby | Greta Garbo |
| Ginger Rogers | George Burns | Charlie Chaplin |
| Bette Davis | Bob Hope | George Arliss |
| Fred Astaire | Ralph Richardson | Clark Gable |
| Katherine Hepburn | Fredrick March | Shirley Temple |
| Fred MacMurray | George Raft | John Mills |
| Barbara Stanwyck | Myrna Loy | Joan Crawford |
| James Stewart | Cesar Romero | Stanley Laurel |
| Ray Milland | Paul Robeson | Ida Lupino |
| Olivia de Havilland | Melvyn Douglas | Oliver Hardy |
| Lionel Barrymore | Hedy Lamarr | Victor MacGlagan |
| Laurence Olivier | Carmen Miranda | Zasu Pitts |
| John Barrymore | James Cagney | Maurice Chevalier |
| Edward Everett Horton | George Formby | Robert Benchley |
| Paul Munie | Pat O'Brien | Ben Lyon |
| Joe E. Brown | Spencer Tracy | Errol Flynn |
| Paulette Goddard | Will Hay | Jeanette MacDonald |
| Joan Blondell | Gloria Swanson | Douglas Fairbanks |
| Jackie Coogan | Virginia Mayo | Gracie Fields |
| Jackie Cooper | | |

# Chapter 2

# 'Jew-boy' to Man

1936 was the year of my *barmitzvah*. On a chosen date sometime during that year I became a man. The whole show was sensational. Certainly as sensational as every other *barmitzvah* in every other Jewish family. I learned my lines by rote and on the day I was word perfect. 'He should be a rabbi,' acclaimed the multitude. Never mind that I didn't understand a word of it and would probably have rejected it had I done so. Mind you, I'd 'intoned it beautifully, and with such feeling! Clearly I should become a rabbi!'

One notable incident did occur. The day before the great day I had broken my arm. A simple greenstick fracture as a result of sky-larking at school. The shock to the family was traumatic. My mother, who never wept as a result of grief, was near to tears. My father looked as he must have done those years earlier when preparing to go over the top. My grandmother wanted the whole thing cancelled . . . 'such a strain on such a young boy.' My grandfather got drunk and stayed that way until well after the party which followed the 'reading'.

The party was the great sensation. It was held at the Casino Ballrooms, E.1. and everyone who was anyone came. The finery had to be seen to be believed. Sequined dresses in such colours as had never before been assembled under one roof. The men wore dinner jackets. Well, some of them wore dinner jackets! There was music during the meal, selections from *The Desert Song* and suchlike. When the feasting, the speeches and the prayers were over, there was then music for dancing. Old Tommy and Daddy Dick thought the prayers a complete waste of time. 'We had enough of all that rubbish in *Schule* today.' The speeches were very forgettable. I cannot remember a word of any one of them, including my own. The meal was really the thing. Never was so much nosh consumed. It was as if they'd all been let out following the blowing of the horn to signal the end of Yom Kippur. I won't go through the menu; it's reproduced elsewhere so that you can make your own judgement. Anyway, it was all quite momentous. It has left me with mostly good memories, but one unhappy one. My *tollus*, the Jewish prayer shawl which had been a present from Grandma, was stolen. On the very day of my *barmitzvah*, in the very synagogue where the ceremony was enacted, somebody had pinched my beautiful new *tollus*. I never felt the need to replace it. Actually I did rather well on presents. After all I was 'Syd's boy' and 'Syd was going places'. I won't try to recall the list of donations, but I know I got seven dressing gowns. Dressing gowns were all the rage in 1936.

Being a Jew in the East End of London in those days was provocative for one particular reason. Mosley was afoot . . . Sir Oswald Mosley the Blackshirt . . . the British fascist who aped Hitler and whose anti-Semitism brought bloody street fights and rioting to London. Mosley was a brilliant intellectual who misread the British character as surely as his alter-ego Hitler was soon to do. Oh! certainly, he built up a following. His 'army' consisted of young, ignorant, out-of-work lads with nothing in their ragged pockets and barely a shirt on their scrawny backs. For a few bob pocket-money and a smart black shirt, he recruited his 'loyal band of followers'. 'Action!' was their battle cry and to enact this emotive hyperbole, they staged their marches. The route was always planned to pass through the most crowded of the Jewish slums. Whitechapel and Shoreditch were favourite confrontation districts. The columns of marchers, carrying inflammatory banners, were flanked by the ever-impartial London bobby protecting their right of 'free speech'. Sir Oswald proudly headed his troops and orchestrated their screeched insults with the aid of an hand-held megaphone. I imagine the objective was to intimidate and terrorise a cringing ethnic minority, but the Jewish cockney was made of sterner stuff. Nevertheless, tension and fear were abroad and at home. The women begged their menfolk to keep out of trouble. 133 Grove Road was a mirror image of Jewish households throughout the East End. Typically, Uncle Tommy, Uncle Lou and my father were spoiling for the fray and I wanted to join in. My mother upbraided my father. 'You're *mashooga*,' she wailed, 'What kind of example to set a young boy?' But they set the example, notwithstanding the occasional black eye. Rarely, if ever, did the parade reach its destination without a fight. 'Never in time and never intact,' would have been a much more appropriate slogan for Sir Oswald's inglorious rabble. The British people rejected Oswald Mosley.* A total and utter rejection of his entire philosophy. Not that they were particularly fond of the Yids . . . they weren't. But neither were they anti-Semitic. The British character is full of complexity. It has more faults than a rusty kettle, but intolerance isn't one of them. Anti-Semitism has been described as 'disliking Jews more than is necessary'. The Brits don't do anything more than is necessary.

---

*Mosley was interned during the war as a Nazi sympathiser. Most of his followers joined the Services to fight and to defeat the dictators. I'm happy to record that the Jews of London and of the rest of Britain fought alongside them.

# Chapter 3

# A Dip in the Pool

My *barmitzvah* confirmed a long held view by both the Zetter and the Stodel families. Syd Zetter was definitely going places and he had a son who would one day, 'please God', take over the family business.

The family business had been running three years by then; its origins are worth recording.

After my father was demobilised and got married, he became what was unkindly known as a 'picture faker'. This entailed travelling around the country and convincing home dwellers to part with precious photographs of their loved ones. For a modest cost, they would be beautifully enlarged and returned to the proud owners in a magnificent frame. It was a highly profitable business with a ready market due, undoubtedly, to the many grieving parents who had lost their sons in the War and whose only memory of them was a faded snapshot. As a war veteran, my father had a natural entrée to those sad families. In all the years in that 'game', he always delivered and he always brought comfort and satisfaction to his many customers.

I want to jump fifty years to tell of an uncanny little coincidence which occurred in 1986. More than anything else, it stirred my fading memory of those early times.

David Isaacs, a colleague of mine, of whom more later, returned from a holiday in China. The borders had only recently been opened to overseas tourists and he and his wife Neta were among the first visitors. He brought back with him a snapshot he had taken in Peking. It was of a shop specialising in fitting and selling picture frames. The name above the door was ZETTER.

Back to the twenties. After a while, like many things, business deteriorated. The sharks had got into the act. Unscrupulous commercial travellers soon soured the market by taking a treasured portrait and a cash deposit, neither of which were ever seen again.

Never mind, ever-resourceful Syd soon got a new line. The Irish Sweep was, forgive me, sweeping the country. Very simply, it was an Irish National Lottery run, partly, for the benefit of hospitals in Southern Ireland. For ten bob, you could buy a ticket which gave you the chance to win fifty thousand pounds. Yes . . . fifty thousand pounds! It was a fortune beyond the wildest dreams. Unimaginable wealth, just by having bought the right ticket. Of course, ten bob was a huge price to pay, so you joined a syndicate, ten of you, and for a shilling each you were up and running.

The system was, and still is, well known. Your counterfoil went into the draw. A huge revolving drum, situated in Dublin, was used and a number of counterfoils were drawn out, the majority of which won consolation prizes of about £100 each. Not bad, eh? A special few, however, were destined for bigger things. These were the 'Horses'. A winning ticket was allocated the name of a horse running in a major classic British race like the Derby. If you drew a 'Horse', you were guaranteed a win of £1,000 whether your horse ran or not. If it did run and came third, your had won £10,000 . . . second, £20,000 and – hold your breath – first, £50,000!

The tickets sold like hot cakes in impoverished post-war England and Syd Zetter was a salesman. I have no idea how he first got into this 'nice little earner' but get into it he did. He became a highly successful agent with his own sales area and a team of agents working for him. His trips to Dublin were regular and rewarding and he really started to make money.

A sequence of events then occurred which were to have the most far-reaching consequences.

A friendly local police inspector invited my old man for a drink one evening and tipped him off about the clamp-down which was about to be enacted to stop the growing sale of illegal lottery tickets. 'Knock it off, Syd,' he'd said, 'Or I'll have to knock you off and I wouldn't like that. You can run your last sweep on this year's Derby, and that's it. And I'm only turning a blind eye to that 'cos I bought a ticket from you myself last week.' The Old Man was certainly upset but, as always, philosophical. 'Something else will turn up,' he told my mother. He feverishly stepped up his sales efforts for his last fling. Part of the system of reward was an allocation of free tickets to him which he could sell for his own benefit. However, Syd always kept one ticket in every book of ten he sold. So, come the Derby, he had a whole stack of ten shilling tickets to himself. About one week before Derby Day he made his last delivery of sold tickets to Dublin and thought that episode of his life was over. It was not to be. Three days later, he received a telegram congratulating him on having won a £100 consolation prize in the draw. The next day, he received another telegram informing him of a further £100 win. Then, two days before the race, the final telegram came. He had drawn a 'Horse'. Royal Dancer, a fancied runner in that year's great classic.

Well, what a to-do. The Press got hold of it. 'Lucky, Zetter, war hero, scoops three winning tickets in the Derby'; 'Lucky 3 for Syd'; etc., etc. The 'phone never stopped ringing. Offers came pouring in to buy the ticket before the race. Begging letters piled onto the doormat. Lucky Pixies were sent by wellwishers, who remembered to include an invoice with their greetings.

I don't think any of us slept much for a couple of nights. Dad stuck to his ticket, of course, and we all crowded round the wireless to listen to the race commentary.

'April the Fifth', a horse owned by Tom Walls, a well known English actor, won it. I forget who came second and third but Royal Dancer was beaten, by a nose, into fourth place.

The gloom that descended on that household was worse than a London fog . . . but not for long. Syd Zetter had twelve hundred pounds from his three wins, a considerable fortune. More importantly, he had hundreds and hundreds of names and addresses of people who liked a little flutter. The Irish Sweep was out, but wasn't there something to take its place?

With the nationwide clamp-down on the Irish Sweep, another harmless flutter was to take its place . . . the Football Pools. The Pools had been around since the early twenties. I understand that they had their origins in Scotland, where small-time bookies had been in the habit of laying odds on individual soccer matches and then groups of matches with consequently bigger payouts to winners. All this went well enough until one particular 'black' Saturday when all the fancied results came up. The bookies either renegued and disappeared, or paid out and packed it in. All that is except a canny Scot named Jarvis. Jarvis was a well travelled man who had once had the good fortune to visit Paris. Apart from other things, he discovered in that great city a betting system called the 'Pari-Mutuel'. Very simply, it established the odds on any bet by first deducting ten per cent of the total 'take' and then sharing the remainder of the 'pool' of money between the winners. Jarvis ran his football betting business in Glasgow on this system and so 'the Pools' were born. They hardly had an auspicious beginning. Jarvis was not particularly successful and the whole concept may have petered out had it not been for one man . . . John Moores. He it was who saw the potential and who in 1923 started his own Pools Company. He called it Littlewoods, that being the birth name of John's partner, Colin Askham (born Colin Littlewoods but adopted by the family Askham). Both Moores and Askham were young men working for the Commercial Cable Company and didn't want the company to know of their extra-curricula activities. So Littlewoods was chosen for the name of the company destined to become the biggest Football Pool in the world.

Littlewoods was founded in 1923, the year I was born. Zetters was founded ten years later. A decade of difference.

I cannot pretend that I remember the actual start of Zetters Pools. I suppose I became aware of it over a short period of time. I do remember my father's first office. It was a single room above Lovells, the sweet shop, in Borough High Street.

The 'Old Man' was immensely proud of his move into the 'real business world'. He worked all the hours that God sent and the family soon became very involved. Every day of every week, family shift workers gathered round the large old kitchen table in Grove Road. That's where the routine of running the business was established.

On Sunday evening, we handwrote names and addresses on envelopes . . . the customers. On Monday, Dad collected next Saturday's virgin coupons from the printer . . . Monday night, we filled them into the envelopes we had addressed and my job was to stick stamps on them. Halfpenny stamps! Dad stuffed them into the nearest pillar box by Tuesday morning and you could be sure they were all delivered within 24 hours! Wednesday, we spent writing out the winner's envelopes that hadn't been completed during the Tuesday. Thursday, the post had started to come back. Completed coupons with postal orders enclosed (average bet a shilling). So Thursday, Friday and Saturday morning we were on post opening. Saturday night was the big night – the football results started coming in. I was sent out several times during that evening to get the *Star*, the *Evening News* and the *Standard*. 'Late night final' the placards announced, but several late night finals were needed before all the results were in. Then checking started. Checking the coupons to find the winners. This went on late into Saturday night and all day Sunday. Then off we'd go again with the same routine. It was a fantastic apprenticeship, but it played havoc with my school homework.

Wide ranging changes have taken place over the years but, in essence, the same work programme is followed to this day.

# Chapter 4

# School Days

I was, of course, at my proper school by this time. By scrimping and saving, enough money was found to send me to a 'posh' school, the City of London School, no less. How I managed to pass the entrance examination, I shall never know. But pass it I did and there was I, a pint-sized East End yid, going into that great palace of learning on the Thames Embankment where all the nobs sent their sons.

My life really got going at the City of London School, 'CLS' as it is always referred to by those of us lucky enough to have gone there. I cannot pretend to have loved it. I have never looked back on that period and thought of it as the halcyon days. I think I was too overawed by my surroundings. I was certainly one of the least promising pupils of my era. Neither was I much good at sport. I hated cricket. I don't think I ever took a wicket excepting, of course, that earlier triumph. I never held a catch and my all-time best innings was five runs. Rugby was a little better: you could get stuck-in and be lost in the ferment. I actually enjoyed my rugby and played enthusiastically throughout school, the army and most notably in those heady post-war years with the 'Old Citizens', the beautifully descriptive name given to former pupils of CLS.

Those were the formative years, the years of puberty. The years when one established friendships which could – and did – last a lifetime. And what years they were in the calendar of this most dramatic twentieth century. I joined CLS in 1934 and left in 1940. Those six years witnessed the birth of the greatest human malady experienced during the history of mankind – National Socialism emerged in Germany, an almost inevitable consequence of the injustices imposed upon a wretched and defeated country following the 1914–1918 World War. So the Nazis came to power under the hypnotic, evil genius of Adolf Hitler.

No hint of things to come was evident when I started at the School. I was filled with nervous anticipation. The very journey was exciting. At first my father took me, but later I was brave enough to go it alone. I caught a No. 8 bus from the corner of Grove Road and Bow Road and through history we travelled. Leaving the East End at Club Row. Past Liverpool Street Station through Bishopsgate. Alongside the Bank of England. Down Poultry into Queen Victoria Street and down to Blackfriars. Crossing the vast expanse of roadway which led to Blackfriars Bridge you came to the Thames Embankment at the beginning of which CLS was grandly situated. I well remember the splendid sight which one witnessed following a heavy shower. An army of council works appeared, as from nowhere, to squeegee the road dry, thus avoiding any serious skidding on the wood block surface.

And so to School. Three streams were in operation at that time . . . Classical, Science and Modern. Like all mediocre pupils I was placed in Modern where a splendid, non-specialist, general education was provided. I was in 'New Grammar'. Our form master was Le Mansoir-Field: a lovely gentle man who tried his best with his kindergarten and undoubtedly won their trust and affection. It was he who prepared us for the greater demands schooling was to put upon us as the years went by. He was French and one of his tasks was to introduce us to that beautiful and useful language. He used to say that, generally, students spoke bad French with a good accent or good French with a bad accent. Then there were the British who spoke bad French with a bad accent. Anyway, we loved him – old Micky Fields – nearly as much as we loved Biff Vokins our second year master. Biff was the epitome of all that was good at school. He was kind and considerate, and he kept good order by having won the respect of his charges. I never saw him angry. If your meagre efforts fell below reasonable requirements, you saddened him and his sorrow hurt so much you determined to strive to do better next time. Biff was a genius and a gentleman. I write of a time over fifty years ago and, to my great joy, Biff is still alive and attending our annual Old Boys' Dinner, as well as other events.

Friendships were being formed, casual associations which changed by the week while others survived time, war and marriage. Roll call always started the day. Arundel, Balls, Bates, Brisacher, Clarfelt, Claringbold and so on, all twenty-three of us. I was always the last. I don't think that was significant. Two boys, Louis Brisacher and George Clarfelt were to become special friends. Dear genteel Louis . . . slight, blonde and beautiful, born of a kindly Swiss father and a dominating British mother. The father died early in the war, when Louis was about fourteen years old. It must have been a deep hurt to him at the time but we knew little or nothing about it. Our friendship developed slowly as the years went by and didn't really become established until the early part of the war when we were evacuated to Marlborough. More of that later. George Clarfelt was completely different. Large, Jewish and typically extrovert. We quickly established mutual accord. His personality overwhelmed those with whom he became involved, including me. We were equally dim academically, and lived not far from each other. Although our association was by far the stronger one, it did not survive, however, and although I occasionally bumped into him in later life, no real bond existed between us. George married well and had five children. Sadly, he died at a fairly early age. I only recently learned of it by chance. There was another friend, Peter Jeffs. Peter was a sheer delight. Fat, jolly, full of fun and definitely a middle-class individual from Bromley – Kent not Bow. Dear Peter was killed in action during the war.

For all my scholastic inadequacies, I began enjoying CLS. I don't think academic rivalry existed there. The exception was the annual general knowledge paper. Everyone looked forward to it and everyone got the same paper, from the Head Boy in the VIth to the minutest newcomer in Modern IIB. We all sat that paper and the competition was fierce. George and I had a bet every year. The loser had to buy baked beans on toast and a chocolate milk-shake (Ugh!) at Lyons teashop by Blackfriars Station. We came out roughly even, but one year he won in a manner I considered to be totally devoid of moral justice. It came about this way. Having come from an East End background, I always avoided the use of bad language and was shocked and saddened at the ready acceptance of the Anglo-Saxon vocabulary by my social superiors. You can imagine, then, my righteous indignation when I discovered why I had lost that year's contest. There was, you see, a new swimming pool being built. The builders were Trollope & Colls. The general knowledge question, worth two marks, asked who the builders were. I hadn't known the answer, George had and collected two marks, putting his grand total just one rotten mark above mine. 'How on earth did you know the answer to that question?' I asked somewhat querulously. 'Everyone knew that one because of their nickname, Trollope & Colls . . . Bollocks & Balls. See?' he said looking very smug.

I still don't like the free and easy use of four-letter words and the like, but I came to know of their value in certain circumstances.

It's odd how these trivial incidents stay in the memory for the whole of one's life. Another such occurred when I had been at the City of London

School for about two years. I had found my feet by then and exhibited a confidence probably bordering on cockiness. This was particularly true in the gym where I discovered, to my surprise, that I was able to perform with great agility. I acquitted myself with some panache and was seen to possess a tough and lithe athleticism. I revelled in this newly revealed prowess. At least I did until one notable day.

There was an inter-house boxing match scheduled. And there on the notice board, to my utter chagrin, was my name. I was down to box for my house, Beaufouy, against Chris Cartledge representing Seeley. I knew Chris. He was about the same weight as me, but stood many inches taller. He was lean, sharp and as tough as nails. He had a boxing reputation in the school sufficient to terrify any opposition . . . and he terrified me. My friends didn't help. Not only was I not given a chance, I was going to be destroyed. Well! I chickened out. I got my father to write a note withdrawing me from the contest. Considering the enormity of my behaviour, the school and my colleagues treated it all very lightly, but I deeply regretted what I had done. Nevertheless, it taught me a salutory lesson which has stood me in good stead ever since – a bloody nose heals quicker than a dented ego!

The war clouds were clearly gathering now. Hitler had reoccupied the Saarland without so much as a rap on the knuckles. Munich and Chamberlain filled the headlines and newsreels at the cinema. 'Peace in our time' was a bigger laugh at school than Laurel and Hardy. Only if you've got cancer, was the schoolboy assessment of that particular oratory.

One incident, typifying the times, remains in my memory. A new boy joined the class, Bischeim. Arundel, Balls, Bates, Bischeim, Brisacher, etc. Bischeim couldn't speak much English. He was a German . . . a German Jew . . . an actual real live *refugee from Nazi Germany. We were all terribly excited about it at first, but we soon got bored when he refused to tell us any gory stories or answer any of our insensitive questions. Bischeim became Beecham and, subsequently, a highly successful and respected British businessman.

I was sixteen in 1939. That summer was the most dreary I can ever remember. Everyone knew it was coming. Russia and Germany had signed a non-aggression pact. The one significant factor that might, just might, have made Hitler hesitate, fear of the Russian bear on his Eastern front, had been neutralised. War was now inevitable.

---

*How notably did we and other countries benefit by that enforced exodus. It is a lesson that should be remembered.

# Chapter 5

# The 'Last' War?

So the summer holidays were a complete washout, that is until late August. Then the excitement began. We were to be evacuated. The whole school was moving to Marlborough. We were to be billeted on the unsuspecting folk in and around that delightful Wiltshire town. It's odd, but I cannot remember how we got there. I think we all caught a train from Paddington. Anyway, get there we did and were then required to pair up with those with whom we wished to be housed. I was delighted to end up with Louis Brisacher.

We were taken on a long, long walk with our small attaché cases and gas masks, almost out of Marlborough, down a pretty country lane to a gorgeous looking cottage. Rest House it was called. We later found out that it had originally been called Pest House. It had once been a dormitory house for those locals with incurable diseases. The news soon got round and Louis and I became the school lepers! Sunday 3 September dawned like any other day. We were getting to know the young married owners who were our hosts. Over a generous breakfast, we heard the news on the wireless that Warsaw had been bombed by the Luftwaffe. (The announcer explained that 'Luftwaffe' was the German word for Air Force.) The German Army had penetrated deep into Poland. Hitler had boasted that the whole country would be quickly overrun in what he called a *Blitzkreig*. This, our BBC man told us, meant 'lightning war'. He went on to tell us that Neville Chamberlain, our Prime Minister, would be broadcasting to the nation at 11 o'clock that morning. We all knew what he was going to say. It was almost an anticlimax and certainly a relief when he said it.

So England, once more, found herself at war with Germany and my doting parents made a decision. Whether it was as a consequence of missing me or because they, too, thought evacuation was a wise precaution, I do not know. Anyway, they decided to leave London and rent a house in Marlborough. All of them, my mother and father, grandmother and grandfather. I was not best pleased, especially when it was made clear I was to move in with them. After some initial resistance I capitulated, but only on the understanding that Louis came too. He was delighted, so a kind of normal home life was re-established.

In a surprisingly short time, school life also resumed normality. Le Mansoir (Micky) Fields reverted to his near-impossible task of convincing us of the importance of declining French verbs. J.E.B. (Jeb) Marsh tried a similar task with English grammar. So, once again, maths, geography, history etc. imposed upon our lives, as if nothing else of importance was happening. The excitement of our new environment soon waned, notwithstanding the superb facilities Marlborough School made available to us, most notably, the Memorial Hall. This contained a spectacularly beautiful assembly hall, theatre and music room. We took music there under a Mr Taylor, a hard, unsympathetic teacher who, nevertheless, motivated those of us with any interest in the subject. To this day, you can still see that splendid building, in the grounds of the school, as you come through Savernake Forest on the A346, down the steep hill into Marlborough. Savernake Forest was, and still is, a spectacular area of natural beauty. Wild horses and deer were prolific and frequently sighted. It very soon became a most favourite exploration ground for the newly arrived London boys. One of the strangest situations we all encountered during our stay there was the almost total lack of association with the pupils at Marlborough School. At the time, my immediate contemporaries and I didn't give a damn. To be honest I don't think we even noticed. But older boys and, indeed, masters were included in what was clearly a non-fraternisation policy. It must have been quite hurtful, but I suppose it was understandable. After all, to have some hundreds of uninvited guests foisted upon you could not have been entirely desirable, especially as the visitors were of a distinctly lower order in the very class-ridden society existing in the thirties. The fact that we were nearly all Londoners certainly didn't help matters. Indeed, there were even rumours that there were some cockneys amongst us. Ahem!

The winter of 1939 was bitterly cold and heavy snowfall covered southern England. The temperature dropped below freezing and stayed there for weeks on end. The streets of that little town were covered with snow and ice and one saw people actually skating along the roads and pavements. School went on as normal, of course. However, whether as a consequence of the weather or of the overcrowding, sickness and disease began to affect classroom attendance. Once started, it spread throughout the town almost as fast as the rumours of its dire consequences. I can claim credit for one particular unpatriotic malady which swept the populace. I developed German measles. Of all things to catch in 1939. German measles! Just about everyone got it. Even Marlbrarians! Then the mumps hit us. 'Flu soon followed and, far more sinister, meningitis. Illness was everywhere and twice a week we witnessed the astonishing sight of Council workers spraying the frozen streets with disinfectant. Whether that helped we'll never know, but we survived. One outcome of all that sickness caused a change in our cosy environment. George Clarfelt had always jealously gazed upon the Zetter household with its obvious home comforts. It clearly exposed his own accommodation for the uncomfortable billet it really was. Now George was an amazing chap who, having determined what he wanted, went for it with a single-minded purpose. The little cottage in Manston where he was quartered was overcrowded and just about everyone there caught something. Couldn't my mother manage to put up just one more boy? Please? Well, of course, she did, notwithstanding the fact that it meant we, too, became overcrowded. Anyway, George was a friend and lively company. He gave the lie to the proposition that two's company, three's none. We all got along famously.

During all this rural domesticity, my father was still attempting to run his Pools business in London. It was all going surprisingly well, but not before surviving – by dint of pure genius – what could have been a mortal blow. Shortly after the start of the war, an Order in Council was enacted which was to have the most far-reaching implications on the Pools industry.

Up until that time, Pools were conducted on the basis of sending out huge mailings to virtually every household in the land. It was understood, of course, that only one in five of those despatched actually returned a staked coupon.

The consequent waste of paper and, particularly, of manpower in the postal services was recognised by the authorities and considered unacceptable during war-time.

There was no wish, however, to close down the Pools industry. It was by then well established, well run and largely honest. It was also seen as having worthwhile morale-boosting benefits for a populace who were, inevitably, going to experience all kinds of deprivation should the war go on for a long time. And who could doubt it? In the autumn of 1939 a delegation consisting of the Moores brothers, John and Cecil of Littlewoods, Vernon Sangster of Vernons and, I believe, Harry Sherman of Shermans and Alfred

Cope of Copes were called to a meeting at the Home Office. To their utter consternation, the Order in Council was explained to them. No football coupons were allowed to be despatched to the general public through the postal services. Pools were NOT themselves being made illegal, just the wasteful use of the postal services. If ways could be devised to by-pass the Post Office, at least for the enormous outgoing mails, then the Pools could continue.

The quandary was quickly and cleverly resolved. Simply by buying sufficient space to reproduce the coupon as a paid advertisement in the popular newspapers of the National Press, the whole distribution problem was solved. Every household took one or other paper. All the punter was required to do was to cut out the coupon, fill it in, find an envelope and post it back to the company. This solution was welcomed by Government, for it was easy to handle, very profitable – through the sale of postage stamps and poundage on postal orders – and was in no way labour intensive. Furthermore, as no coupons needed to be printed, there was a huge saving of paper.

One problem, however, still remained. There were seven major Pools companies: Littlewoods, Vernons, Shermans, Copes, Murphy's, Bonds and Strangs. The smaller, war-time newspapers just didn't have the space to accommodate all that advertising. So 'Unity' Pools was born: an agreement to amalgamate the seven companies under one title with appropriate shares to each, for the duration of the war, was concluded. Littlewoods, assisted by Vernons, ran the show. All the others sat back, did nothing, and laughed all the way to the bank. Great if you were in the club but disaster if you were not. Syd Zetter was not. It looked like 'curtains' for Zetters Pools and all the other little Pools companies. I think they all packed up . . . except for Syd Zetter, for whom there had to be a way.

Solly Littlestone was my father's accountant. A gentle man, an indifferent accountant, but a wise and committed friend. Solly and my father were at their wits' end. Here was this lovely little business, six years old and having survived all the start-up problems of an unknown, underfinanced company, at last getting on its feet and making a fair profit, then along comes this bloody war to put the kybosh on it. How unfair, how totally unreasonable. Well, it was not to be.

Solly was also the accountant for a small newspaper, specialising in sport, called the *Sporting World*. The two brothers who ran it, Phil and Maurice Wolff, were about to be called to the Colours and were desperately concerned that their newspaper would vanish from the street and its title be lost forever.

So a plot was hatched. My father would take it over and publish it every week until the end of the war when it would be handed back to the Wolff brothers. For the duration of the war, Zetter's coupon would appear as a paid advertisement in the paper. However, the circulation of the *Sporting World* was negligible and was not normally bought by any Zetters Pools client. The Order in Council only prohibited the use of the mail services for the posting of Pools coupons. It did NOT prohibit the posting of newspapers. So every week a free copy of the *Sporting World* was sent through the post to every Zetters client. The fact that it contained an advertisement which enabled the punter to complete his pool bet, did not offend the law. It worked a treat. Zetters continued right through the war with a coupon based on regional football games. Unity Pools thrived and so did Zetters and so did the *Sporting World*. I was, and am, inordinately proud of this episode in the history of the Company. It is, of course, splendid to record that both the Wolff brothers survived the war and in 1947 the *Sporting World* was handed back to them. It staggered along under their stewardship for a short time, but eventually disappeared from the bookstands.

(That is the story of events as described to me by my father. I cannot vouch for their complete accuracy, but I do know that 'Unity' Pools ran throughout the remaining years of the war.)

Back in Marlborough the first war-time Christmas was nearly upon us. The school broke up and Louis and George went home to their parents in London.

The Zetters and Stodels were, of course, comfortably settled in their Marlborough home in George Lane and, like the magnet that Christmas was to our families, down to Wiltshire they all came. Or at least many of them. It was going to take a lot more than the bloody war to stop our annual festivities. And it all happened. The turkey and the pudding. The fruits and nuts. The crackers and decorations. Frank Heard played the piano and Lou Stodel sang 'O Sole Mio'. It was all so nearly normal.

But there was a war on and some six thousand miles away, in the South Atlantic, the first major incident of the war at sea was being enacted.

A powerful German pocket-battleship, the *Graf Spee*, had been operating in those southern seas and causing heavy losses to British merchant ships. Three small British cruisers, *Achilles*, *Ajax* and *Exeter* had, by quite brilliant anticipation, intercepted the *Graf Spee*. Although seriously outgunned, they had caused her sufficient damage to make her break off the action and flee to Montevideo, a neutral port on the River Plate in Uruguay, for urgent repairs.

The news was electrifying. War at Sea! A clash between the British Navy, reputedly the most powerful naval force the world had ever seen, and the mighty German battleship, said to be capable of outgunning any ship afloat. The BBC gave us running commentaries on the action and the whole Zetter household – and, probably, the whole nation – were glued to their wireless sets. Blow-by-blow accounts were delivered as at a sporting event and I suspect this might well have been the first time civilian populations were given itemised news of war actions as they were happening.

Well, we'd all heard how three brave little ships had outwitted the vastly superior enemy vessel and made it break off and run. The *Exeter* had been seriously damaged and put out of action. The *Achilles* and *Ajax* were also damaged, but were still capable of bringing their guns to bear. They chased their enemy into neutral waters and laid siege just outside the three mile territorial limit. All this was going on during the run up to Christmas and was the dominant topic at home. We had more naval strategists in George Lane than there were at the Admiralty. The sense of involvement created by the BBC was the foretaste of future broadcasting. The Captain of the *Graf Spee*, Captain Langsdorff, had become an instant, 'villainous' celebrity. He had a difficult decision. He was well aware that under international law he had just forty-eight hours of sanctuary after which he, his crew and his ship would be interned or forced to set sail. What would he do? Come out and join battle – and the odds were still on his side – or end his war in the comfort of a friendly neutral country? Bets were laid. Tactics were debated. We all had our theories and the war became very exciting.

In the event, he transferred most of his crew to a German merchant ship, sailed the *Graf Spee* out into comparatively deep waters clear of the shipping lanes and scuttled her. He then left a patriotic suicide note addressed to his Führer and shot himself. Oddly enough, there was a feeling of frustration by the general public, but really the outcome could hardly have been better. The pride of the German Navy lay at the bottom of the sea and no further British lives had been lost. First blood to us. It's somehow bizarre to recall the warm feeling we all felt at having satisfactorily concluded that episode. 'Now we can really enjoy our Christmas,' we all said to ourselves.

# Chapter 6

# Back to the Smoke

During those Christmas holidays I had been invited to spend a few days with Louis in London. They had their posh hotel in Queensboro' Terrace, Bayswater and Louis and I shared a magnificent bedroom which even had its own bathroom adjoining. That was a blissful time. We ate colossal meals in a huge kitchen – breakfast, lunch, tea and dinner with portions to satisfy the appetite of a giant. We lazed around most mornings. Went prostitute spotting in Shepherds Market after lunch. Went to the pictures in the afternoon and then again most evenings. One evening my father collected us and took us to the Hackney Empire. Monsewer Eddie Grey was performing and I still think he was the funniest man I ever saw. Another treat was a visit to Lyons Corner House at Marble Arch. This glorious palace of eating, midst untold luxury, was one of several such establishments which thrived before, during, but not after, the war. (They somehow lost their way in the post-war years.) Our visit was memorable and I can recall my intense pride at being among all those 'toffs'. (In reality they catered for the upper working- or lower middle-class masses and did it superbly well.)

The prospect of returning to Marlborough was not welcoming: that quiet, dreary little town with nothing to offer but schoolwork and dreaded exams. It was the spring term of 1940 and the 'phoney war', as it so absurdly had become known, was at its height, by which I mean nothing was happening anywhere. Poland had been brutally and swiftly overrun by the Germans and the Russians, Hitler getting the lion's share. The memory of our famous victory at sea had soon faded. No other shots were being fired in anger and it was truly 'all quiet on the western front'. How dull! We had been in

Marlborough for over six months and I was getting fed up with it. I was also deeply concerned about my obvious inability to cope with my studies.

I was poor at every subject with the possible exception of maths. School Certificate was hanging over our heads like the sword of Damocles and I knew I hadn't a ghost of a chance of achieving a satisfactory result. I lucidly debated with myself the value of this doubtful diploma. I was aware, of course, that it was the principal purpose of all those years at school. Nevertheless, I won the argument. It would be of no possible use to me even if I were lucky enough to get it. I really don't know, all these years later, whether I was right, but I don't think I was. I think it was my first important mistake. Anyway, having convinced myself, I then set about convincing my parents. It was like pushing against an open door. The prospect of returning home was so joyful, so overwhelming, that they agreed with alacrity. London, their beloved London, beckoned.

All over England families who had so recently evacuated in fear were now streaming back. After all, the war was benign, wasn't it? The prophets of doom were wrong, weren't they? Eight months of conflict and no bombs had dropped on our precious England. The Jerries had sorted out their Polish problems and peace talks were in the air. The French sat in their Maginot Line and the only missiles they were hurling were *petanque* balls. London was by now a boom town. Other than the black-out, you'd hardly know there was a war on. No shortages existed. There was plenty of everything. No perceivable rationing had been introduced. Everyone had pockets full of money and was spending it. The theatres were playing to packed houses. Cinemas were showing the latest Hollywood epics. *Gone with the Wind* was playing in Leicester Square and there were queues for seats for every performance. So the Zetters were going home. The decision made, my father's organising ability readily coped with the logistics. I was to leave school and go into a job.

One week later I had an interview with Lloyds Bank (my father's bankers) and was hired, starting two weeks later, at £3 10s. per week, at the Head Office in Lombard Street. Remember, that was for a boy not yet seventeen years old and with no qualifications. Well, there was a war on wasn't there? Young men were flocking to the Colours and vacancies existed everywhere. What else had to be done? Well, apparently, the lease we'd held on 133 Grove Road had gone so we had to rehouse. As a temporary measure, we all moved in with Auntie Clara and Uncle Jack. Auntie Clara lived in a large house in Cassland Road on the edge of Victoria Park in the East End of London. I imagine she must have had lodgers who had moved away as three bedrooms were available to the returned evacuees: me, my mother and father, Grandma and Daddy Dick. In the event, our stay there was to be of very short duration. Clara was the eldest and undoubtedly the most controversial member of the Stodel family. Dear, dull, meek, middle-aged Clara was controversial? How could this possibly be? Simple. She'd married a Catholic! Not just a *yok* (may the good Lord forgive her) but a Catholic already! It says something for the human spirit (and indeed for animal magnetism) that this timid little lady could defy the pressures of a fervent Jewish household and marry the man of her choice. And yet, on reflection, the history of the Stodel family was diverse and extraordinary. Of the nine children, Clara had wed her Catholic; Jane had wed her Aussie (Uncle Joe). Annie (who I never knew very well), married a merchant seaman, of all things. I don't think he was a Catholic, but they produced countless children until he was lost at sea and presumed dead. Millie, Sophie and my mother married nice Jewish boys and Tommy had married fat Aunt Leah. Straight out of the Old Testament she was. Sweet old Lou Stodel found his comfort with his ex-butler friend Frank Heard, and the other son had died unmarried. I cannot believe theirs was the normal pattern of family behaviour for those days. I am sure it must have stemmed from old Sarah Stodel's background, but I don't know it and neither can I find any reliable information.

Anyway, back to our plans to return to London. One desperately unhappy consequence of leaving Marlborough was the break with Louis. I didn't mind too much about George, but I was very worried I might lose track of my best friend. In fact I did, almost. It wasn't until 1947 that we resumed our friendship.

Leaving school turned out to be a little sadder than I had anticipated; I said my farewells to all the masters who had had the misfortune to teach me. I suppose they looked at this teenager and knew that it would not be very long before he wore a uniform. Leaving my friends was also rather sad and was marred by an unhappy event. It was Sunday and Mrs Brisacher had been driven down to Marlborough by Curly Smith. He was her manager, driver, handyman, general factotum and nephew-in-law. She dominated him as she dominated everyone, but he was of immense value to her after the loss of her husband and he certainly benefited very handsomely from the association. (Curly stayed with Louis long after the death of Mrs B. He now spends a happy retirement, sunning himself in Barbados.) The arrangement had been made for me and my father, whose car was off the road, to be given a lift back to London by them, as I was to start my new job at Lloyds Bank the following morning. My mother and the old people were to stay in Marlborough until Louis and George could be rehoused.

Mrs B. took a party of us boys to lunch and my parents had elicited a promise for us not to be late. After all, it was winter, the days were short, the roads bad and I was starting my new career the next day. Clearly, I needed to be in London in plenty of time for a good night's rest. In the event, Mrs B's lunch lasted an eternity and was then followed by a grand tour of the town with visits and extended conversations with all traceable masters. I could feel the tension mounting in Louis and he knew the same was true of me. Our return, in the dusk, to George Lane was fraught. My mother was pale and tight-lipped. My father was lucid in his condemnation of her total lack of consideration. A major row resulted. She had clearly wanted to show her disapproval of my leaving school and leaving Louis in the lurch. This was the way she chose to do it. My parents were absurd in their reaction. Louis and I were the sufferers. He spent the last days with my mother most unhappily. I was deeply distressed at the unnecessary stupidity of adults. I didn't see Louis (or Mrs Brisacher) again for seven years.

Chapter 7

# The Blitz

London was lovely. My job at the Bank was wholly undemanding and great fun. I was on the 'Walks'. It simply meant walking around to a number of fringe banks in the City and collecting from them, each day, the cheques which they wanted specially cleared. I then listed them, struck a balance and passed them through for clearing. It was so easy, a child could have done it, but it did give me a wonderful opportunity of exploring the Square Mile with its fascinating alleyways and narrow streets. I loved finding new routes between banks and became quite expert at it. The street names were so emotive they stirred within me a pride of London . . . King William Street . . . Cheapside . . . London Wall . . . St. Swithin's Lane . . . Milk Street where in 1666 the first great fire of London started and Pudding Lane where a monument was erected to mark where it finished. I was to come to know those places and many more in the next eighteen months which I spent at the Bank. Before long my father brought my mother and the old people home from Marlborough and we settled in with Auntie Clara. My father seemed pleased enough with the Pools business and the success of his newspaper the *Sporting World*. I loved life at the Bank. I was beginning to meet girls and discovering what they were for. Spring of 1940 was in the air and all seemed right with the world.

Then Hitler invaded Norway. Within days of Chamberlain saying that 'Hitler had missed the bus' Nazi hordes had invaded Norway. It was a master stroke, carried out brilliantly and efficiently. The British managed to get a task force together and under the protection of the Navy, we effected a landing at a place called Narvik in the far north of Norway.

It was too little, too late, of course. Oh, there were some spectacular naval exchanges. Outrageous claims were made of the heavy losses we were inflicting on the enemy. In spite of our obvious propaganda, we were furious that Germany had managed to occupy that long strategic seaboard and so pose a threat to our North Sea and the Northern Atlantic approaches. We all believed that Hitler had won a spectacular victory.

Our judgement was almost certainly too critical and probably wrong. There were major consequences which were to have untold benefit to our war effort. Firstly, the Norwegian nation boasted a huge merchant fleet. Most of their ships were at sea during the invasion of their beloved country. Without exception, every single vessel opted to join the British Merchant Navy and pursue the war against the hated Germans. Secondly, very serious losses were, indeed, inflicted on German naval forces. As a result, later that year, Hitler was unable to transport the Panzer divisions across the Channel to invade England. Finally, it led to the defeat of Neville Chamberlain in the House of Commons and the appointment of a new Prime Minister . . . Winston Spencer Churchill.

The 'Phoney War' was over. Within weeks Germany was to prove the massive power of her armed forces.

Holland, neutral Holland, which had even avoided involvement in the First World War, was overrun by German forces. Belgium very quickly followed. The 'Glorious Defeat' at Dunkirk and the fall of France taught us the real meaning of *Blitzkrieg*. So we were all alone. Only the British on their little island stood between Hitler and European, if not world, domination. And yet, none of us seemed too disturbed at all these disastrous events. There was an excitement in the air. After all, the nucleus of the British Army, having been successfully evacuated from Dunkirk, was intact. The Navy had acquitted itself as Britain expects. And the RAF? Well, we were yet to see, but our confidence was beyond belief. We had, of course, begun to realise what the war was all about. My strongest memory of those turbulent days was of rumours of the imminent invasion. None of us took them seriously. Nobody really believed the Krauts were going to be so stupid as to try a landing in Kent. It was a joke. We almost wanted them to have a go. They never did.

The summer was lovely. I was enjoying myself at the Bank. We were comfortably settled with Auntie Clara and everything seemed to be returning to normal again after all the excitement. On 9 July, I was seventeen years old and life was sweet.

On 10 July the Battle of Britain began. Not very dramatically at first. Actually, all we knew of it in London was what we heard on the BBC news bulletins every evening. 'German aircraft attacked an RAF airfield in Southern England. Spitfires and Hurricanes of Fighter Command engaged the attackers. Twenty-seven enemy planes were shot down for the loss of eight of ours.' The next day similar bulletins were issued ending with the tally . . . 54 of theirs down to 17 of ours. And so it went on, day after day, with ever-increasing losses to both sides, but always 3 to 1 in our favour. The excitement mounted . . . realisation dawned . . . this was *the* battle. Just as H.G. Wells had predicted in *Things to Come*, a war in the air was actually happening. To be given the daily score was like taking down the football results with your side winning every time. In fact, we were betting on the numbers at the Bank and the news broadcasts never had more listeners. The stories of the 'dog fights' over Kent and Sussex were on everyone's lips. People were taking the train down to the south coast to watch the vapour trails high in the sky. Broadcasts of the air battles, as they were being fought, raised the emotions to a fever pitch and we knew, we really knew, the outcome would decide the war. And we were winning! Day after day it went on, throughout July and into August. Rumours abounded. 25 August was going to be Invasion Day; that was the odds-on favourite. I bet half-a-crown to three bob against, and took a girl out for a drink with my winnings.

London was still untouched. The raids were still concentrated on our airfields and the sound of war was still unheard in the capital. On Saturday 7 September, the latest Hollywood epic, *Confessions of a Nazi Spy*, was showing locally. Edward G. Robinson was the star and although the cinema, the South it was called, was a real flea-pit, it was only five minutes walk from home, so we went. My father was busy so I took my mother, grandmother and Auntie Clara. It was a great film. The first half anyway. We'd just got to the part where the democracy-loving Americans were clobbering the nasty Nazis who had infiltrated high places, when the siren went. I never knew how the film ended. A message was projected onto the screen telling us that the air raid sirens had sounded and advising us to leave the cinema 'in an orderly fashion'. We did. On our walk home we met my father scurrying to meet us.

In our small garden, an air raid shelter had been erected. I don't think I'd even noticed it before, but I did now. It was an Anderson shelter, a corrugated iron construction named after Sir John Anderson, the Minister for Home Security. The thing was half buried with the spare earth spread over the top of it. It uncomfortably seated about eight persons, four each side and proved to be surprisingly effective against all but a direct hit. Anyway, we all got into it, my mother, my father, the old people: Sarah,

Daddy Dick, Auntie Clara and Uncle Jack, and me. We heard our first bangs. Nobody knew if they were bombs or guns, but as they seemed a long way off it didn't matter too much. After about an hour the 'all clear' sounded. We all trooped out and, by common consent, through to the street outside. It was thronged with people all agog and gazing skywards. There were vapour trials in the clear blue skies and the outline of a descending parachute.

At that time, I was a member of the newly formed Local Defence Volunteers, later to become known as the Home Guard, and much later, immortalised as 'Dad's Army'. I had been issued with an old rifle, a first World War .303 Lee Enfield. So I dashed in for it and was prepared to do battle. The fact that the poor fellow was at least 5,000 feet above us drifting swiftly out of range and was probably one of ours and, in any case, I didn't have any ammunition, was all gently pointed out to me by my father. There was a feeling of euphoria in the air: 'Seen the buggers off,' was the generally expressed view. But my normally optimistic father didn't seem to share it. That night we discovered why. We'd all gone to bed fairly early. I was in a deep sleep when my father woke me. The sirens were sounding and we all trooped down to the shelter. It was dark, the weather was mild, but we were shivering a little. We heard what my father identified as gunfire in the distance. It got nearer and then we heard a sound to which we were going to become very accustomed. The droning, throbbing sound of heavy aircraft . . . German bombers. Their bombs had simple devices attached to their vanes which caused a shrill whistling noise as they fell. It really was very scary. You heard first the whistle and then the explosion . . . there were a lot of them that night. The first raid only lasted about an hour. The 'all clear' sounded at about 2 a.m. So we all trooped to the kitchen for the inevitable cup of tea. Almost immediately the sirens sounded again, so back we went to the shelter for about another hour of the same medicine. When that was over my father and I went onto the streets, but this time we saw a very different scene. A factory nearby, Bergers the paint manufacturers, was ablaze. Fire engines and ambulances were screeching their way in all directions. A house a hundred yards or so down the road had been demolished and the war had come to London.

At 6.35 a.m. that morning I was astonished to be woken by my father. 'Come on, son, it's Monday, time to get up and go to work.'

'After a night like that?' I most querulously replied.

'I'm afraid there's going to be a lot of nights like that,' he said.

God, how right he was. The No. 8 bus ride to the Bank that day was epic. Packed as usual, of course, and the stories! Everybody had a more hair-raising tale to tell. Our route was circuitous to say the least, for there was terrible damage everywhere. Collapsed buildings blocked many roads. Fire hoses snaked over many others. Craters needed negotiating and it was amusing to hear an argument between helpful passengers directing the bus driver as to his best diversion. The Bank was buzzing with chatter. We all vied with each other to claim the most horrific experience. Fortunately, the work ethic eventually asserted itself as it was to do for the remainder of the war.

Anyway, it appeared that the East End had suffered the brunt of the night's raids and that turned out to be the pattern that was to ensue. We spent every night, for the next week or so, in the shelter listening to the whistles and bangs. One night, we'd taken a portable wireless in with us and rather foolishly tuned-in to a German station broadcasting in English. It was Lord Haw Haw, as he had become known because of his upper class singsong intonation. Lord Haw Haw was an Englishman. His name was William Joyce and he was an ardent supporter of Adolf Hitler. He served the Nazis throughout the war with his propaganda broadcasts to the British Isles. His message to us that night is worth recalling. There we were, sitting huddled, tired and frightened in our air raid shelter. This is, roughly, what he said: 'Fellow Englishmen sitting huddled, tired and frightened in your air raid shelters. I know you're there. You were there last night and the night before and you're going to be there tomorrow night and the night after and next week and next month and so on and so on. The German bombers have you at their mercy. And why? Because the Jew-lover Churchill refuses to make peace.' He failed to damage morale. Instead, he made us angry, a much healthier reaction than intended. I did actually wonder if Churchill really was a Jew-lover and found the prospect rather pleasing.

It was clear that life style would once more have to change. The Government urged those who could leave London to do so. Our first very temporary move was to Auntie Millie. Millie Green was my mother's sister, the youngest member of the Stodel family. She was married to Syd Green, a kindly man, and they had one son, my cousin Tony. They lived in Hendon, which was a green and pleasant suburb, largely populated by British Jews on their way up the financial ladder. Situated as it was, north of London, it was, and ironically remained, comparatively unscathed by the Blitz. The attacking aircraft came over the south and east; they dropped their bombs in those suburbs, with the braver elements of the Luftwaffe penetrating to central areas. Few flew beyond and, indeed, had no need to. We slept on the floor and settees for a few nights, the old people taking the only spare room.

My father, in the meantime, had found a flat for us in Aylesbury, Bucks.

Far enough away to escape the onslaught, but near enough to commute. He was still using his car. Petrol was rationed by then, but not too severely, so one way or another we managed to get to work every day.

Conditions at the Bank were changing. The vaults were turned into dormitories for those who couldn't travel. It was apparent that much of the damage being caused was as the result of small incendiary bombs setting fire to the buildings on which they fell, so a fire patrol was instituted. All staff, male and female, senior and lowly junior, were required to take turns on a night duty roster. For approximately one night a week, we became night watchmen on the large roof of Lloyds Bank, Lombard Street. We soon learned that the roster could be so manipulated as to produce a desirable companion to share the duty. As a consequence, those nights on the tiles transformed what would otherwise have been an onerous task into a labour of love.

It is extraordinary to recall the titillation which the Blitz induced. Debate was the order of the day. 'Experts' on air warfare abounded. Their opinions enlivened the times. There was, for example, a strongly held view that one could identify the nationality of the aircraft overhead by the sound they made. Quite heated arguments developed on whether it was one of theirs or one of ours. Even the Government joined the dispute. An Air Chief Marshal broadcast a message to the nation telling us that he, with all his vast experience, could not tell the difference between friend and foe simply by the noise of their engines. As for me, I could never quite understand the controversy . . . if it dropped a bomb I reckoned it was one of theirs! The raids continued unabated throughout that beautiful autumn. The weather was perfect and seemed to be on Hitler's side. We almost felt ashamed to be out of it all in our Aylesbury retreat, so my father and I joined the local LDV (it still wasn't called the Home Guard). We were on duty one night patrolling the blacked-out streets of that respectable little Buckinghamshire town. It was mid-November and a fine frosty night with not a breath of wind. As we trudged on our way, we could hear the heavy bombers flying overhead. It was almost eerie and most definitely frightening. They seemed to take an eternity to pass over. Then, after a while, we heard them again. 'Someone's caught it,' said my father. 'They are on their way home now.' The next morning we heard the news. Coventry had almost been wiped out.

Our daily journey to and from London was getting tedious. It was also more and more difficult to get sufficient petrol. The flat in Aylesbury was very cramped for all of us and it became clear that another move was imminent. London, for all its dangers, still acted as a magnet on the family and, particularly, me. I reminded my father of our short stay with Auntie

Millie in Hendon. Noisy maybe, but they still weren't being bombed. Couldn't we start looking for something in the northern suburbs? As it happened, our daily journey took us along the A41 to the North Circular Road, over Hampstead Heath and into London. Hampstead Garden Suburb was *en route* and it was like nothing else I'd ever seen. A beautiful, tree-lined neighbourhood just a few miles from central London with houses that must have rivalled those in Hollywood. Most of them lay empty, their owners having evacuated. Many more were for sale and prices had never been lower. One particular house caught our eye. It was large . . . it stood well back from the main road . . . it had a good garden . . . it was about five years old, in perfect condition, and it was cheap, as I recall, around £2,500. We moved into 20 Lyttelton Road, London N.2. before Christmas 1940. It really was a splendid house with six bedrooms and bathrooms galore. Enough, in fact, to house other family members seeking respite from the pounding they were getting in the East End. Nat and Sophie Spiers (née Stodel), with their nineteen-year-old daughter Sadie moved in. She oozed sex appeal, did Sadie, and golly wasn't I aware of it. It's perhaps fortunate that, after a short stay, she left home to join the Auxilliary Territorial Service (the Women's Army).

Life was transformed . . . we had a real home. I had a bedroom to myself, a super room with privacy, space and my own wash-basin with hot and cold running water. From the house, it was a ten minute walk to East Finchley tube station on the Northern Line. Just eleven stops to The Bank and, from there, one minute to Lombard Street.

It's true the raids went on almost every night, but we really ignored them unless they became too heated. My father had installed another type of air raid shelter. This was an indoor, all metal construction about 8' × 8' and standing roughly 3' high. It was called a Morrison Shelter after a famous Socialist politician, Herbert Morrison. He was a real 'lefty' but, nonetheless, the Home Secretary in Churchill's Coalition Government. (Party politics really didn't exist during that stage of the war.) We used it occasionally. Several people could crawl between its steel layers and it was quite cosy, depending on the company. Fortunately, we were never called upon to test it for its effectiveness against bombing. There were no air raids on Christmas Day 1940. We knew there wouldn't be and there weren't. The Zetters had a party of course. It wasn't quite like old times, but we made a brave effort and we enjoyed it.

1940 ended with a bang. Or more accurately with fire. On New Year's Eve, the second 'Fire of London' was ignited. The Germans had discovered that incendiary bombs were causing far more damage than high explosives so the pattern of bombing changed. I was still doing my weekly fire watch stint at Lloyds Bank. That evening the sirens sounded quite early, about 8 p.m. I think. It was the start of the big fire raid that wiped out a considerable part of the central city area of London, particularly around the Bank, Moorgate and London Wall. I don't know how many of us were on duty that night, but I do know we put out dozens of bombs with our little stirrup pumps. The flames from buildings all around lit up the whole sky and you could actually feel the heat of them. I do believe that, between us, we saved the Bank's building. Had similar patrols been in places elsewhere, the damage would have been substantially less. The raid was over by about 11 p.m. but the destruction was the greatest we suffered of any single raid during the war. The area wasn't rebuilt until the 'sixties', when it became known as The Barbican.

A few weeks later a frightful blow befell us. The business was flourishing. It's astonishing, but war, bombing, black-outs, shortages, none of them affected the Pools business. Every week the coupons were delivered by the Post Office. Football was played, winners were paid and life went on. The operation had expanded and was now situated in smart little self-contained offices in Newington Causeway. We were all to blame for what happened, of course. We should have learned the lesson of the 'big fire' and had a night watchman. The building was obliterated. Nothing was left. Not a single item remained and there, in the middle of that smouldering cavity that had been a two storey office block, was the nose cone of an anti-aircraft shell. My father looked at it, said, 'I hope it brought down the bugger who did this,' and kept it as a paperweight. I have it on my desk to this day. Good luck always rode alongside my father. The building was destroyed on a Saturday night, but Saturday's coupons had already been checked. The winning coupons had been taken home to deal with during Sunday. The following Saturday's mail had been despatched and staked coupons wouldn't start coming in until at least Tuesday. Zetters were still in business. Certainly, enormous logistical problems remained, but we were able to continue without even one week's interruption. In fact, within weeks, my father had taken a suite of offices above Beales, the bakers, in Holloway Road. There he remained until the end of the war.

I was eighteen years old in July 1941. I don't think a birthday was ever more solemnly greeted by any parents anywhere. I could join the Colours. 'What's the hurry?' my mother wanted to know. 'Can't they manage without you?' 'You're going to make the difference?' 'So now we're going to win?' And so on and so on. All from my mother, noisily supported by my grandmother of course. My father never said a word . . . he knew. He was distressed, but he knew I was going to join up. By the middle of August I had won the argument and by the end of the month I took the decisive step.

During one lunch hour, I made my way from the Bank, along Moorgate to the City Road where a recruiting office was situated. Not any old recruiting office, mark you, but one which I had long since earmarked as the place where I was going to join the army. It was a castle. Truly it was, and still is, a little castle. In fact, it is a most attractive castellated stone structure, being the headquarters of the Honourable Artillery Company. Throughout the war it remained open for the signing-on of young men and women to serve King and Country. There was quite a queue in front of me and it was some time before I reached a sergeant sitting at a scruffy desk. My interview was brief and to the point. I requested a posting into the Tank Corps.

'Why tanks?' he asked.

'I'm small,' I replied, 'and I'd rather drive into battle than march.'

He ignored my weak attempt at witticism. 'You'll get a letter calling you for your medical,' he growled. 'Next.'

So I went back to the Bank, only to be reprimanded for returning late from lunch.

'Don't you know there's a war on?' grumbled my department manager. 'God, I don't know what the young are coming to these days,' he complained aloud, to no one in particular.

It's a long, long time from August to September when you're very young but, eventually, the letter arrived. 'Report for medical examination 14.00 hrs Monday 23rd September 1941 H.A.C. Barracks, City Road, Islington. Allow 2 hrs.' Well, having enquired what '14.00 hrs' meant, I then had to see my manager to get the afternoon off.

'Good God, boy,' he said. 'You know bloody well it's monthly audit day and we're short staffed. Well, be back in the office by 4.30.' As he walked away he looked up at the ceiling and appealed to his maker. 'Don't the youth of today have any consideration?'

The medical was precisely as described in countless films and novels. Even to the 'coughing' test, which I found most unpleasant. It was the first time anyone had ever touched them. One gets used to it as the years go by! Anyway, it seemed that I was A1 and the waiting game started once more. The war had entered an entirely new phase by now. Hitler had invaded Russia (June 1941) and, while his early successes were spectacular, we all had the feeling that this time he'd bitten off more than he could chew. Everyone was quite absurdly optimistic. The bombing had stopped . . . clearly the Luftwaffe had moved east! Rudolph Hess, Hitler's deputy, had flown to Scotland and given himself up. And even if the Russians couldn't stop the German army, the Russian winter most certainly would. It was against this background that I impatiently awaited my call-up papers. I was terrified it would all be over before I could get into uniform. This was the autumn of 1941.

# Chapter 8

# Khaki Career

In November it came. 'Report to The 58th Training Regiment, RAC, Bovington Camp, Wareham, Dorset.' The Royal Armoured Corps! What joy! What bliss! What a marvellous chap that recruiting sergeant had been! He had actually listened to me after all and granted my most fervent wish. On the great day my parents took me to Waterloo. Even their distress (my father actually cried) could not diminish my excitement. Arriving in Wareham wasn't quite as welcoming as I'd expected, but there was a real 15 cwt. army truck waiting to pick up the fairly obvious group of young hopefuls who'd got off the train. We were driven to Bovington Camp, given a meal, issued with four blankets each, put into a Nissen hut and told to go to bed.

At 6 a.m. the next morning we were rudely awakened. After a good breakfast the first day began. It started with the issue of our pay books. In reality, this was our identity document, a kind of passport known as PB64 which was to stay with us throughout our army life. It contained brief personal details, a form of last will and testament and our army number. Once issued, never changed and never forgotten. Mine was 7948797. Our next stop was the MO where we were injected, vaccinated, re-examined and given a dental inspection from which most poor lads did not emerge unscathed. Finally, to the barber where 'short back and sides' took on an entirely new meaning. At last we were kitted out. This was immensely exciting and we were all like little boys with new toys. However, an additional and somewhat sobering item was given to us: a cardboard box in which we were told to put every stitch of civilian clothing. The boxes were to be addressed to our homes and handed in to the post room for despatch. The final contact with civilian life was thus severed.

All our new gear had to be marked or stamped with our army number, including two identity discs which were to be hung around our necks on a length of cord (I still have them). The rest of the day we were to spend cleaning, blancoing and polishing our beautiful new things in preparation for an inspection on the morrow. No group ever set about this task with more keenness, energy and enthusiasm, than did those young volunteer recruits. The next day, no group had ever been more maligned and castigated for 'lack of effort'. This absurd policy of denigration became more and more apparent during our 'stretch' in Bovington.

The next six months were a nightmare. I couldn't believe such harsh, unbending treatment of dedicated volunteers was either sensible or neces-sary. Having said that, the training was brilliant. Of course, they had time. Our war was only taking place on one front . . . Egypt/Libya. And the Eighth Army were more than holding their own. So time was on the side of the British forces. Men could be trained and prepared for war without the need to hold a front line and, in the meantime, the Germans were being really stretched in Russia.

Our programme was so comprehensive. In six short months, I learned to drill and to fire a pistol, rifle, machine gun, anti-tank gun and tank gun. I could throw a hand grenade. I could drive anything from a motor-bike to a two-ton lorry or forty-ton tank. I could send and receive morse code (at which I proved to be exceedingly adept), read a map, cook, sew and find my way through a mine field! Which, metaphorically, describes Bovington precisely. If you survived six months in Bovington without a serious blemish on your military character, you were either very clever, very lucky or were a fancy boy for one of the establishment and so enjoyed protection. I nearly fell at the last fence. On the morning of the long-awaited 'passing out' day there was to be a kit inspection. The Commanding Officer, aided and abetted by the Adjutant, the Regimental Sergeant Major, our own sergeant and his corporals were to inspect our kit. I, along with my colleagues, thought it would be a comparatively routine affair, simply to check that all items were properly marked with our army number. We could not have been more wrong. There were about thirty of us and we had all received a posting to our respective field regiments. The object of the inspection was to ensure that we were despatched to our destinations with the complete regulation issue. Woe betide the soldier found to be in the least deficient.

Between leaving Bovington and reporting to our new unit, we were due to receive seven days privilege leave. Seven whole days of sheer heaven after six long months of sheer hell. As soon as the inspection started, this glorious prospect was clearly seen to be in dreadful jeopardy. Of the first rank of ten men inspected, six of them were put on a charge for 'losing army equipment', namely, a needle missing from the hussif ('housewife' – the name given to the sewing repair kit) . . . a button missing from a khaki shirt . . . a stud missing from the sole of a boot, etc., etc. These grave offences would undoubtedly mean not only the loss of leave, but a black mark indelibly stamped onto your army record. We couldn't believe what was happening to us. The second and third ranks waited in an agony of suspense and trepidation and with just cause for, in their turn, the second rank were decimated. It was getting worse, if anything, for they were made to remove their battle dress blouses and shirts to reveal army issue underwear. One poor devil wore a civilian vest . . . I don't think he was ever heard of again! I was the last man in the third rank (we were in alphabetical order). I trembled for I only had two pairs of socks instead of the regulation three pairs. Two pairs were on display all right, but the third pair had been nicked. Then it came. The order I had dreaded. 'Rear rank, boots off!' screamed the RSM and slowly and surely that fearful inspection team moved inevitably towards me standing there in my bare feet. Now I shall never know what moved our troop sergeant to act as he did. It may have been to save his own skin, but I like to think he was a kindly man whom I had impressed with my enthusiasm during training. Anyway, he stood as best he could shielding me from the approaching enemy and whispered to the soldier in the second rank, who had already been inspected, to chuck me a pair of his socks. What a risk we took, all three of us, but most particularly the sergeant. He, honestly, would have lost his stripes and God knows what would have happened to me.

That afternoon I caught a train to London for my first seven day leave. After a blissful week at home I reported to my new unit. Brigade Headquarters, 11th Armoured Division, Rottingdean, Sussex. This was the real army. Tough and efficient . . . and the mindless 'bullshit' of our training regiment soon became a thing of the past. We were equipped with Centaurs, our newest tanks, boasting 25-pounder guns capable of matching anything Jerry could put against us. At least, that was the confident claim of our officers. Confidence, in fact, was the order of the day. The war really had turned in our favour. Pearl Harbour had happened while I was in Bovington and the Yanks were now in the war. Russia was, indeed, crippling the German Army, while the British 8th Army in Egypt were building an invincible force under the direction of a new commander, General Montgomery.

We couldn't wait to test ourselves in battle. I had only been with the 11th for two weeks when I joined a tank crew as wireless operator. I was warmly accepted and enjoyed the field training. We were ready for anything and eager to go. Then I caught impetigo! After just a couple of months with this crack unit, I was *hors de combat* with this horrible complaint. Impetigo is a ghastly skin disease which, while not serious, is very infectious so I was sent to an isolation hospital in Tunbridge Wells. It took about three weeks to recover (penicillin hadn't yet been discovered).

On the morning of the day of my discharge from hospital, I felt elated at the prospect of returning to Rottingdean. I was very soon deflated by being given a travel warrant to the 51st Training Regiment RAC, Farnborough, Hants. There had to be some mistake. That wasn't my unit. In any case, I was a fully trained soldier, a member of a tank crew and I'd been in the army for eight months. I couldn't go back to a training regiment full of rookies. Oh yes I could, said the army. The 11th Armoured Division were on their way to join the Eighth Army in Egypt. I was on my way to Farnborough to await an onward posting to another field unit. Farnborough was dreadful. To fill in time while the army decided what they were going to do with me, I was put onto a despatch rider's course. That wasn't too bad, but the intolerable return to the 'bullshit brigade', after the relaxed style of a field unit, was almost beyond endurance. I came nearer to serious trouble in Farnborough than in all my five years' service. I was saved by my posting. I was to proceed to the First Battalion, The Royal Gloucestershire Hussars, Ogbourne St. George, near Marlborough, Wiltshire. I couldn't believe it. Near Marlborough! Near the City of London School! I wondered how many friends were still there. It seemed an eternity ago since I'd left, but it was only a couple of years. I determined to pay a visit at the first opportunity. The Royal Gloucestershire Hussars. Golly, didn't it sound swell? It really was, too! A real county regiment if ever there was one and a new experience awaited me.

I'd suffered the persecution of my first training regiment. I'd thrilled at the professionalism of the 11th Armoured. I'd felt doomed on my return to the other training regiment. Now I came across the Colonel Blimp army. It was a joke. It out-spoofed any Ealing comedy. Fred Karno would have loved it. The officers were mostly large landowners and gentlemen farmers, all vastly experienced at riding to hounds and the 'blasted war' wasn't going to stop them. The sergeants tended to be from the racing fraternity. The tanks were generally accepted to be a confounded nuisance. Far too noisy and caused too much damage to fields and hedgerows to be used too often. Everyone was absolutely charming. Discipline was non-existent. I had arrived at my Alma Mater. It really was like being welcomed into a new school or university. The Commanding Officer, Colonel the Lord Leigh of Ashford, welcomed me to the Regiment and 'hoped I would be truly happy with them'. I think it was his normal practice with new arrivals and earned him the nickname of 'Happy Harry'. He asked what I'd like to do and suggested that, perhaps, I would enjoy being a despatch rider. At least, it showed he'd done his homework. 'Anyway, try it,' he said kindly. 'If you're not happy after a few weeks, come and see me and we'll try something else.' I kept him to his word. I didn't like motor-cycling, mainly because I wasn't much good at it. I'd crashed a couple of bikes. I wasn't hurt, but the bikes were written off. Nobody minded, of course, but I was clearly accident-prone on those infernal machines, so I opted for a change. I wasn't too keen to get back into tanks, having found them claustrophobic. However, I had noticed a small group called the reconnaissance troop. They were equipped with the Daimler Scout Car, a wonderful little vehicle. It was fast, it had a straight eight cylinder engine and a fluid fly-wheel. It had preselector gears and could move as fast in reverse as it could go forwards. This, then, was for me and, of course, 'Happy Harry' obliged. Now while it was true that I could operate the radio set and read a map I was, nevertheless, somewhat surprised to be made a car commander right away. I soon learned why. The previous commander had been killed in that very car by that very driver just the previous week. I was the replacement! I couldn't help feeling that maybe Happy Harry wasn't quite as naive as he appeared.

Anyway, I settled in easily enough and, for the first time since I joined up, I began to get to know and like the people around me. There were ten cars in the troop, each with a car commander and a driver. We were split into five pairs, and an NCO (lance corporal or corporal) was in command of each pair of cars. There was one sergeant, Sergeant Bill Boyland, and one officer. Bill Boyland was a great chap, a local Gloucestershire man of course (they all were, the hierarchy!) and one of the few effective leaders in that entire Regiment. Lieutenant Wallace was the officer. 'Nellie' Wallace, as he was of course known, was a true blue. A real aristocrat, if ever there was one and we all of us thought the world of him. Mind you, we did wonder how many officers at that stage of the war kept a pack of beagles on camp and 'followed' them at least once a week. Then there were the junior NCOs and the other ranks, the troopers. I immediately felt relaxed and happy in their company. I was to spend the next two years with the RGH and made good friends, some of whom would last a lifetime.

In Ogbourne St. George, we all lived in Nissen huts. The Recce Troop had two, ten men in each. My companions included a number of interesting

characters with whom I became friendly. There was Owen Bathe . . .
pleasant and bright, about twenty years old and very witty. Then there was
Jack Cartwright . . . clever and scholastic. Jimmy Halliwell . . . upper class
and clearly going places. Frank Judge, a real London cockney . . . older
than the rest of us, he must have been all of thirty (it was said of Frank that
you could trust him with your life, but not with your wife). Johnny Harris, a
Bristol boy . . . ex-Territorial, poetic, socialist, lucid and sensitive to a fault.
John was to become a very close friend. Arthur Askew . . . Arthur was a
frisky youngish Yorkshire lad. He'd joined the army before the start of the
war and claimed to have been at Dunkirk. Probably on a day trip we all
thought. Arthur was the greatest womaniser I have ever met. Finally, Jim
Clarke . . . intelligent, correct, confident and hardworking. The expression
'salt of the earth' might well have been written to describe Jim Clarke. He
will appear more and more throughout these pages.

I was truly happy in the RGH. In spite of all its unbelievable inadequacies
as a fighting force, or maybe because of them, we all loved it. There was an
amazing camaraderie and loyalty. It's hard to believe that one could feel
any pride for such a ragtag and bobtail outfit, but proud we all were. I did,
in fact, make my way to Marlborough to look up my old school. I didn't
come across any boy I had known but a few of the masters recognised me.
They were very kind and one of them, Jimmy Riddle (yes, honestly, that was
his name), took me home to his lodgings for tea. Other than that, the trip
was no success. Everyone looked war-weary and fed up. I was glad to get
back to my army mates and I never repeated the visit.

In the late summer of 1942 the Regiment moved. All of us, the whole
darn shooting match. And what a move . . . from the rolling plains of
Wiltshire in south-west England to the craggy peaks of Northumberland in
the far north-east. Why on earth it was done I do not know, for it was a
huge logistical exercise and must have cost a fortune. Our final destination
was Bamburgh Castle. What a spectacular billet! This imposing edifice
perched high on the cliffs overlooking the North Sea and Holy Island. We,
the recce troop, were actually housed in the castle. The scout cars could
easily negotiate the twisting roadway. There was plenty of room for parking
in the courtyard and they provided a jolly handy taxi service for the Officers
Mess, all of whom were comfortably housed within those solid walls. Mind
you, so were we, and it was by far and away the best billet going.
Altogether, it was glorious up there. The weather was still perfect and the
beaches along that coast are among the best in the British Isles.

We were in the 'advance party' and, a day or so after arriving, an incident
occurred which allowed me to benefit handsomely from this vacation venue.

Captain Wallace, as he had now become, took me aside one morning.

'Trooper Zetter,' he said, 'The CO has given us a job to do. We are to reconnoitre the surrounding countryside and submit a list of all the bridges in our operational zone, giving their weight-bearing capacity. We need that information, you know, otherwise our armour is immobilised. What?'

'Yes sir,' I said, feeling sure there was more to come. He didn't react so I chanced a question. 'How then are we to do it, sir?'

'Ah yes, of course,' he nodded. 'Well, you see, there's a yellow metal circular disc, about the size of a dessert plate you know. You will find one affixed to every bridge. Each will have a large black number painted on it. That number gives the weight, in tons, which that bridge will bear.' He handed me a local one inch ordnance survey map. 'That's the area. I want every bridge completed by the end of the week when the armour is due to arrive. Coming up by rail, you know. The Colonel's relying on us, so don't let us down, there's a good chap. Off you go.'

Well, it looked like an impossible task . . . somewhere near two hundred square miles . . . hundreds of bridges over thousands of road miles.

My driver was now Arthur Askew. (I'd managed to 'lose' the danger man who had been my original driver. He'd had a couple more near misses, so it was suggested he'd do a better job in a tank.) We set off, with every good intent, along the coast road towards Beadnell, crossing just one bridge at Seahouses. True enough, there was the yellow disc; it had a '40' on it, so I jotted it down. The day was getting unseasonably hot, so we stopped at a quiet beach in Beadnell Bay, stripped off and swam in the cold but inviting sea. We then ate our sandwiches and snoozed in the warm sun (having a zizz, we called it). By the end of that day, I'd collected fewer than ten bridge numbers.

The next morning dawned on another beautifully sunny day. I'd had a restless night knowing that something was expected of me and I'd better produce the goods. So I determined to set aside all temptations and make a real effort to get the job done. That is, unless a thought I'd had in the night worked out. We got away early and, much to the surprise of Arthur, I'd put on my best uniform, instead of my denims. A quick query at the local police station in Bamburgh directed me to Alnwick as being the administrative centre for the area. At Alnwick I went into the Town Hall. A polite enquiry produced gold. Yes, of course, they had a list of all the bridges in the surrounding countryside. Yes, of course, the weight tolerance was recorded. Yes, of course, I could make a copy of them. For all they knew I might have been General Rommel, but then, I don't suppose it would have mattered too much if I had been. We had a marvellous week, Arthur and I.

Swimming every day. Sightseeing in the Peak district. Over the border into
Scotland. It was the best holiday I'd had for years. At the end of the week I
handed in the list. 'Nellie' Wallace was delighted, especially when he told me
a day or so later how pleased the CO had been. The following week, I was
promoted to lance corporal – the highest rank I achieved throughout my
service career.

The 'track' vehicles eventually turned up, having completed their long
journey from the south. We were all at Bamburgh Station to meet them. It
was then our task to lead them to the tank park on the edge of town.
Bamburgh Station lay about three miles to the west of the town itself. It was
on the main line from Edinburgh through Newcastle and eventually on to
London, so it was always busy. The tiny station boasted an even smaller
siding. Consequently, the exceptional length of that particular train meant
that it extended over the level crossing, thus closing the road in to and out
of Bamburgh. The unloading process was slow, as each tank needed to be
carefully driven down the ramps from the low loaders. The tracks were
slightly wider than the ramps, so great care was needed. All was going well
enough until a wood yard, alongside the station but outside the crossing,
caught fire. Nobody knew why, but it went up in flames. The rather ancient
fire engine from Bamburgh arrived very speedily and for all its great age
would have quickly dealt with the merry blaze. Unfortunately, it was
trapped on the wrong side of the crossing by our tank train. The officer in
charge was a certain Major Hicks-Beach. As well as having Royal connections, he was also a highly respected barrister in civilian life and seemed
certain to become a successful QC when the war ended. Brilliant lawyer he
may have been, but he tended to get rather excited when under stress. To
make matters worse, he always developed a pronounced stutter in such
circumstances. Can you imagine a 'silk' with a stutter? Well, Hicks-Beach
got excited and took a hand in directing the poor chap who was giving hand
signals to the tank driver to assist him down the ramp. The more agitated
became the Major, the more he yelled, and the more he yelled, the more he
stuttered. The poor hand-signaller became so flustered that his signals
became wild and unclear. The consequences really were inevitable. The tank
slipped sideways off the edge of the ramp and movement was no longer
possible. By the time the recovery vehicle had righted the tank and enabled
it to unload, the wood yard had burnt out. We all wondered who would
have defended the tank driver if he'd been sued!

We stayed in Bamburgh for a long time. The popular view was that the
War Office had put us as far away from the war as possible. There was
certainly a general belief, within the regiment, that the 1st RGH was being

excluded from the intensive training in which the rest of the British Army were engaged. The preparations for the invasion of the continent of Europe were under way. It seemed we were not to be included. There was, however, a kind of mixed emotion in our attitude. Nobody wanted to be a dead hero but, after all, we'd joined up to help to do a job and we wanted to play our part in the doing of it. For many of us, the dilemma was to be resolved without the need to take any precipitate action.

Christmas 1942 happened in Bamburgh. Some of us were due to go home on leave until misfortune, in the form of a blizzard, changed the plans. We were snowed-in and nobody got away. Well, almost nobody. The roads were impassable except for 'track' vehicles. After all, we were a tank regiment, weren't we? And tanks have tracks! An officer – a very senior officer – commandeered a tank to drive him through the snow drifts to Newcastle some fifty miles away in order to catch his train to London and his Christmas leave. For the first and only time in the RGH, there was real disapproval from the men and murmurings of class resentment. Understandable as that may have been, I think it is fair to record that all coins have two sides.

We were cold in our rooms in the castle, the meagre and antiquated central heating being inadequate to meet our requirements. So, we provided our own heating. One of the lads had bought a small stove in a shop in the High Street. They were, in reality, electric cooking devices about six inches in diameter with a coiled wire element. If you left it on twenty-four hours a day you created a really cosy fug in those little rooms and never mind the uneconomical cost of electricity. Before long we all acquired one of those desirable home comforts. Well, of course, fuses started blowing. However often we replaced the fuse wire, bang it would go again. Thicker and thicker wire was brought into use, but to no avail. The system was clearly not designed to carry such a load. Finally, in utter frustration, one of our drivers, a chap called Ronnie Trigg who boasted some electrical skill, put a six-inch nail across the fuse circuit. The mains fuse in Bamburgh blew and the entire population for miles around was effectively blacked out.

By spring, we were on the move again. South this time to Yeadon, an ugly little town on the outskirts of Leeds. We were not there for more than a month or so and the episode is entirely forgettable except for two incidents. The first concerned one of our drivers . . . Ernie Purdey. Ernie was a most likeable fellow, but not too well disposed to army discipline. He wouldn't have lasted five minutes in any other regiment, but even the RGH had certain basic requirements which Ernie had the greatest difficulty in meeting. He was my driver at that time and we were with the 'advance party' at this new location. Having sorted out suitable billets for ourselves and then for the rest: tank crews, transport, etc., Ernie and I wandered into the town. Now, while it truly was an eyesore of a place, the people were a sheer delight. I don't think I ever came across more hospitality than was thrust upon us that night. Ernie decided to extend his enjoyment of this hospitality for rather more than one night, but there was a price to pay. He wasn't on parade the following morning. Never mind, somebody covered for him. The cover was extended to a second day. The problem arose when his name appeared on a guard duty roster on the third day of his absence. Having ascertained that neither the duty sergeant nor the duty officer were likely to know him, we drew lots for who would take his place. I lost! That evening, I presented myself in drill order with rifle and bayonet, in time for the guard parade, as Trooper Purdey. Everything would have been fine had the blasted idiot not put in an eleventh hour appearance himself. He turned up on parade totally dishevelled, unshaven, improperly dressed, without a rifle and looking like something the cat had brought in. There were no dreadful consequences, of course. I was ticked off and made to complete the guard duty. Ernie was told to get a good night's rest and to present himself for a medical examination in the morning. The benign tolerance of the RGH was once more amply demonstrated.

The other incident was rather more environmental. We were stationed on the perimeter of Leeds aerodrome. It was then a RAF bomber station and, at that stage of the war, was receiving deliveries of the newest Lancaster four-engine bomber. They were so factory fresh that their giant Rolls Royce engines hadn't been 'run in'. So, for hours and hours every day, seven days a week, they ran them in virtually outside our Nissen huts. They didn't have decibels in those days, but one wonders what the count might have been.

You can imagine the joy with which we greeted the next movement order. Thetford, Norfolk was our destination. In the spring and summer of 1943 Norfolk was a delightful place. (I suspect it's always a delightful place.) Our camp was at West Tofts near Thetford. 'Toft' means level surface. Very flat, Norfolk! The entire surrounding area including Swaffham, Mundford, Brandon, Lakenheath and the northern extremities of Bury St. Edmunds had become a military training ground and restricted zone.

It was ideal 'tank country', with its long lines of spruce and conifers and its firm sandy soil. We knew it as the 'Christmas tree and sand' land. It was buzzing with armoured units, all busily occupied with the task of getting ready for D-Day. 'Schemes', as the training exercises were called, were a continuing occurrence and there were even some villages that had been evacuated so that house-to-house street fighting could be practised. I do hope the pre-war owners and occupiers were properly compensated when it was all over. Top Brass abounded . . . there was an embarrassment of four-star American generals and red-tabbed British staff officers seeming to hide behind every fir tree. We were clearly being assessed. We stayed there, busily doing our best until the late autumn. As the days started to draw in, we were sent to Hatfield Peveril in Essex. Nobody quite knew why, but it was obviously well away from all that military activity. Soon afterwards, it was learned that the Regiment had been selected to protect the area north of the Thames at Tilbury. Apparently, a top secret installation called 'Mulberry Harbour' was being assembled there and it was thought that the Germans might, they just might, risk a parachute drop of Storm Troops to sabotage the project. Soldierly pride took a bit of a knock when we further discovered that our support infantry was to be supplied by the local Home Guard.

Mulberry Harbour was a brilliant idea, said to be the brain-child of Winston Churchill. It was a pre-fabricated structure, floated across the English Channel on buoyancy tanks. Once in position off the landing beaches in Normandy, the tanks were flooded leaving an instant pier stretching far out into deep waters. Millions of tons of front line material were unloaded in this way. Mulberry Harbour was used to supply the Allies until a suitable port was captured. Its remains can be seen to this day.

It now appeared certain that we would not, as a regiment, take our part in the imminent invasion. It's hard to describe our feelings. Two words I suppose would cover it. 'Relief' – 'regret'. With hindsight, I could probably add a third – 'anger'. I do believe we were angry at what appeared to be our rejection by the War Office. Oddly enough we thought they were wrong. Of course, it was recognised that our military skills and professionalism fell rather short of what the shooting war required. But we more than made up for that by the affection and loyalty that just about everyone had for everyone else in the RGH, including the officers. We'll never know, but I rather think we'd have acquitted ourselves commendably.

Hatfield Peveril suited me very well. I could always hitch a lift on the busy A12 into London. Just a couple of hours after leaving camp, I was at 20 Lyttelton Road. Many a day pass and many a week-end pass came my way. And many a trip home took place without the luxury of a pass. I frequently took army chums with me, mostly Johnny Harris or Jim (Nobby) Clarke. (Why are Clarkes called Nobby?) London was positively effervescent. The West End was crammed with military personnel. Rich Yankees in their swell uniforms mingled with British Tommies with their much envied battledress. Poles and Free French. Gurkhas sporting fierce knives. Indians

with turbans. Aussies and New Zealanders. Airmen, sailors, soldiers
crowded the pavements and the girls never had it so good (or so often).
Competition was fierce, but we did well enough.

I was a lance corporal. I am aware, of course, that that was not
considered to be an exalted rank. A single stripe on a sleeve was not very
sexy. But then I didn't have a single stripe on my sleeve. For reasons that I
never quite understood, lance corporals and, indeed, corporals in the RGH
wore two stripes on one sleeve only, with a gold metal crown above them. I
believe it was simply a throwback to the cavalry days when a cape covered
one arm. Now there was a story, widespread and widely believed, that a
double stripe on one sleeve, topped by a crown, was a special award worn
only by something or someone called a Kings Corporal. The holder of this
most prestigious title was said to have performed some truly outstanding
service for King and country. It was a myth . . . a total fallacy. I never found
any basis for truth in such a story. But those in the know – 'the military
experts' – loudly proclaimed to their eager audiences in the pubs and clubs
of war-torn London that this little chap shyly sipping his pint over at the
bar was that rare and special breed of man, a Kings Corporal. The country
was hungry for heroes. The rewards for being so perceived were great. I
wasn't about to disillusion anyone.

The first day of 1944 came near to being my last. It was cold, so that
evening a group of us gathered round the combustion stove in the middle of
the hut and plied it with the plentiful supply of wood we had collected. The
metal casing glowed red with the heat and a relaxed and pleasant atmosphere prevailed. Someone, as was the normal practice, placed an old
four-gallon petrol can, filled with water, on the stove so that those wanting
to shave in hot water could do so. Those cans were dreadful. They were
made of the thinnest tin and almost all of them leaked. God knows how
many millions of gallons of precious wartime petrol just seeped away. One
also wondered how many cans had purposely been punctured in order to
provide a ready source of black market petrol. Having said that, empty cans
were useful for all kinds of things, including makeshift washbasins, and for
heating water. Our can was doing well. Just about on the boil it was, when
somebody quietly said, 'It's still sealed.' It took the briefest of moments for
the frightful ramifications of that statement to sink in. If it was still sealed, it
was full of petrol, it was on a red-hot stove and it was almost boiling. One
could almost hear the thoughts thundering through the minds of all those
around. 'Evacuate the hut and wait for the explosion.' 'Try to damp down
the fire.' 'Call out the guard!' Suddenly big Frank Judge stood up, lifted the
hot can from the stove by its crude wire handle and then, as cool as you like,

carried it outside. It was a brave thing to do. Perhaps it was foolhardy, but it was very brave.

I was on guard duty on the night of 5/6 June. It was just as well really, because nobody got any sleep that night. The bombers didn't stop going over. Our bombers. The RAF and the Yanks. Non-stop wave after wave of them. Something was up. The next morning we found out . . . D-Day. The Allied forces had landed in Normandy. Colonel the Lord Leigh called a parade. The whole regiment were to muster at noon that day. There were about three hundred of us lined up in our various troop formations when the Colonel marched grimly onto the parade ground. He told the Regimental Sergeant Major, RSM Lonsdale, to order us to break ranks and get as near to him as possible. He had something to say and he wanted all of us to hear him. This is what he said: 'I am a shit.' Those were his first four words and, in a stony, sombre voice to a dumbfounded gathering, he repeated them. 'I am a shit. I have let you all down. This Regiment will not be joining the invasion forces. The trained men will be called upon, in small groups, to be sent to regiments in the field to replace casualties, as will the officers. I will be leaving you today, to join a brigade ready to embark for France. I have begged the War Office to let me take you, my Regiment, to join the battle . . . they have refused. Thank you all of you, for serving under me. Whatever happens, I shall always remember you. May God bless you and see you safely through to the end of this terrible war. Please forgive me. Goodbye.' That is, as near as my memory serves, what he said. We were nearly in tears. Grown men were choked and the ribaldry with which we had hitherto reacted to our situation didn't seem quite so funny any more. An unexpected occurrence then took place. Frank Judge broke ranks, strode up to his Commanding Officer, saluted and said, 'Can you take me with you, Sir?' We were astonished. Wise-boy Frank: 'Never volunteer', 'Keep your head down', 'Stay out of trouble' and the rest, went to war.

A couple of days later, Captain 'Nellie' Wallace called a few of us, one at a time, to see him. He had decided that he was not going to wait around to be called to an unknown, decimated unit where he would be a complete stranger and almost certainly drop a rank. He had volunteered to join a very special group. It was secret . . . it was to do with communications . . . it was doing an exceedingly important job and he could take some of his men with him. It would entail a short period of intensive specialised training, well within our capabilities. He was sure we would rise to the challenge. He approached Arthur Askew, Owen Bathe, Jack Cartwright, Nobby Clarke, Johnny Harris and me. Every single one of us decided to go. By the end of the month we had bid a sad goodbye to the RGH. We were sent to a secret establishment near Crowborough. Not far from London, but don't get excited. No leave . . . no passes. It was a large country house and we were somewhat surprised to find that it was run by civilians . . . BBC personnel no less! There were also a goodly number of SAS characters around and our surprise turned to apprehensive astonishment when we were issued with red berets. We were in the Special Air Services. By this time 'Nellie' Wallace had disappeared out of sight. We never saw him again. God knows what happened to him, but, as we were to learn, he hadn't let us down. Actually, I met him for lunch at the Savoy some forty-five years later, but that's another story.

Our specialised training turned out to be a crash course on high-speed radio operating and learning the intricacies of cypher techniques. A few weeks later, we had all passed what proved to have been a preliminary suitability test. We were told that we were being sent to our field unit where, after further training, we would be on active service. We were excited and, to a man, very nervous at what might be a distinctly dangerous destination. To add to the cloak and dagger atmosphere, we were required to sign the Official Secrets Act. So it was, with considerable trepidation, that we opened our travel documents. They instructed us to proceed to Richmond in Surrey! Richmond on the District Line, change at Earls Court for Piccadilly Circus.

Our unit was called 'Phantom'. Phantom was unique. Its parameters were wide indeed. Highly skilled communications experts belonging to Phantom were to be found in almost every operational army unit from front line troops to GHQ, from underground partisans in Europe to London. Its reputation in high places was renowned and small units were 'lent' to both the American and the Canadian forces. To be in Phantom was to be considered élite. Richmond was wonderful. For three weeks, an even more intensive training régime followed in order to discover what each of us did best. Nobby Clarke, Jack Cartwright and Owen Bathe were the cypher experts. Arthur Askew, Johnny Harris and I became wireless operators. We were good at it. As an example, commercial transmission of morse signals by Reuters was said to be at 17 words a minute for normal messages and 22 words a minute for urgent stuff. We regularly worked at over 30 words a minute and I once received a message timed at 34 words a minute. Our billets were in those beautiful houses on Richmond Hill overlooking the Thames. Our 'Mess' was in the Richmond Hill Hotel. It had been and is now again, a superb hotel opposite Richmond Gate into Richmond Park. How incredibly incongruous to find oneself on active service, for that indeed is what we were, in such great comfort and such splendid surroundings.

In Phantom I had discovered yet another type of army. This time, rank had to be earned and class played no part in the earning of it. This was a democratic army, where ability and effort won promotion and respect. Phantom boasted some VIPs including Major Niven. David Niven was charm itself, friendly with everyone and everyone's friend. He told unrepeatable stories about Hollywood, but I hope what he said about Dorothy Lamour was true. A very relaxed régime was in place, which meant that, when you were not receiving, sending or deciphering, you could go where you pleased, when you pleased. The broadcasting and receiving station was in Richmond Park, just behind King Henry VIII Mound above Pembroke Lodge. It was a closely guarded and tightly restricted area, well out of sight of prying eyes. We worked eight-hour shifts round the clock, four hours on the set, four off. We used five-letter, one-time codes, and it's very hard accurately to transmit and receive high speed messages which don't make sense until decoded. It was demanding, but never onerous work and when you were off you could really enjoy the advantage of the venue. I went home fairly regularly, but the real draw was a theatre, just off Leicester Square, that had been allocated to the Allied forces in uniform. Glenn Miller – of most wondrous memories – was the star of stars and he performed for us at that glorious fun place, the famous Stage Door Canteen. His music was magical. To have been there, to have seen him on the stage live, is a privilege for which I shall always be grateful. The fondest and saddest memory I have is of his farewell concert just before Christmas 1944. The whole auditorium was packed with troops of many nations. We loved him and his music. We did not want to let him go. The next day his plane disappeared on the still dangerous flight to Paris. He was never heard of again.

The German secret weapon was now in use . . . the rocket bombardment of London. It had started with the 'V1': the 'Doodlebugs', the Londoners called them, and was shortly followed by the 'V2'. The 'Doodlebug' was a pilotless aircraft packed with high explosives. Aimed at London, it was designed to run out of fuel over the capital, whereupon it then crashed and exploded causing terrible damage and loss of life. The V2 was a pure rocket with the same objectives and results. Oddly enough, frightful as they were, nobody bothered too much about them. Their launching sites were on the west coast of France and Belgium. They were not to function there for much longer, for they would be overrun.

As is the way of things, time ticks by, situations change. Nobby Clarke went off on compassionate leave following the death of his father. Arthur Askew was posted, as were the others in the cypher group. That left Johnny Harris and me. We were still doing our stint in Richmond Park. It had been a worthwhile job all right but, as the front line moved further away, the less there was for us to do.

The war was entering its last stages. An assassination attempt on Hitler had failed, which was a tragic pity; it would have saved many lives. Arnhem also failed, but we still crossed the Rhine. The Germans tried a 'last ditch' offensive in the Ardennes and that failed. Christmas 1944 gave time to take breath and prepare finally to finish it off in 1945. So it was. The Russians were on the outskirts of Berlin. We were deep into Germany. Hitler committed suicide and suddenly it was all over.

When Richmond had been closed down, Johnny and I were sent to Calais for a short time. From there we went through Belgium into Germany, ending up at a small spa town in the north called Bad Oeynhausen. Everybody was concerned as to whether the war in Japan might require our services. In the event, that ended with a bang (or rather two bangs) so that was it. With the end of the hostilities, most units lazed away the time waiting for their longed-for demobilisation. Johnny Harris, having been in at the start of the war and being about three years older than me, was out very early. I was, as a result of my radio skills, sent around Germany with a small group collecting and exchanging information on displaced persons and their sorry like. My travels took me from Köln (Cologne) to Dortmund, from Hanover to Brunswick (Braunschweig) and Fallesleben where the Russian tanks had met the British. I was also sent to Nuremberg in time for 'the trials'. Hermann Goering was in the large Court House where they were being held. I passed his cell the day before he bit the pill.

To see Germany was to disbelieve what you were seeing. The devastation in those towns was total. How anyone survived is beyond understanding. The black market defied description. Almost anything the Germans had left to trade, they traded. The currency was cigarettes, coffee, soap and sugar. With these commodities you could buy personal jewellery, personal favours, even property. I knew an ordinary soldier who bought a small, but working cinema for 10,000 cigarettes. Talk about Players Please! Even more astonishing was the disturbing feeling of sympathy for that most wretched population! I hated myself for it. How could I, of all people, have any kind of compassion for these murderous Nazi swine. The non-fraternisation policy was imposed upon us all and really there was no problem in its observance. But we never played our role as conquering oppressors. We were cool but not unkind. They'd lost the war and their survivors rightly suffered the consequences. They had paid dearly for the crimes of their leaders and for the condoning of them. I was deeply affected by what I was witnessing and with what I was involved. I spoke a little German and that was put to use. I turned people out of their houses at four hours notice, so that our men could be housed. Decent, honest families in their spotless little suburban homes were ejected. Heart-rending scenes were common-place. Protestations of innocence of Nazi support were loudly proclaimed. It seemed there had been no Nazis in Germany. Tears flowed freely and there were times when I found it nearly impossible to keep back my own. Nevertheless, it was a job that had to be done and it was done as fairly as war permits. The occupation was brilliantly executed. The defeated army was fed, put to work, housed after a fashion and received justice. Indeed, more than that . . . much more. With the memory of the mistakes made following the 1914–1918 war, huge investment was earmarked by the West, which effectively meant the USA, to rehabilitate the losers. I wonder if this was the only war in history where the victors paid reparation to the vanquished.

It is interesting to conjecture what our fate would have been had it gone the other way. Maybe a victorious Third Reich would have been magnanimous. But the Jews, the Catholics and others are glad it was never put to the test. Anyway, there was one thing we were all absolutely certain about. Notwithstanding all the help Germany were getting, they were a totally beaten and divided nation. They would never again rise in our lifetime. That's what we all believed in 1946!

My last few months were spent near Frankfurt with the American Army. I was seconded to Control Commission Germany at Hoechst where I was reunited with Owen Bathe, Jack Cartwright and Nobby Clarke. I forget how we all managed to get together again, but we did. We were a small British unit operating in the now American Zone of Germany and we were known as GHQ Liaison Regiment. There really wasn't much to do. We enjoyed the unbelievable benefits of the PX Store, the American equivalent of our NAAFI. The comparison is frankly absurd. A PX Card was the passport to Aladdin's Cave, a veritable cornucopia, and probably reflected the degree of dissimilarity between the British people at home and the Americans. Luxury items of clothing, jewellery and watches were all available. Canteen food of amazing variety, quantity and quality were on sale as were chocolates, sweets, ice-creams, cigarettes, cigars, tobacco. Even exotic fruits like bananas and oranges were in abundance. All these things were there. Our small British contingent thought we were in fairyland, but couldn't help feeling ever so slightly aggrieved at the injustices that circumstances sometimes produce. The poor British squaddy in North Germany with his one bar of chocolate a week and his meagre cigarette ration. He'd had a pretty rough war, too. His fruits of victory were far less bountiful.

There was one thing we didn't have in Hoechst – that was British newspapers. Major A.W. Laurie, the CO, sent for me one day and said that he understood I spoke French. Detecting something to my advantage, I nodded my assent even though my French only extended to an enquiry as to the whereabouts of my aunt's pen. 'All right, Zetter,' he said. 'I want you to go to Paris. Fix yourself up with travel documents and proceed to W.H. Smith's in the Rue Rivoli. They've just opened up again. There's a train every morning from Paris to Frankfurt. Get our British newspapers on it. Think you can do that?'

'Yes, I think so, sir,' I said.

'Right, off you go,' he said. 'It shouldn't take you more than a day or so. Be back by the end of next week.' What a kindly man!

Because of the enormous damage to rolling stock, I knew the three hundred miles journey would take about fifteen hours, so I had booked myself a sleeping berth. They were only supposed to be used by officers, but there wouldn't be any British on the train and I could cope with Americans. What shattered me a bit was to find myself sharing a compartment with a general. He was friendly and delighted at my presence. One wonders as to the reaction of a British general at having to share a night cabin with a common soldier. Anyway, we got along famously. We chatted easily and I was introduced to the beneficial effects of bourbon. When I finally climbed into my upper bunk I was ready for a sound night's sleep . . . and had one.

The next morning, over breakfast in the dining car, my general told me that he was Commanding Officer in charge of transportation. He gave me his card and said I should contact him at his Paris office if I ran into any problems getting my newspapers onto the train. Shortly after breakfast the train pulled into the Gare de l'Est. That was the first time I saw Paris and my heart was most certainly young. I quickly found the modest little hotel for which I had a voucher. It was in the Rue Fauberg St. Honoré, near to the reopened British Embassy, and very centrally situated. It was a Friday morning so I decided to set about my task right away. With a bit of luck I might even get it done that day and have the week-end and most of next week to myself. I went first to W.H. Smith, just ten minutes walk along that spectacular Rue Rivoli. My arrival was expected at some time and I received an open arms greeting. The manager actually entertained me in his private office and, over coffee and biscuits, I passed on Major Laurie's newspaper list. No problems. A couple of days late, obviously, but providing I could fix the transport arrangements we would have our daily papers delivered every day. So back to the Gare de l'Est where I was directed to the Office of the Train Commandant, SHAEF (Supreme Headquarters, Allied Expeditionary

Forces) Paris, France. A youngish American major eventually saw me late that afternoon. He was busy and very put out that a no-rank nonentity should bother him with trifles. He told me, in no uncertain terms, 'that his train was made up of Americans, by Americans and for Americans, and not for effing Limeys.'

I took a deep breath and, with all the reasonableness I could muster, I said, 'One parcel, Sir, delivered to the train in Paris every morning and collected from the train itself the next day in Frankfurt. That is all I'm asking.'

'Well ask someone else, now eff off, I'm busy.'

So I did. Both! I went to my general. Sadly, he'd gone for the night, but the sweetest American WAC (Womens Army Corps) made an appointment for me for early Monday morning. I asked what she was doing over the weekend, but no joy. Nevertheless, I managed to pass the time without too much difficulty and first thing on Monday I was back at those swell offices. He listened to my tale of woe and lifted up his telephone. After a brief conversation which I will not record, he dictated a note which I was to show when I returned to the Gare de l'Est. Needless to say, the arrangements were speedily concluded. I went back to W.H. Smith to report my success and for the following three mornings went to the station to ensure it was working according to plan. During my free time, I spent every waking hour sightseeing in Paris. What a town! What a spectacular town! Each day produced an even more glorious experience. The nights, too, were not without enlightenment.

My last months in Germany did not drag. Life was so easy and conditions so good that we were all enjoying ourselves. The non-fraternisation policy had been relaxed which, of course, meant that associations were being formed. Fresh-faced young fräuleins with knee length socks and short skirts became irresistible to most of us. To my regret, I was an exception although it was a close run thing. I had, you see, resolved to reject these people. There was one girl, however, who nearly broke my resolution. Heidi, we'll call her. Heidi worked for the Americans: to be precise, the Coca Cola Company. Every day she drove her converted Volkswagen van, loaded with 'Coke', to our small British unit and left us a crate of that delectable drink. Quite free, of course, that is until we began to get an insatiable taste for the stuff. Then a small charge was introduced and gradually increased in regular stages. My first experience of successful marketing. Heidi was a delight. She flirted, charmingly and provocatively. She was the object of every man's desire. And she set her cap for me! I was the butt for a great deal of coarse humour and I was most certainly tempted as never before. Heidi was a gorgeous young Bavarian, with the fairest of hair and the bluest of eyes . . . the 'Perfect Aryan', and there's the rub. How recently had she been educated to detest my origins? Hadn't I every reason to loathe hers? She remained warm and friendly until I left and could never understand why I never went beyond my polite responses. I don't think I could either.

The great day came. Demobilisation Day. There were no dramatic farewells. No parties or celebrations. It was an everyday occurrence. Major Laurie asked me if I wouldn't consider signing-on for a short term of duty. 'Just three years and a strong probability that you'd get a commission,' he said, 'and if you then decide to continue you can be sure of a good career in the army. The war may be over, but it'll be years before we win real peace.' A very wise man was Major Laurie. Anyway, I said my goodbyes. I couldn't fiddle a trip through Paris this time. This time the system took over. I had an interminable journey into the British Zone to connect with an overstuffed train to Cuxhaven. There we needed an ice-breaker to get out of the harbour for our troopship cruise across the North Sea to Hull. From Hull I went to Guildford where I was fitted-out with my 'civvy' suit, ration cards, identity card and some other papers including a letter from the War Office reminding me that I'd signed the Official Secrets Act and that I was still a reservist, likely to be recalled at any time. 'Z Reserve' it was called. I wondered if it was personally targeted at me! I ignored the 'spivs' outside the centre offering a fiver for 'the whistle & flute'. I caught a train to London with my very last free travel voucher and five days after leaving Hoechst I was home.

# Chapter 9

# Happy Days are Here Again

Home. Just five years and twenty-six days after that sentimental farewell at Waterloo Station I was back home. Untouched by war, physically at least. I hadn't killed any Germans and they hadn't killed me. It seemed a fair bargain. I won't bore you with the excitement of my homecoming, but it was wonderful and emotional. They were all still there: Old Sarah, my grandmother, Daddy Dick and, of course, my doting, delighted mother and father.

I was twenty-three years old. What was I going to do with the rest of my life? My father's business had also survived and he clearly and desperately wanted me to join him. So much so, that he made me an offer I couldn't refuse and which turned out to be the wisest thing he ever did. He suggested that I might like to bring into the company with me one of my army friends. There were two obvious candidates, Nobby Clarke and Johnny Harris. I made the right choice. On 7 January 1947 Mr Jim Clarke and Mr Paul Zetter joined Zetters International Pools Limited. The business was located in a small building in Euston Road near Great Portland St. Station. It has long since been pulled down, but it was a pleasant enough place to start my commercial life. My father had bought me a brand new $1\frac{1}{2}$ litre Jaguar as a coming home present, so I knew he was doing all right. That was doubly confirmed when I found that he was running a pre-war Rolls (how I wish we'd kept it) and a chaffeur to drive him around.

To my great surprise I found that I liked the business. I was truly finding it interesting. Where were we in the league table of Football Pools in 1947? Well, near to relegation I suppose. Unity Pools had by now disbanded and

63

the members had all gone back to running their own businesses. In order of
size these were Littlewoods, Vernons, Shermans, Copes, Bonds, Strangs and
Murphys. These seven re-formed a pre-war trade group called The Pools
Promoters Association. Outside that cosy grouping there were some hundreds of other firms, whose promoters thought that running a Pools
company was a licence to print money. Of these the best of the bunch were
I.T.P., Kenco, Ireland's Own, Soccer, Empire, Screen, Western, GIC and
ourselves.

Jim Clarke ('Nobby' was never heard of again) was placed with Mac
Dawson. Mac was a pleasant, brainy little man. His responsibilities were
wide, covering accounts, banking, wages, overseas business and advertising.
It seemed a bit overwhelming, but, as the turnover of the entire company
was only about £3,000 a week, it wasn't too much of a workload. My father
just gave me a desk in his office and told me to listen, take in all I could and
learn the business. He gave me no particular job to do, but was insistent
that I accumulate knowledge and understanding of the whole Pools industry. He also required Jim and me to learn permutations. We were taught by
a very clever young woman called Joyce Price. She was not only good at her
subject, she was a brilliant teacher. Jim was a natural. With his recent
coding expertise, he mastered the mathematics of pool betting and perm
entries with ease. I, too, became reasonably adept at this new science. So
both of us, in our own ways, began to settle down into civilian and
commercial life. Jim had come home to a wife and family. I was still single
and fairly determined to remain so, for the time being anyway.

The winter of 1946/47 was a particularly bad one. The weather was
dreadful. My joy at not having to spend another winter in Germany soon
evaporated when I experienced the blizzards that blew across the British
Isles. I also began to see the hardships that the population at home had
been, and still were, suffering. Rationing was still firmly in place. Food,
sweets, clothing, petrol, cigarettes, all were in short supply. Constant power
cuts, lasting for hours, were commonplace and frankly, life was bloody
grim. Far worse, indeed, than conditions had been in Hoechst.

By April, spring was in the air and I felt the urge to try out my civilian
status and my new Jaguar. I rang Johnny Harris in Bristol and proposed an
excursion to France (I was still aglow with memories of Paris). Dover to
Calais (and how we remembered our previous visit). Two innocents abroad
and all to play for. We each had our full legal currency allowance . . .
seventy-five pounds in travellers cheques plus ten pounds in cash. As it
happened, we needed every penny and more, so wasn't I lucky to discover
an extra few pounds that had fortuitously found their way between the

pages of a novel I'd taken with me!

With a longing for the sun on our backs we headed south. Two days hard driving, on almost empty roads, found us in Nice. The sun was there all right, but the town was distinctly tatty. The first night, we stayed in a tired old hotel (Les Trois Épis) on the Promenade des Anglais. The next day, feeling disappointed and a bit let down, we set out to explore the coast. Driving along the lower Corniche towards Monte Carlo our spirits soared. Anyone having driven that route will know why. I had never before, or since, seen seas more blue, prettier bays and beaches, more charming villages and such a profusion of the most colourful flora, and all within a few miles (kilometres). We detoured around beautiful Cap Ferrat and along to the aptly named Beaulieu. It was a hot, sunny day, unseasonably so, but we didn't know it. The sea looked tempting so we determined to stop at the nearest beach and try it out. Eze-bord-de-mer was it. We swam and sun-bathed until hungry, then we made our discovery. Just opposite to where I'd left the Jaguar, I noticed an hotel and restaurant with attractively laid tables in a small courtyard. It was the first sensational meal I'd ever eaten. I wish I could remember what we had, but I know it was a feast. 'L'addition' when it came astonished me and delighted John. Relieved, may be the more appropriate verb. It was a few shillings, or rather francs, including the wine.

By this time, the proprieter had joined us for coffee and cognac (on him). He was only a little older than us and had just opened up. He was a Parisien, married with one small daughter. They'd sunk their meagre savings into this place and we were about their first customers. 'Wouldn't it be magnifique if, perhaps, we could stay a few days. Non?' 'Oui!' we both said in unison and we moved in that afternoon. So I discovered M. et Mme. Robert Squarciafichi, The Bananerie and France. All three were to play their part in my future happiness. We stayed about ten days, then drove to Paris with a fair amount of money in hand.

The hotel in Fauberg St. Honoré was still there, but this time we had to pay. Paris accounted for the rest of our funds in a couple of days and although still 'formidable', we both had a hang up on the Côte d'Azur.

My return to the office was deflationary. I couldn't remotivate the original interest I'd felt for the business and I felt unsettled and unsure of myself. I drove my father to the office every day and sat at my desk listening and learning, but not doing much. Jim Clarke seemed far more settled. He'd really taken to the business like a duck to water. It was at about this time that I received some literature from my old school association. They described their activities, including those of the Sports Club. So I joined the

'Old Citizens' and started playing rugby. This, more than anything else, rehabilitated me. Louis Brisacher was back, having spent an exhilarating war flying Spitfires. 'Nothing too hairy,' he explained, 'Most of the time in South Africa, teaching other poor sods.' We immediately re-established our friendship, which survives to this day.

The OCs turned out three reasonable fifteens and had some good fixtures. I started as a hooker in the 'B' team and progressed backwards to become a fairly regular wing-forward in the 'A', with an occasional game in the 'first'.

Our home ground was at Sunbury-on-Thames. Having attended a couple of practice/training sessions, I was excited to receive a card advising me that I had been selected to represent the Old Citizens B XV at Sunbury on the following Saturday. I proudly drove myself to the ground in my shiny black Jaguar. My pride very quickly evaporated. For there, on arrival, I was horrified to see dozens of cars driving in to the entrance and hundreds of people swarming around. 'Good God,' I thought, 'I'm not going to make a spectacle of myself by playing in front of this lot.' I needn't have worried. They weren't there to see me. Our ground, or at least part of it, was an overflow car park for Kempton Park racing. Pity, really; I had a good game that day.

The Old Citizens were a major influence on my return to civilian life. Rugby was naturally an important part of it, but far more was the associations it enabled me to develop. For the whole of my army service, I had been very distinctly one of the lower order. I was classified as an 'other rank'. The Army's 'class' system considered their world to be made up of commissioned officers and others. I am not making a judgement, just observing a fact. Indeed, far be it for me to be critical of the social structure into which I had been born and brought up, for I was in the process of improving my status within it. It had started at school, my posh school, the City of London. Money had made that first step possible, not forgetting, of course, the self-sacrifice my parents made to supply it. The war and my lack of military ambition had been a lengthy hiccup in the process. Now the Old Citizens had me back on course. In their ranks I mixed with young business men, doctors, accountants, lawyers, representatives from all the professions and I was an equal. I didn't have to call anyone 'Sir' any more. There were even those who called me 'Sir'. I didn't like it very much; it was something I had never before experienced. With one notable exception, when I actually hated it. That was the time when I'd been a Scout Car Commander in the RGH. My car had broken down on one of the exercises and we'd lost contact with the troop. As soon as we were mobile again, I'd set about finding them. I'd located Brigade HQ easily enough and went into the 'ops' room to make my enquiry. A sergeant was poring over a map so I asked him politely if he knew the whereabouts of my Regiment. My public school accent had always been a joke with my own chums; now it was an embarrassment. The sergeant, who had his back to me, sprang smartly to attention, turned quickly whilst saluting and said, 'Yes, sir.' He then saw that I was a low-life lance corporal. Poor chap, he didn't know where to turn. He just flushed with either embarrassment or anger and, tight-lipped, pointed to a spot on his map where the RGH were to be found. I said, 'Thanks, Sarge!' and got out as quickly as I could. From that day, until much later in life, I invariably adjusted my accent to suit the occasion and the company.

I have, mind you, always been conscious of class differences but have vigorously striven never to be seen to be superior by any of my fellow men. Nevertheless, it was a joy to be treated as an equal by the middle class society into which I had now moved. I could and did make friends with the kind of people whom I would have been saluting only a few months earlier. It was a new world to which the Old Citizens were helping me adjust. During this period I first met David Isaacs. David and Louis were already good friends when I joined the Club. They were both 1st XV star players, particularly Louis. He was a wing three-quarter and filled the position to perfection. Fastidious, as ever, he avoided the hurly-burly and hated the thought that he might get his gear muddy. Which is probably why he earned the reputation of scoring a try every time he was given the ball. The very thought of being tackled was an anathema to him. David played at stand-off and a greater misnomer would be hard to imagine. He was involved everywhere. He got stuck into the game with energy and enthusiasm and, like Louis, he used his head as well as his hands and feet. Unlike Louis, the individualist, David was a superb member of a team. These descriptions apply to their characters either on or off the rugby field.

David was, at that time, working for his father in a wholesale/retail business based in a most appropriate area near Houndsditch. Louis was helping his mother to run their splendid little hotel in Bayswater. Dr Ward was an Older Citizen. All of twenty-seven he must have been when I first met him, much respected for his playing abilities and intellect, I was particularly pleased to enjoy his company and earn his respect. Ben Ward was a radiologist. He had arrived at this prestigious position by a combination of bad luck, good luck, and skill. He had been unlucky to develop tuberculosis while still training for a medical degree. After his cure, and during the very long convalescence then required, he was fortunate to have met a colleague who suggested a career in radiology. It was fascinating work, not too physically demanding, and would enable him to stay in medicine. His commitment and ability did the rest. Ben and I became firm friends; a most unlikely duo we were. He was so good at everything, bright of mind, successful, lucid. He flattered me by his friendship.

Back home, the slings and arrows of outrageous rationing were still evident. If anything, things were getting worse. Bread, which had never been rationed during the war, was now in short supply. Petrol seemed to be more plentiful, but only on the black market. Currency for overseas travel was severely curtailed. In fact, it dropped to the absurd level of just £25 per person at one stage. Restaurant meals did not escape the grim austerity of the times. A legal limit was placed on the charges that could be made for food. Five shillings! Be it at the Savoy or Joe's Café, your eating bill could not exceed five bob, twenty-five pence in today's currency. Even forty years ago you couldn't have much of a bust-up for that. There were many who said the Conservatives had purposely lost the General Election knowing the misery in store for us in the immediate post-war era. I never took that view, I don't think they were either clever enough or perhaps, devious enough, to have thought it through. In the event, the Socialist Government of Clement Attlee were in a 'no win' situation. Morale was dreadful. Nobody expected overnight recovery after six years of conflict, but there was bitter resentment that having won the war, we were losing the peace. As far as I was concerned, I suppose I joined the general disaffection, but not with any great intensity. I was back with my family, I was making wonderful new friends and the world was my oyster.

My father and I were developing a very good working relationship. His style and personality dominated the office and I was very content to stay in his shadow. The staff all loved and respected him. It wasn't too surprising, for he was, after all, a very sweet man, but also, most of them turned out to be relatives! I came across more aunts, uncles and long-lost cousins in that little building in Euston Road, than I knew existed. They swarmed within that place like bees around a honey pot.

Lou Stodel, dear Uncle Lou, was the Manager. It was all very cosy and worked after a fashion, but efficient management was not Lou's great forte. The Company ticked over but the prospects for growth were hardly exciting. Back home, my grandfather Daddy Dick died of cancer. He had smoked heavily all his life, so it's fairly remarkable that he lived to a very reasonable eighty-four years of age. He'd been ill for about a year and my mother said he'd waited for me to come home. Three weeks later my grandmother died – of no particular illness; she just went to sleep and didn't wake up. She had also turned eighty and they had been married over sixty years. Clearly she decided there was no further point to living. It was a sad time, for we were a close family. My mother was most affected and lonely at first. Things improved when dear old Auntie Clara moved in with us. She'd lost her husband Jack, so the solution was obvious and sensible. Doesn't it further show, however, the outstanding tolerance and kindness of my father!

A young doctor called Michael Lyons had been attending the old people. He lived nearby in the fashionable Bishops Avenue and was the family doctor. Michael was just a few years older than me and we got along famously from our first introduction. He was an orthodox Jew and a highly motivated Zionist. He tried to influence me on his two pet concepts and failed on both counts. Nevertheless, we clearly had a liking and respect for each other. He had a third passionate ambition. He wanted to leave General Practice and become a specialist in diseases of the eye. The significance of this was not initially apparent to me. Only later did I learn that such diseases were very prevalent in the Middle East. Michael was planning to spend his life in that area, thus fulfilling all three elements of his philosophy. His plans included me but I did not know it then.

He had a good, local practice which included some interesting neighbours of ours in Lyttelton Road. On one side, there was a snobby French couple, very aloof and rather superior. We never got to know them! Alongside them, were the Muzikants, a wonderful, extrovert Dutch family with two voluptuous daughters about my own age, who scared the pants off me. Not literally! On the other side were the Morgensterns. Isn't that a beautiful name . . . it means 'Morning Star' in German. Kurt and Hilda Morgenstern with their daughter, Helen (originally Helle), were German-Jewish refugees. They also seemed a bit up-market to us and, at first, kept themselves rather to themselves. After a while, I discovered that they were more shy than snooty. On the spur of the moment I invited Helen, over the garden fence, to make up a four to go to Goodwood Races. It turned out later that she hadn't a clue what Goodwood was, but she accepted with alacrity. Dick Langton and Josephine (Dick was a Old Citizen and Josephine his fiancée) were the other couple and, unbeknown to me, they had invited Josephine's cousin, Henrietta. The five of us had a super day!

Helen was about eighteen years old and I dated her occasionally. She was a student at the Hornsey College of Art and my father and I gave her a lift to college whenever we saw her waiting at the bus stop. Our families came from vastly dissimilar backgrounds, as different as Emmentaler and Cheddar. Kurt, for all his rather domineering appearance, was astonishingly naive. Born into a weathy family environment, he refused to believe the evidence of his own eyes. They had lived in Fürth, near Nuremburg, and even after the horror of the *Kristalnacht* and Hitler's ominous Nuremburg Rally, he would not accept the tragedy that was being enacted all around him. In the spring of 1939, within months of the outbreak of the war, he was incarcerated in Dachau. His wife Hilda bribed a guard to let him walk out. Finally, even he realised their inevitable fate, if they didn't get out of Germany. Quickly assembling a few portable possessions, Kurt, Hilda and seven-year-old Helle caught the train to Holland and, mercifully, on to the haven of Great Britain. Kurt remained essentially German all the years of his long life. It is to his credit that he considered the Nazis as a minority of madmen and not in any way typical of the true German character. I had no wish to disillusion him, so I never argued. I wonder if history has yet reached a conclusion?

In the meantime my commercial education was gathering momentum. The Pools industry had had a chequered history. I have already touched on the origins, more particularly those of Littlewoods. Those giants, and indeed the rest of us, owe our continuance to a mixture of chance and what might best be described as divine intervention. The circumstance dates back to 1934. After a number of skirmishes, during which a Royal Commission (1932–3) recommended that pari-mutuel betting should be prohibited, the Government of the day acted. A Betting and Lotteries Bill (1934) included a proposal to prohibit pari-mutuel betting . . . the Pools! This was greeted with a groundswell of disapproval and the whole Bill could have failed had the Government not given way and dropped the offending clause. Widespread newspaper comment questioned the strength of the opposition to that particular facet of betting legislation. There was considerable critical observation as to the power of effective lobbying by commercial interests. It is a matter of history that two subsequent Royal Commissions came down in favour of the Pools . . . moderately so in 1949 and much more positively in 1978. So it seems the older we get the more respectable we get. There's nothing new in that!

The 'Old Man', as my father had become known since the death of Daddy Dick, was now involving me far more in the day-to-day running of the business. He was subtle and clever in the way in which he would defer to my opinions. All very flattering for a young man and was, undoubtedly, the main reason for stimulating my interest and contribution. One particular noteworthy event is a prime example of the result of this policy. After my fairly slow involvement at the office I had, by now, moved up several gears. The fairly undemanding weekday activity didn't bother me but the weekends were another story. We checked coupons Saturday evening and most

Sundays, too. The Old Man never insisted that I go in, but somehow I knew that I had to. Many a Saturday, after a game of rugby, it was not much fun to see the boys preparing for an evening of drinking and debauchery while I went off to check football coupons in the Euston Road. Mind you, I was free in the summer. There wasn't any checking to be done in the summer. No football was played and we all ran Pools on jockeys. They were wholly unpopular, so the handful of coupons received could easily wait until Monday morning for checking.

All very fine if you were bent on fun every weekend but who was going to pay the bill! I fairly soon established that we, in common with the rest of the industry, lost in the fourteen summer weeks, about 50% of the hard-earned profit we had made in the other thirty-eight weeks of the year. Nobody liked Jockey Pools because the coupon had to be posted by Friday at the latest and declarations of runners and riders were not published until Saturday. People didn't like betting blind. Now, much as I enjoyed my freedom of weekend activity, I still thought it was a daft way 'to run a railroad'.

One day, in the early spring of 1948, I was wandering around the office when I saw a French coupon. Or rather, not to be misunderstood, a coupon printed in French. Upon enquiry, I discovered that these coupons, and there were quite a few of them, were Belgian. They were printed and distributed over there by an agent of ours in Brussels. I was tickled pink to learn of this exciting facet of our empire, but astonished that people living in Belgium would want to bet on British football. 'Why not?' asked the Old Man. 'After all,' he explained reasonably, 'English punters bet on Scottish football and vice versa and if you think about it, London is probably nearer to Brussels than Glasgow. No, it's obvious, a bet is a bet, give people 'form', results and leagues tables, and they'll do the Pools, especially the Football Pools. We get coupons from several overseas countries, that's why we're called Zetters International Pools.' The logic was unarguable and it set me thinking. If foreigners bet on our game, wouldn't the Brits bet on foreign games during the summer period, rather than the disliked Jockey Pools?

Football was becoming popular all over the world. All we needed were the fixtures well in advance and we were up and running. The Old Man was delighted with the idea and told me to investigate the possibilities. Well, one obvious contender was Brazil, for the whole of South America were football crazy and nowhere more so than in Brazil. Fixtures were well organised, well known in advance and their leagues were based on the British system. It was perfect.

The trouble was that, when I finally obtained all this information, the British season was nearly over and we'd never be able to get the Brazilian

fixture programme prepared and a coupon printed and despatched in time
for the start of our summer season. We had, in fact, our normal, unpopular
Jockey coupon already prepared, to which we had added an additional
feature. Very early in my enquiries, I had received details of the Swiss
football programme. There were only a few games, and their season ran just
a few weeks longer than our own. However, by using those matches and
asking clients to forecast the half-time and full time results, we were able to
cobble together a Ten Match Results Pool, which we included on the
summer coupons. It ran for only four weeks, but we took more money on
that little experimental Pool than we'd ever taken on any summer Pool
before.

The Old Man was ecstatic. He couldn't wait for the next year's summer
Pools. 'Just imagine the entire coupon, including a Treble Chance Pool, on
Brazilian football,' he rhapsodised, 'It will transform the business'. One
thing bothered me. Something the Old Man had said earlier . . . 'Providing
people had 'Form', results and league tables, they'd love betting on football
matches.' With the Swiss Pool, we'd printed one small league table on the
coupons and the results were included in our dividend advertisements in the
press. All very well for a few games over a four week period, but we could
never do that with a half a dozen league tables, and over forty match results
every week for fourteen weeks, and no newspaper would dream of doing so
editorially just for Zetters Pools. Zetters really were virtually unknown,
evidence the fact that nobody noticed our Swiss Pool. This innovation was
to herald the greatest advance in the Pools Industry since Pools began. It
was the forerunner of the fifty-two-weeks-a-year Football Pools operation
and was responsible for every firm in the business being able to run at a
weekly profit, instead of a serious loss for 30% of the year. And nobody
even noticed it!

Yes, Zetters were totally insignificant. No newspapers would print the
'form' for foreign matches just because Zetters featured them on their
coupon. Who the hell were Zetters? If the major Pools ran them it would be
a different story. I was tempted to suggest to the Old Man that we tell the
'big boys' in the PPA but apart from the vanity of wanting to be seen to be
the originators, if they all did it, surely our business wouldn't enjoy
anything like the improvements in turnover we all anticipated.

We compromised. A large, independent football pool called Shermans
had recently quit the PPA following a major national scandal. It had to do
with the severe paper rationing in force at the time. Shermans were accused
of bribing senior Civil Servants and even Ministers of the Crown, in order
to receive a larger paper allocation. A tribunal was set up under a certain

Justice Lynskey. The Lynskey Tribunal sat in judgement for many weeks, and many reputations were gravely sullied by the time it was all over. It was an unsavoury incident, and brought no credit to any of the parties involved. Its origins stemmed from the dissolution of Unity Pools. Fierce controversy had arisen as a result of the shareout of clients lists, particularly between Shermans and Littlewoods. Shermans always believed they were short-changed. Consequently, when official paper allocations were made, based on the mailing list of the companies, Shermans were doubly incensed. They set about redressing what they clearly saw as a grave injustice. The upshot was the withdrawal of Shermans from the PPA. Whether they were pushed or fell from grace is not recorded. In the event, they were the only large Pools promoters not belonging to the élite gathering. This had all taken place sometime before my summer Pools inspiration. Shermans were our obvious 'White Knight'. I telephoned their Head Offices in Cardiff, and after some difficulty was connected to a Mr Arthur Penny, their Managing Director. His reaction was immediate and positive. The chief executive of that giant corporation came to London the very next day to see my father and me. He accepted the concept of Pools in the summer based on overseas football and he acknowledged, with gratitude, the reasons why we had approached them. He undertook to put their weight behind the effort still required to get 'the show on the road' and guaranteed that we would get widespread newspaper support in publishing forecasts, league tables and match results for the games on our coupons. To his and Shermans' immense credit, they did all of that and, even though we eventually issued our coupons contemporaneously, they never once claimed to be the originators.

Nevertheless, our own role was not over yet . . . not by a long shot. There was one more twist to this tale. We were, by now, well into the winter season of 1948/9. Mr Penny had sent two of his more senior people to Rio de Janeiro and they returned with the full Brazilian fixture programme for 1949. We had each compiled our summer coupons in great secrecy, featuring Brazilian football matches, and eagerly awaited the season due to start in May. In February, the best laid schemes went awry. Shermans received a cablegram from the Brazilian Soccer Federation advising them that the entire fixture programme for 1949 and 1950 had been cancelled owing to the World Cup due to take place in Rio in July 1950. It was a bombshell. If we wanted South American football, it seems we were going to have to wait for at least two more years.

It was unacceptable. There had to be an alternative. The Old Man described the requirements perfectly. Find somewhere in the world where it's winter during our summer, and where they play football. The place was obvious, but did they play football in Australia? I hot-footed to Australia House and talked to Australians. Yes, of course, they played soccer. Amateur soccer but well organised, proper leagues and loads of matches from May to September. I contacted Reuters who could and did supply a fixture and results service . . . and still do, over forty years later!

That summer, both Shermans and Zetters issued the first coupons on Australian matches. It was an instant, overwhelming success. We had hiccups, of course: the worst flooding ever known caused the cancellation of scores of matches for several weeks at the season's start; a paucity of drawn matches and the great disparity between clubs made forecasting much too easy, so there were too many winners and dividends were too small; the very poor standard of football and reports that in some games, piles of clothes were used to mark the goal posts, caused considerable ridicule from some quarters. None of it bothered us; we had achieved our objective. It is worth recording that several national and most provincial newspapers gave prominence to Australian football so our Shermans ploy worked well.

Australian football put Zetters on the map. It is also true to say that Zetters put Australian football on the map. We were delighted with the outcome. It improved our business, our profitability and, more importantly, our status within the industry. Three years later, every Football Pool in the land, including all members of the PPA, were using Aussie fixtures, and still are to this day. Turnover on summer Pools now averages 75% to 80% of turnover of winter Pools, notwithstanding the fact that millions of people stop doing their Pools coupons while they are away on summer holidays.

What was it my father said in 1948? 'A bet is a bet; give people "form", results and league tables and they'll do the Pools.' How right he was.

The successful use of Australian Football came at a most opportune time for Zetters, improving our status – as it did – at a most testing time in the affairs of the Pools. It would not be an exaggeration to claim that it may well have saved the Company.

In 1948, the whole industry was in turmoil following the introduction of a tax on Pools. The Chancellor of the Exchequer, Sir Stafford Cripps, had, in his budget of 1947, imposed a 10% Pool Betting Duty on gross weekly turnover, to take effect from January 1948. Everyone was in an unbelievable tizzy. My father who was, in any case, so opposed to the Labour Government as to be almost paranoid, likened it to the worse excesses of fascisim. 'Is this what we fought a long and bloody war for?' he asked bitterly of all and sundry, neither wanting nor expecting a reply. More surprising, in fact, was the reaction of the 'big boys' in the PPA, Littlewoods, Vernons etc. They ran a massive anti-tax campaign, circularising everyone on their multi-million mailing list. 'IS THIS THE END OF THE POOLS?' they queried boldly on a red and white leaflet. It was an even sillier question than that of my father, in that its rhetoric reached an infinitely wider audience. I won't pretend I was a 'smartarse', but I just couldn't understand what the fuss was all about. Let me explain. Pools dividends were, and still are, arrived at by deducting expenses and profit, then sharing the balance between winning clients. The effect of the new Pools Betting Duty was that, instead of approximately 80% being returned to winners, henceforth it would be 70%. I just couldn't see how that could destroy the industry. In any case, there were three aspects of this new tax which I firmly believed would act very much in our best interests. Firstly was the fact that the Pool industry had now been recognised and accepted by Government . . . we had become respectable! Secondly, it was to herald the end of credit betting. Until that time, Pools Companies had, by law, been obliged to receive their bets without payment on the first week. Payment could only be made on a subsequent week or bet. It sounds daft, doesn't it? It was! Anyway, the Chancellor, in his wisdom, wasn't going to risk any bad debts for his Pools Duty so 'cash with the coupon' became the order of the day. Lastly, and to my mind far and away most important, was the perceived value of the Pools Revenue to the Exchequer. Surely, I argued (but only to myself) no Government will ever forego this easy-to-collect tax or *allow its source to be compromised*. All the time the money rolls in, we won't have to fear a National Lottery. Well, here I am some forty-odd years later . . . still a Pool Promoter and still no National Lottery, although the threat of one is still ever-present. Maybe I was right. What I hadn't considered, I'm bound to admit, was how successive Chancellors, in successive Governments, saw the Pools as a milch cow. Pool Betting Duty has doubled and more than doubled again, reaching an unacceptable 42.5% by the 1980s. As a consequence, the return to the punter today is a paltry 25% of stakes. The high level of tax is grossly unfair. It has destroyed almost every small Pools company because, together with restrictive Pool betting laws, it favours the industry giants. There were some hundreds of Pools Companies operating when the Chancellor introduced his tax. Many of them folded immediately, rather than face the embarrassment of accountability. Only the brave and the hardy have survived.

# Chapter 10

# Fast Living

For the first time in my young life I was experiencing the joy of freedom. Whether consciously or not, I was establishing a pattern of pleasure which spilled over from home to office to playtime and leisure. I was enjoying rugby. I went fishing. I was taking out girls. I was making new friends and I was driving my own motor car. I loved driving. Just to be behind the wheel of a vehicle was like being in command of a force. If you controlled your force with skill you experienced a sense of achievement. I drove my Jaguar whenever and wherever I could. The petrol rationing was frustating but, by careful husbandry, a bit of scrounging and some rule bending, the mileage on the speedometer mounted appreciably. There was also extra allowance of petrol coupons to competitors in motor sport. I tried various activities of this kind, including hill climbing, treasure hunts and even one day rallies.

Grand Prix racing was a rapidly growing spectator sport, immensely popular in England and made more so by the super-stars we were beginning to produce. Reg Parnell delighted the crowds at Silverstone, an ex-RAF airfield adapted to provide our first post-war Grand Prix circuit. It was he who inspired many of us to support the brave attempt to build a successful British racing car. Countless thousands responded to a fund-raising effort which actually resulted in the creation of the BRM (British Racing Motors) and the production of racing cars bearing that name. I don't think a BRM ever won a Grand Prix, but it certainly played a major part in the eventual success of British cars and British drivers. Young Stirling Moss was thrilling us enthusiasts with his flair, brilliance and obvious potential. Here was a world class driver, the first of the many. I don't think I missed any major car

76

race meeting and the more I saw the more I loved the sport and the more I wanted to be involved in it.

I decided that car racing was out of the question for me, but serious rally driving was not. My Jaguar, good as it was, was not good enough for what I wanted. It was underpowered, appalling through the gears and boasted a soft suspension. All very fine for passenger comfort when driving to the office, but road holding and cornering at maximum revs made it feel like a dinghy in a force ten gale. It also, believe it or not, suffered a stigma. That beautiful, very British car, with its fine sporting pedigree and which catered so well for the business men with a love and a yen for motor sport, attracted a most unpleasant label. It was known as the 'Jew-boy's Rolls Royce'. Isn't that dreadful? Shame on me, but it turned me off.

I searched the pages of *Motor* and *The Autocar* looking for the right replacement vehicle. I found it . . . an Allard. A brand new arrival on the scene of British motoring, made in England by a brilliant British engineer, Sydney Allard, it was exactly what I was looking for. It was a sports coupé with leaf and tongue suspension, strong enough to give a hard ride and a road-hugging performance. Broad based and with an eleven inch road clearance, it made light of any road surface; in fact, the worse the road, the better the ride. Best of all, the Ford V8 engine with a three speed gear box gave the car fabulous acceleration (in 1950) of 0 to 50 m.p.h. in 6 seconds. It looked like a dream and it handled like a dream. It was the Venus de Milo of motor cars and the most eye-catching vehicle on the road.

Equipped with such a breed anything was possible. The first full scale post-war Monte Carlo Rally was due to take place in January 1950. I applied and was accepted for a place in the world's No. 1 motor rally. I was overjoyed, especially when it eventually dawned on me that I was actually representing my country at a major international sporting event.

The 'Monte' had over four hundred competitors. We each had to complete 3,500 kilometres in 72 hours. There were several different starting venues throughout Europe including Lisbon, Munich, Oslo, Palermo (in Sicily), and one in Great Britain, Glasgow, which is where I started. Each starting point had a different route, of course, which eventually converged on Paris. We would, by then, all have covered the same car-breaking and crew-exhausting distance.

I chose Ben Ward as one of my co-drivers and another friend called Frank Lee. Frank Lee was a sophisticated business associate rather than a close friend. He was quite a lot older than me, very reliable, a good organiser and with some mechanical ability. He also drove very well. Ben was a steady safe driver, a good friend and a doctor. He might be useful! We

drove to Glasgow on Saturday before the Sunday start, proudly sporting
our two red Monte Carlo Rallye plaques with our number 67 boldly
emblazoned in white. That evening we went to the cinema. *Marius* was
showing, the first of the now famous Raimu trilogy of *Marius*, *Caesar* and
*Fanny*. An outstanding film and certainly a cinema classic. Nothing could
have been better devised to put us in the mood for France. The next
morning we presented ourselves to Rallye Controle at the RSAC in
Blythswood Square. Having checked in, the Allard was positioned in its
starting place around the Square. Several crews were already enjoying the
hospitality of the splendid Club House and soaking up the atmosphere
while awaiting 'the off'. Large crowds were gathering outside. The tension
and excitement were novel experiences for the three of us. Weather
bulletins, covering our whole route from Scotland through Britain and the
whole of Western Europe, were being distributed. Navigators were poring
over their maps and the whole place was buzzing with activity. Extreme cold
throughout the journey was forecast. A daunting prospect, there being no
car heating in those days. None of us relished the thought of being wrapped
in duffle coats and sweaters for three days and nights. A more immediate
concern, however, was the black ice reported over Shap and through Wales.
Ben's priority objective was to get to Boulogne. 'Once we're over there,' he
said, 'I'll consider we've successfully reached our destination.'

We did a bit better than that.

The starter's flag waved us off to cheering crowds all the way out of
Glasgow, on our journey through eight countries in the next three days.
Despite the bitter weather, we had the roof open and this attracted more
than our fair share of popular support. It also made it easier for the back
seat passenger to jump out for a quick pee, which Ben seemed to want to do
every other mile. Folkestone, our last control in the UK and our embarka-
tion port, was reached in plenty of time and entirely without incident. An
advantage of having started in Glasgow was the benefit of being in rally
limbo for the couple of hours it took to load the cars and cross the Channel.
It was fun to watch them being hoisted on and off the ferry. They used a
kind of wheel-clamp sling on each wheel attached to a frame, hoisted up and
lowered by a crane. It all went like clockwork but, of course, took a great
deal longer than the drive-on/drive-off vessels shipping today's vast tourist
traffic. We also enjoyed a comfortable breakfast during the crossing.

The first casualty occurred at the Boulogne control check point situated
just on the exit of the town. A couple of nice English girls, driving a
Sunbeam Talbot, checked in late. How on earth could they be late at that
point? After all, we'd all been unloaded in plenty of time. Well, the poor

lasses had decided not to have breakfast on the boat. As soon as they were unloaded, they drove to a café for a longed-for French omelette with all the trimmings. They thought they had loads of time, at least an hour in hand. They'd forgotten to put their watches forward one hour. We were all a bit male chauvinist at the time and thought it hugely funny. But it was really very sad, especially as I think they eventually arrived in Monte Carlo with hardly any other penalties.

We went on our way to the next control in Luxembourg, about a six-hour drive. Frank drove while I dozed in the back and Ben sat contentedly sipping from a bottle of vin rosé that had been thrust at him by an excited French spectator. He was supposed to be navigating but then it wasn't very likely that Frank would lose his way on that section.

You may be wondering who Frank Lee was and what he was doing in my car on the way to Monte Carlo. Frank Lee was the UK Controller of Radio Luxembourg. We had become friends, because Zetters Pools were advertising on that popular radio station and Frank had been particularly helpful with our programming schedules.

This, then, was to be his first session at the wheel. The plan was to really burn up the kilometres in order to get there ahead of our scheduled arrival time, that being 22 hrs. 12 min., on 23 January 1950. A slap-up meal was to be laid on to set us up for the long night stint through Belgium and Holland.

It didn't quite work out that way. The roads were narrow, difficult and icy. There were major road works with diversions in the town of Luxembourg; it was difficult, therefore, to get to Frank's Broadcasting House. When we finally did so, all we had time for was a quick snack of pâté de foie gras, washed down with a glass of champagne and off we went again.

Liège at 1.15 a.m. lacks charm. Amsterdam six hours later bustled with early morning traffic. The Hague was memorable for one particular reason . . . we were now heading south. Brussels welcomed us with cheering midday crowds reminiscent of the liberation. It was dark again by the time we got to Rheims. We could have bathed in the freely flowing champagne had we been of a mind, but the fatigue and the icy cold was beginning to get to us. The *bonhomie* was abundant all right; we just weren't able fully to appreciate it.

Paris bucked us up no end. We were in plenty of time for efficiently organised ablutions and the lavish hospitality at the control point just near the Arc de Triomphe. It was also the last evening. Only one more night and tomorrow we would see the Mediterranean. Easy really. We only had to cross the Alps at night, during the winter on minor roads in a blizzard at an average speed of 50 k.p.h.

The long run to Nevers was difficult, but we arrived with over half an hour in hand. On the next long and tricky section to Lyon it started snowing. The Allard was handling like a dream in those difficult conditions. Ben quietly mentioned that we were passing many more cars than were passing us. I don't think we had adrenaline in those days, but something was causing the blood to flow through the veins a bit quicker. Over 3,000 kilometres completed without penalty. Less than 500 kilometres to go with just four more control checks. The night was nearly over and the dawn of our final day was imminent. In less than nine hours we were due to be in Monte. Then we hit the hill! Fifteen kilometres short of Lyon (and we were still ahead of the clock) there is the Col de la Luère. The road was narrow and twisting. It was north facing, taking the full blast of the blizzard and it was a mess of rally cars. They were strewn everywhere. There was clearly only one way to take it . . . at speed. I tried . . . I put my foot down and went – not far though. Vehicles were all over that tight little road and we were soon brought to a standstill. Out we piled and in the foulest of bad humour, set about the cold, wet, dirty task of fixing the chains. We knew that our speed, acceleration and worst of all, our manoeuvrability, would, from then on, be drastically impaired. As we were toiling, a glare of blazing headlights came storming up the hill at a rate of knots. Well, he was going to have to stop, whoever he was. There wasn't enough space for a bike, let alone a car. Oh, wasn't there! Through a narrow gap between two trees, into a field and back onto the road again a hundred yards up and beyond the snarl up. That was Sydney Allard in the car of his own manufacture. It was the most spectacular piece of driving I have ever seen and none of us were surprised when he went on to win the Rally. Meanwhile, back at our traffic jam it seemed to take an eternity to get the chains on and negotiate our way out of the mess for the run into Lyon. We were late, of course, but so was everyone else apart from Sydney, it seemed. So we were still in reasonably good heart as we set out for Valence, especially seeing the sunrise over the Alps on what we hoped would be the last day of our rally. We did have one hiccup on this section, but managed to survive it. There are two roads from Lyon to Valence; the main N7 and the more tortuous N86. They run either side of the spectacular Rhone/Saône valley. We had been advised to take the lesser road, the N7 being clogged with the formidable *camions* making heavy weather of the snow conditions. It went very well until we came to a road junction just outside Valence. We knew we had to cross the river at some stage and thought this might be the place. Minutes were precious, we dared not make one single mistake and there was no signpost at the junction.

Fortunately, there was an elderly gentleman standing by the side of the road. We screeched up to him, I wound down the window and in my best French yelled, 'Direction Valence. s'il vous plaît.'

'Comment?' he enquired politely.

'Valence, Monsieur! Direction Valence!' I shouted with ill-disguised impatience.

'Je suis desolé monsieur mais je ne comprends pas,' he murmured with infuriating solicitude.

By this time several other rally cars had stopped behind us all equally unsure of their route and clearly hoping car 67 would get it sorted out, but quick! 'Connaissez-vous la ville de Valence. VA-LENCE?' I enunciated beseechingly. By this time the cars behind were hooting angrily and we were going spare, as he sadly shook his head.

'Show him on the blasted map,' said Benjie.

I hurriedly stabbed my finger at the name printed boldly on the map, while he laboriously took out his glasses. After some agonising moments he smiled sweetly. 'Ah, Valence. Bien sûr, monsieur, certainement,' and pointed us towards the right road. Many years later I told this story to a French lady. She was not amused. 'The emphasis is on *Va* not *lence*,' she explained tersely.

We were still, of course, in the mountain region and even though the storm had blown itself out and the weather was now beautiful, the roads were treacherous. Nevertheless, the car was handling surprisingly well and we were making good progress. Next stop Digne, then Grasse, gateway into, or in our case out of, the Alps. We would actually be able to see 'La Mediterranée' from Grasse. At Chateau-Arnoux, a tiny village near Digne, a French *camion* I had been trying to overtake for the last few kilometres, suddenly stopped. I didn't. Not of my own volition that is. Many hours later, my sadly reshaped Allard limped ingloriously into Monte Carlo – out of luck and out of time. We were somewhat mollified to discover that of over four hundred competitors, only five had finished the course within their stipulated time. Some satisfaction, but in car 67 we all had the same infuriating thought. If only that blasted truck hadn't chosen that moment and that place to stop for whatever it was it needed to stop for. I wonder how many other crews said, 'If only . . . "?

Frank Lee flew home next day and Louis Brisacher flew out to join the post-rally festivities. We, none of us, liked the hotel into which we'd been booked, so I took the boys five kilometres along the coast to the Bananerie at Eze-bord-de-mer. Robert Squarciafichi greeted me with open arms, especially when a number of other British competitors followed our example. A real fillip to him at what was normally the quietest season of his year.

The Bananerie was, in fact, unofficially adopted thereafter by the British contingent, for which Robert was always grateful to me.

I cannot claim to have achieved notable success with my first venture in international sport, but, in every other way, it was wonderful. I continued rallying for some years and competed in several more Montes. Ben did one more. Louis Brisacher and David Isaacs joined me a couple of times and I drove once with another crew.

We never did win any prizes, but usually managed to be thereabouts. One of our better efforts came in the Rally Sestrière, where we were the first British car (out of sixteen) and nineteenth overall out of a hundred and ten starters. Rather more momentous was the spectacular round hotel, sticking up out of the snow in Sestrière like some giant gasometer with windows. The rooms went all round the perimeter with the core of the building housing services and lifts. A gentle spiral slope separated the lifts and the rooms. One particularly boozy evening some clown produced a couple of bicycles and a game plan. Two teams were to take part in a relay. The object was for each player to grab a bike, cram it into a lift, go to the top floor and cycle down the slope. He then handed it to the next competitor who repeated the exercise and so on until the winning team emerged. It turned out to be a fiasco, of course, but luckily no innocent was bowled over leaving their bedroom and there were no serious casualties.

After one fairly uneventful Monte Carlo Rally, we decided, purely for cultural purposes you understand, to drive home by way of Paris.

The journey was free of anything untoward other, that is, than a major catastrophe . . . the horn didn't work! The car horn, I mean. Now, if you don't think the malfunction of such a vital piece of equipment is a 'major catastrophe', then you never drove in Paris in the fifties.

We tried various garages *en route* to get it fixed . . . all to no avail. Finally, in the shabbiest looking, most run down *maison mécanisée* near Fontainebleau, we found salvation. The wizened proprietor quickly dismissed any possibility of an actual repair. 'But, despair not,' we thought he said. With a merry twinkle in his eye, he disappeared into his little shed. After some moments, he reappeared with a hooter. Yes, that's right, a vintage, brass hooter, complete with a black rubber bulb on one end and a trumpet on the other. He gazed at the sleek, modern Allard, clearly weighing up the compatibility of the two anachronisms. Then, having decided the first test had been passed, he honked it. A slight frown crossed his brow and he honked again. Clearly the sound it made was unsatisfactory so, shaking his head almost angrily, he disappeared back into the shed. After three such attempts, he was finally satisfied that both appearance and tone met with his approval and he proudly presented us with this most beautiful hooter 'avec mes compliments, messieurs'. Our hooter saw us through the worst of the Parisian traffic – with some style, I'll tell you. It is to my everlasting regret that I allowed that superb relic of better days to leave my possession, along with the Allard and so many other treasures.

I also took part in the first RAC Rally of Great Britain. Ben once more joined me and this time Jim Clarke made the third member of the crew. The RAC Rally of Great Britain is to the Monte Carlo Rally as Clacton-on-Sea is the the Côte d'Azur. They both have a coast line . . . there the similarity ends. The Monte is won and lost on the long open road sections, particularly in the Massif Central and the Alps. The RAC depends upon speed and manoeuvrability tests on special closed circuits. The road sections are just routes from one such venue to the next. This soon became apparent when Ben Ward, Jim Clarke and I set out on the '1st RAC' in June 1951. Ben and I were old hands, or thought we were; Jim was an excited new boy. I had sold the Allard (to Ben) by this time and now owned an AC. Not the fancy racing model, but the ordinary saloon. It was a fine car and although its straight, six-cylinder engine was under-powered, the road holding was superb. With a low centre of gravity it surpassed most of the opposition in difficult driving conditions and had sufficient engine capacity to cause no problems on the easy road sections. In fact, there was seldom need for fast driving on the RAC and I can only remember one occasion when we had to do so. Somewhere in Scotland we had a niggling doubt as to whether we were on the right road. I drove at top speed, on the premise that if you think you might be going the wrong way the sooner you find out the better.

The AC was not really the ideal vehicle for the RAC. Acceleration, particularly on hill tests, was poor. Manoeuvrability through chicanes left much to be desired. Ground clearance over the rocky tracks of Scotland and Wales had us worrying about the low-slung sump. There was, however, one trial at which we excelled: ten laps of Silverstone at an average speed of not less than 60 m.p.h. It doesn't sound very difficult now, but most cars, including the AC, only had a top speed of about 90 m.p.h. Tight corners around a circuit, crowded with ordinary cars driven by inexperienced drivers, created a demanding test. One problem, which both Jim and Ben foresaw but which I made light of, was keeping an accurate tally of completed circuits. To humour them, I agreed to their plan to put ten sticky paper tabs on the dashboard and pull one off at the end of each circuit. As further insurance, they would stand by the track, at the finishing point, to time and check my progress. How right they were. After about five laps, I'd completely lost count and, in the exhilaration and concentration of the drive, had neglected to pull off the tabs. At what I thought was my ninth lap, I reckoned I would just about manage the tenth within the allocated time when I saw Jim and Ben waving like mad for me to come in. It seems I'd completed ten with time to spare. In the event, practically every other car cocked it up. We were one of about a dozen without penalty. The furore and weight of protest from several hundred defaulters intimidated the rally officials to such an extent that, much to our chagrin, they excluded the Silverstone Test from the final reckoning. Nevertheless, we enjoyed the trip. We'll always remember the breathtaking landscapes of the west of Scotland. The startled faces of mums and dads as about a thousand screaming tyres tore into the quiet summer resort of Dunoon. The puzzled official, at a traffic census we were unfortunate enough to encounter going into the Mersey Tunnel: 'Were we really serious about going from Brighton to Bournemouth on this road?' The reputation we quickly acquired for our navigational skills (Jim's really). It became commonplace to find a whole line of cars following us through the Highlands and later through Wales with not one of them keen to overtake and become pathfinder. The fury with which we reacted to an unbelievably stupid marshal who, on our arrival in Bournemouth, gave us twenty penalty points for what he called 'car damage'. All it was, in fact, was a deep scratch just below the driver's door. It had obviously been caused by a rock being thrown up by the front wheel when traversing a cross-country section. We should have protested, but none of us were of a mind to. The irony was that, had I not insisted on having the car washed and polished before final check in, the scratch would not have been seen because of the mud. It was a good rally and has become one of the most important on the International calendar. It was my penultimate effort.

Rally sport was becoming more and more professional. Car manufacturers were engaging top flight drivers and supporting them with well staffed mobile workshops. Tyre companies had teams positioned all around the routes with rapid wheel change equipment and tyres to suit all driving conditions. Prize money zoomed and big money sponsorship transformed the sport. The days of the amateur were over. I had enjoyed some wonderful years but, with the changed times for the fun driver, I decided to leave the sport. Actually I left on a happy note. My last Monte was with Louis and David. We had a good rally and finished within time. As usual, we stayed at the Bananerie. One evening, just before dinner, Robert called us together and, a little mysteriously, told us to get the car and follow him and Madame in their Citroen. He drove about two kilometres towards Monaco and then turned off the road, through wrought iron gates, down a narrow, twisting drive. Descending a few hundred metres we arrived at a large, white villa, situated on a small peninsula surrounded on three sides by the sea. This, Robert told us, was Cap Estel; it was their new hotel opening later that year. Over a very liquid dinner that night, Robert and Madame excitedly told us of their plans to turn Cap Estel into one of the most luxurious hotels along the Côte d'Azur. They went on to make us an offer. If and when any one of us should marry, they would invite us to spend the first week of the honeymoon at Cap Estel as their wedding present. Two years later, it was an offer I had the greatest joy in accepting. If you look today in the Guide Michelin, you will see that Robert achieved his well deserved luxury rating.

The Monte, of course, came right in the middle of the rugby season. Never mind, we only missed two games at the most. We more than made up for it. At the end of each season it was the habit for most clubs to go on an Easter tour, usually to a pleasant coastal area not too far from London. Three fixtures were arranged Friday, Saturday and Monday against good local sides we would otherwise never get to play.

This was always the highlight of our rugby year and frequently cemented developing friendships. The club would typically book a suitable small, two-star hotel-cum-pub and it was clearly preferable if we were able to take over the entire establishment for the long weekend. The party was always boisterous. Considerable quantities of alcohol were consumed, mostly beer, but behaviour never, in my experience, reached unacceptable levels. If, occasionally, there were other guests unfortunate enough to be staying in the hotel, the worst they would have suffered was noise and rude songs. Quite often the latter were very well received, particularly by middle-aged spinsters.

A typical rendition, causing blushes and giggling, went:

> There was a young lady from Yale,
> who offered her body for sale.
> For the sake of the blind
> she tattooed her behind
> with the list of her prices in Braille.
>
> *That was a cute little rhyme* etc.

The first such tour I went on was to Battle, Sussex. I think we played Hastings, Eastbourne and Lewes. I've no recollection of the results. I suspect we did well, but it really doesn't matter. We ate well and we drank well. We used the traditional dartboard for inventive new betting competitions. Card schools played well into the early hours for dramatically low stakes, poker being the most favoured game. There were always a couple of tables of bridge fours for the clever ones like Leon Israel, Teddy Langton and Benji Ward, of course. The singsongs normally followed the evening meal. 'The Ball of Kerry Moor' and 'The Bloody Great Wheel' are two of the more vulgar songs I remember, but not well enough to be able to reproduce the words here. Then came the jokes, the ruder the better. Did you hear about the shipwrecked sailor whose only companions were a young pig and an alsatian? The fierce dog took a shine to the pig and the sailor couldn't get near to it. One day a beautiful maiden was spotted offshore and saved by the sailor. In gratitude she offered him any favour. 'Good,' he replied, 'Take the dog for a long walk.' There were others less subtle.

Peter Jones, a young architect, then did his party piece 'the one-armed fiddler'. It was well prepared and when first seen nearly brought the house down. He would dress up as a country yokel . . . not difficult for he looked like one. He'd stuff one arm into his clothing leaving an empty sleeve in his shirt and jacket. He placed a conveniently positioned pint of beer on a chair in front of him. Then, with a replica of a violin procured from I know not where and strapped to his body, he hummed 'Tavern in the Town' and got us all to sing along with him. As the singing got under way, the middle finger of his hidden hand poked out from his trouser fly and into his pint of beer. You had to be fairly well lubricated to find this amusing, but we all were, so that was all right.

I discovered on this tour that Ben shared my passion for angling. I was delighted, therefore, to take up his suggestion of a fishing trip to Southern Ireland later that summer.

A remarkable occurrence was to take place beforehand. Michael Lyons, our family doctor, asked me to dinner one evening. Over our meal, in Blooms Kosher Restaurant in Whitechapel, he made me a proposition, becoming progressively more enthusiastic as he unfolded his story.

The new State of Israel had been born. They, too, had experienced their 'blood, toil, sweat and tears' but a Jewish nation was now an established reality. This, for Michael, was as great a happening as the birth of Christ must have been – and still is – for countless Christians.

His fervour was almost infectious. He described how the desert was being turned into a land of milk and honey. How a new democracy was being born into an area which had never before experienced freedom. How twentieth-century pioneers, with the benefit of a five thousand year culture, were creating a haven which Jews from all over the world could call their homeland. Suspecting that this lecture was not without motive, I asked why he was telling me all this.

He paused for a moment, then came his bombshell. He told me that he had achieved his ambition to become an eye specialist. That he had been offered full funding to open a specialist clinic, for diseases of the eye, along the Mediterranean coast near Caesarea. That such diseases were prevalent in the Middle East and so the work was vital. That he needed an administrator and he would like it to be me.

I was dumbfounded. Why me? What did I know about it? In any case, I had only recently returned home after being away for years. And I wasn't an Israeli and I certainly wasn't a Zionist.

'Every Jew, all over the world, is now an Israeli, if they want to be,' he said. 'You are unmarried, free, young. You have no responsibilities. You can do as you please and go where you please. To be your own master, doing one of the most worthwhile jobs for humanity in a new country. This is an opportunity in a million. Grab it with both hands.'

'But I know absolutely nothing about hospital administration,' I said.

'You don't have to have been a sailor to become First Lord of the Admiralty,' he said, quoting one of my father's favourite sayings. Well, on and on he banged with convincing persuasion. Finally, he said that I should think it all over. He would be going to Moorfields in Brighton later that summer for the final ceremony, after which he would sell his house and practice and leave for Israel by the end of the year. I could let him know by the early autumn; that would be time enough.

My immediate reaction was to reject it out of hand. But as the weeks went by the idea began to intrigue me. What Michael had said was truly emotive. Add to that my love of the sun and the sea, and the whole concept began to have the makings of an irresistible appeal.

The down side of course, was my parents, particularly the Old Man. His greatest aim was for me to take over the family business and it seemed to him that he was going to realise it. My start had been auspicious, what with Aussie football etc. I was clearly enjoying the life and he really could now foresee the day when I would make his dream come true.

I was, however, coming to terms with that one major snag. 'After all,' I argued to myself, 'I wouldn't be burning my boats. I could go over and set it all up. Once it was up and running there would be nothing to stop me coming home again.' I had almost convinced myself to go for it. I decided not to tell anyone just yet but to go on my fishing trip to Ireland with Ben and make my final decision when we got back, just after my twenty-ninth birthday in July. So it was. Ben and I went off to Waterville in County Kerry, with my promise to Michael Lyons that he would have my decision by the end of the month. It was a promise I was not destined to honour.

Waterville was just perfect for the two of us. We stayed at the Butler

Arms Hotel. Accommodation was primitive, but cheap, as was the village and, indeed, the entire country. The Irish people were friendly and cheerful and appeared genuinely pleased to welcome us Brits. The fishing was overrated, but still brought great pleasure. It had long been my wish to go salmon fishing and I was told they abounded in the rivers all around me, but I needed a licence to go after them. This I could procure from Mrs Reilly in the village post office. The post office seemed to be the only shop in the village and sold just about everything.

At 9 a.m. sharp on Monday morning, the advertised opening time, I was waiting outside the firmly locked shop door. At 9.35 I heard the door being unbolted and there was Mrs Reilly, clearly a little put out to find such an early customer before she was ready for the hustle and bustle of her busy day. 'What is yer wanting?' she queried in that most delightful of all dialects. I told her I wanted a salmon permit. She was visibly taken aback.

'Have you caught yourself a salmon then?' she wanted to know.

'No, Ma'am,' I said politely, 'I want the permit so that I can go and try.'

She sighed at the unbelievable ineptitude of the 'bluidy foreigners' and said, 'Off you go, sonny; if you catch yerself a salmon and get yer name in the local paper, come back and oi'll back date yer fishing permit.'

Sadly, I didn't have need to return to her, but we caught some nice trout and had the good fortune to have Johnny Sullivan, the senior boatman (gillie) thereabouts, to take care of us. I have caught many fish over the years, with Johnny's help, including some splendid salmon. He drank too much but, in every other way, was a sheer delight. I was greatly saddened to hear that Johnny went blind before he died some years later.

The holiday was the greatest possible success. I loved the country and will always be grateful to Ben for introducing it to me. It was so different to those glorious fleshpots in the South of France and yet it had so much to offer. The sea was clean and crystal clear. The mountains were prettier than the Alps . . . they're green! The beaches were sandy, varied and if there were more than a handful of people on them, well, another quieter one was just around the bay. The food in the hotel, while not attempting any gastronomic surprises, was plentiful. Breakfast, lunch, a massive tea with cakes galore, and dinner, of course. The bedrooms were pretty ghastly. An elaborate American lady was heard to remark that she wouldn't keep a dog in a room that size at home. But they all came, victims of the undoubted charm which the Irish quite genuinely exude. Billy Huggard, youngest son of the proprietors Mr & Mrs Huggard, ran the establishment with great panache and sensitivity, attracting a loyal and remarkably up-market following. Charlie Chaplin, a keen angler, was for many years a devotee and he typified its cosmopolitan popularity.

It was a lively place, where young and old seemed to be able to mix easily. Several nights during the week, Billy ran a popular game on their ancient billiards table . . . it was called 'Rolling the Red'. A crowd gathered round the table and you paid sixpence to join the game, winner take all. The game was started by whoever drew the short straw rolling the white ball by hand from baulk to try to hit the red ball on its spot. If you missed you were 'out' and you'd lost your sixpence. If you hit, the next predetermined player had to gather the white ball and hit the red with it before the red stopped rolling. Failure to do so put you 'out'. It was enormous fun and the last survivor won the jackpot to cheers and boos from the many losing spectators. After all that jollity, things quietened down and little groups – and couples – drifted off to engage in other games. The Butler Arms and the Huggards have a significant niche in the Irish Hotel industry and a warm corner in my heart.

Arriving back home after this wonderful holiday, I was concerned to find my normally happy parents distinctly subdued and far from their usual jovial selves. Over supper that night I discovered why. Michael Lyons had been killed in a car crash on his way to Brighton to receive a diploma from Moorfields Eye Hospital. I have often wondered whether a hospital for diseases of the eye ever did open in Caesarea.

On 31 December 1952 I went for a haircut. Not a notable event you might say and you'd be right. But I recall this particular visit for a very particular reason or, more accurately, three reasons.

My barber's shop was situated in Percy Street, just off Charlotte Street where we then had our offices. I had established a 'regular client' relationship with Dave, the Jewish proprietor. He, for some unfathomable reason, considered me to be an expert on all things sporting. I presume it was because he knew I was involved with Zetters Pools, which surely must mean I was an authority on all sport!

Anyway, we were discussing the imminent New Year and he posed the question: What great sporting achievement will we see in the following twelve months? For no recallable reason, other than to create a dramatic effect, I dredged up three unlikely occurrences.

Stanley Matthews (later to become Sir Stanley) had been the most stylish player never to win a Cup Finalist's medal. He was playing for Blackpool at the time and, while they were a good side, they were certainly not thought to be a team of any great distinction.

Gordon Richards (later to become Sir Gordon) was undoubtedly the greatest flat racing jockey the 'sport of kings' had ever known. Yet Gordon Richards, now fast approaching the end of his career, had never ridden a Derby winner.

Len Hutton (later to become Sir Leonard) was one of the finest batsmen to grace our cricket scene since W.G. Grace himself. He was the captain of an unknown, little fancied eleven, at a time when England had just about forgotten what it was like to win the Ashes.

So what three sporting triumphs did I forecast in that barber's chair on the last day of 1952? Yes, that's right. Matthews for a Cup Winner's Medal . . . Richards for a Derby winner . . . and England, skippered by Hutton, to win back the Ashes. As I write this some forty years later, I can hardly believe it. But it happened! Three great British sportsmen won the major event of their chosen professions all in the same year. Now if only I'd been a betting man what a sweet little three way accumulator that would have made!

The barber, by the way, thought I must live in Oz.

Chapter 11

# Land of Hope and Glory

1953 was a memorable year. It was the year of the Coronation of Queen Elizabeth II. The build-up to this momentous occasion had been dominating the newspapers for some time and, frankly, I was bored sick with it all.

June 2nd was designated as the great day and the powers-that-be had decided that the times were opportune for a restatement of Britain's glory. What better way could there be than the crowning of a new young monarch. A Queen to reign over the largest group of nationalities, of diverse creeds and colours, that the world had ever seen. Our post-war problems were receding. Winston Churchill was back where he belonged at Number 10 Downing Street. All it now needed was a spark to rejuvenate the British people . . . and that spark was to be the Coronation. A Coronation which would herald the dawning of the new Elizabethan Age.

The parade was to be enormous. Thousands of soldiers from our far-flung Empire would take part. Whole regiments of splendid soldiers, dressed in their most elaborate uniforms, would march to the stirring sound of martial music. Mounted troops and military bands would vie with each other to create the greatest visual and audible impact. Horse-drawn carriages, stuffed with dignitaries of varying hues, would punctuate the procession and the very important ladies would do their utmost to out-feather the Hussars in their choice of headdress. All the world would come to London and expensive, temporary stands would be erected all around the route. I forget the precise details, but roughly it went from Buckingham Palace, through Admiralty Arch down Northumberland Avenue to the

Embankment, Parliament Square and Westminster Abbey. There the Queen would be crowned midst such pomp and ceremony as few people had ever witnessed. Then the triumphant procession was to travel through the West End of London – Marble Arch, Oxford Street, Regent Street, Haymarket, along the Mall and back to the Palace.

Well, as I say, I wasn't terribly interested in the whole thing. However, I awoke early that morning, looked out of my bedroom window and saw that the rain was absolutely tipping down. I turned on my bedside radio to hear an early morning news bulletin. The BBC news reader, with a throb of patriotism in his voice, announced the conquering of Everest by a British expedition. In fact, it was a Briton, Colonel Hunt, who led the expedition, but the successful climbers were, of course, Edmund Hillary (later Sir Edmund), a New Zealander and Sherpa Tensing from Nepal.

Anyway, it was all stirring stuff on the very day of the Coronation. But what about the weather? If anything, it was getting worse and likely to continue so according to the forecasters. I couldn't help feeling a little sorry for our new Queen. All that work and effort to put on a good show and only a few idiots would turn up in this downpour to cheer her on her way. Well, I thought, I'll show willing. I quickly bathed and shaved and, after a quick cup of coffee, got into my car and set out to shout my encouragement as Her Majesty majestically, if somewhat soggily, rode by.

I thought Trafalgar Square would be reasonably convenient for me. At St. Giles Circus, I was a bit put out to be stopped by a policeman. A very senior policeman he was. 'And where do you think you're going?' he asked. 'I'm going to London to see the Queen,' said I, rather too flippantly. He nearly had apoplexy. He explained to me, with a studied pretence of patience, that all roads leading to the procession route had been closed for many hours. The millions of people watching were in place and had been all night, so I would be well advised to turn around and make myself scarce. Well, it was still bucketing down with rain and I was tempted to take his advice. But to give up at the first fence somehow didn't seem very British on this most British of days.

I couldn't believe there wasn't some way. I had a rough idea of the route so I decided to drive to my old school at Blackfriars, dump the car and walk along the Embankment to the junction of Northumberland Avenue where the procession was to pass. All this went well enough until I started my walk. Hundreds of potential spectators were walking towards me, away from the big event, clearly being unable to gain any access. Asking around, my fears were confirmed. It was quite impossible to see a damned thing. Apparently, an enormous wooden barrier had been erected under Hungerford Bridge and it would have taken a battering ram to breach it. I was, by now, beginning to get quite wet. The parade was due to pass fairly soon and my chances of seeing it looked distinctly dodgy. Still, I'd come this far, I may as well walk the last half-mile and maybe I could slip around the barrier in some way. When I got there, my heart sank. It wasn't a barrier, it was a fortress. They'd built this huge fifteen-foot edifice abutting the bulwarks beneath Hungerford Bridge on the Charing Cross side and clear across the road to the Thames. Enormous solid wooden gates blocked the roadway. Had they been the gates debarring King Kong he'd never have made it to New York. Anyway, there was I with this impenetrable obstacle between me and my Sovereign, the rain pouring down and me feeling utterly frustrated. I was just about to give up and go home when something caught my eye. There were a number of ships tied up along the Embankment. A young sailor was coming down the gangplank from one of them and he was carrying a ladder. His purpose was instantly obvious. He was going to use it to get to the top of the barrier. It was a long heavy ladder, so I immediately gave him a hand, of course! Up we shinned and sat on top of the wall. We were under the bridge, so out of the rain. He even shared a bar of chocolate with me while we awaited the great Coronation Procession. Nobody saw it that day with greater satisfaction than I. History records the great event. The splendour of it all. The laughing Queen Salote of Tonga, dripping in her open carriage as she gaily waved to the crowds and me. The horses . . . the bands . . . the colours . . . world dignitaries . . . the gracious Queen and her young husband on their momentous journey. I saw it all and it is truly a wonderful memory.

There is an interesting sequel to that story. I had returned home after the procession had passed and was in plenty of time to see the crowning ceremony in Westminster Abbey, on the family television set. Television was quite new. Only the BBC and only black and white of course, but it was beginning to become very popular. The televising of the Coronation certainly boosted its growth. We, of course, had a set and proudly invited friends in to view. Helen Morgenstern, the girl from next door, whom I had once taken to Goodwood Races, was there. She was growing quite pretty now so, when the TV was over, I asked her if she'd like to come into Town with me to mingle midst the excitement.

The hordes of people were unbelievable. I do believe there were greater numbers even than on VE (Victory in Europe) night. It was all so good-humoured and friendly. The rain had finally stopped and just about everyone was making for the Palace. We found ourselves in The Mall, still in the car, but inexplicably, the only car in that great throng. A police motor cyclist beckoned us, most respectfully, to follow him. I've no idea who he thought we were, but he took us through the milling crowds towards the Horse Guards, where, believe it or not, we could safely park.

On the way, a very famous and popular character – Prince Monolulu – approached us. The self-styled 'Prince' Monolulu was a well known racing tipster. A huge, black man wearing tribal clothes and feathered head-dress, he stood out in any crowd. Quite why he selected us, I do not know, but he did. He bowed formally and in a deep, brown voice said 'Mazeltov'. Eight months later Helen and I were engaged to be married.

In 1954 I married the girl next door, Helen Lore Morgenstern. We stood together under the *chupa* in the synagogue at Upper Berkeley Street, London W.1. The wedding party which followed was notable for a number of reasons. I suppose my main impression was the dissimilarity between the respective families. On the one side, the Morgenstern set with their pronounced German accents and upper middle class pretensions. On the other, the Zetter multitude with their recent East End origins still transparently apparent. Never mind, it all went very well, both the formalities in the synagogue and the subsequent reception in the smart marquee in my new in-laws' garden in Hampstead Garden Suburb. I heard later that, after the departure of Helen and me, a number of guests (on the groom's side, of course!) got well tanked up, but it didn't matter very much and I do believe a good time was had by all.

I had asked Louis Brisacher to be my best man and was disappointed when he declined. Something about religious difference he said but, truth be told, it was his reluctance, because of unimaginable shyness, to make a speech. In his stead, David Isaacs did the honours . . . splendidly, of course. He cut quite a dash in his morning dress. Tall, handsome and witty, he charmed everyone in sight. He was also wonderfully generous in lending us his car for our honeymoon. Following the frugal disciplines which came with my engagement, I sold my beloved AC and replaced it with a Standard 8. Unbelievably, the best price I could get for my superb hand-made classic motor car, raised only enough to buy one of the cheapest production-line vehicles on the road. If only I'd been brave enough (or well off enough) to have kept the AC. I think it would have been worth a small fortune today (1990).

Never mind, the Standard turned out to be a thoroughly good little car which we enjoyed for about three years and 50,000 miles. I then went up-market to a Standard 10!

I do not intend to go into any detail about our first night as a married couple, except for the hotel where we spent it. In those happy days, it was both possible and advantageous to fly, with your car, to the Continent. Several companies ran this service, including an excellent organisation called Silver City Airways. One of their routes was from Lydd in Kent to Le Touquet and I had booked the car and ourselves to catch the 9 a.m. flight on the morning after the wedding. The best hotel I could find nearby for our honeymoon night was the very romantic fifteenth-century Mermaid Inn in Rye, just a few miles along the coast from Lydd. I had taken the trouble to visit the hotel some weeks earlier, to inspect and book their best room, which featured a magnificent four poster bed and all the trimmings one would expect in such a setting. By the time we had escaped from the reception and driven down to the coast it was quite late and we were eager to get to bed. (Well, it had been a long day!) Imagine my fury at being shown up to a poorly furnished, dingy attic room. I didn't make any fuss. Today I would, but I was young, nervous and inexperienced and just let them get away with it. I've always suspected that they never honoured my original booking because a better offer showed up and they were not bothered at what my reaction might have been. Needless to say, we have never been back to The Mermaid. It was, in fact, the only hiccup on an otherwise perfect trip. We caught our flight the next morning and twenty minutes later were in Le Touquet. From there we headed south in David's Triumph TR2. This stylish little touring car might have been made for such a journey and such an occasion. Just for fun, but largely to show off a bit to Helen, we took the Monte Carlo Rally route from Lyon southwards. The route over the Massif Central, then back to Valence (of fond memory) and finally through the passes in the Alps, was breathtakingly beautiful and most decidedly scary. One hairpin bend after another, up and down precipitous mountains. I'd never before driven that section in daylight. The very memory of the same journey at night, during the worst of winter conditions and driving against the clock, gave me the colly-wobbles. Helen found the whole thing desperately exciting, but made me promise never again to do the 'Monte'. I readily did so, albeit with reluctant relief.

Our honeymoon was spent, of course, at Cap Estel. Robert Squarciafichi, true to his word, welcomed us to his most spectacular dream hotel on the shore of the Mediterranean. Everything about it exceeded expectations and three glorious weeks later we were back in London. This, then, was the auspicious start of thirty-six years of married bliss and still counting.

# Chapter 12

# The Halcyon Years

Getting married, setting up house, having children. How ordinary, how boring, how mundane, how marvellous! Notwithstanding the fact that nearly everybody does it, that it is probably the greatest common denominator in our society, in my strongly held opinion; it still is the very essence of civilisation. Far beyond religion, race or colour, the family unit takes pride of place. Why should this be? What is there that is so very special about it all? I don't know. I shall never forget my wedding day, but what's so unique about that, millions of people get married. Our first home together is as fresh in my memory as the newly painted kitchen on the day we moved in. The staggering emotion of having my first child born has only once been matched and that was when my second child was born.

However much I had loved my thirty-one years before 1954, that year was my watershed. My pre-marriage existence falls into a completely different category compared with all that happened thereafter. So what did happen thereafter? Well, as I said, much the same as happens to nearly everyone. The traumas that all young couples suffer when they first try to learn to live together. If you survive, and happily most do, they turn out to be 'the halcyon years'.

Our first home was a delightful terraced house at 29 Frognal, Hampstead. It was newly built. In fact, we bought it during construction with a promise that it would be ready for occupation in good time for our return from the honeymoon. It wasn't, of course, so we spent five frustrating weeks living with Kurt and Hilda Morgenstern at 18 Lyttelton Road, Hampstead Garden Suburb. It would be silly to claim those weeks were ideal or happy –

they were not. Like all young married couples, we wanted to be on our own. We wanted to spend our evenings curled up together on a settee doing outrageous things. We wanted to stay in bed until lunchtime on Sunday morning. We wanted to be sloppy around the house. What we most certainly did not want was to be under scrutiny or to be polite and well mannered. Kurt and Hilda did their best and I'm grateful for the chance it gave me to know them a little better. Kurt was a well meaning man brought up to believe, to truly believe, that man was lord and master in his own house, whilst Hilda was brought up to accept that doctrine without question. They really were a typical German upper middle class Victorian family. He was bombastic, demanding, self-centred, naive, rather silly but very kind. She was meek, obedient, an efficient housewife to her fingertips and a preparer of food the very memory of which still makes my mouth water. She was also a lovely, intelligent woman who very sadly was to die too early at a youthful forty-six years of age. A short, mostly unhappy life.

Frognal, when we finally moved in, was the perfect start. It was a pretty house in an ideal location and it cost me the princely sum of £3,500. Quite a lot in 1954. We remained there for four years during which time my daughter, Carolyn Jane, was born in the October of 1957 at the Westminster Hospital. Our very fashionable gynaecologist was Roger De Vere . . . 'divine De Vere' as he was known. He was also a good fishing friend of mine. When I asked him the weight of my new baby daughter, he replied that they hadn't yet weighed her but 'if she'd been a salmon, she'd go about seven pounds!'

Our garden in Frognal was just about as small as a garden can be. Two deck chairs were cosy, three was a crowd. So, as both Helen and I loved the country, and wanted a good garden for our offspring, we decided to move. We found our way to Hadley Wood in Hertfordshire. In Avenue House, Beech Hill Avenue, we found the perfect family home for the next sixteen happy years. I'd sold Frognal for £5,000. Over 40% profit in just four years! Avenue House cost me £8,000. A mind-boggling amount but, with a 50% mortgage and interest rates at 6%, just about manageable. We bought a minute Yorkshire terrier we called Pip because it seemed appropriate. We acquired a Swiss nanny we called Rita because that was her name. Both of them became much beloved family favourites. Rita was as Swiss as Gruyère and the perfect addition to the Zetter household. Her Swiss reserve soon melted and she became a natural member of the family.

Rita loved Carolyn and cared for her with a fastidious attention to hygiene and good manners. Helen added the requisite maternal qualities and I spoiled her rotten. It was a formula that proved hugely successful. We built a swimming pool right at the back of our handsome half-acre garden.

Helen took the view that, delightful as it was during the summer, for most of the year it was an eyesore, so it should be out of sight. Isn't that sensible? It perfectly typifies her down to earth common sense.

Carrie started school in Barnet when she was just three years old. It was a convent school called St. Martha's and was run by mostly Irish nuns. Why on earth, you might ask, did we choose a Catholic school? Our respective parents certainly did – ask I mean. There were a number of reasons. Firstly, neither Helen nor I were religious. Helen, in fact, positively shunned public acknowledgement of her Jewish ancestry. Understandable, perhaps, when you remember the first seven years of her life had been spent in Nazi Germany. There, she was able to conceal her origin, without rejecting it, owing to her Aryan appearance. I, too, was not the archetype Hebrew, but more disposed to claim allegiance than Helen. Not the faith, of course, the race, the Jewish race.

God forgive me, but I just cannot accept or believe the practice of Judaism or, indeed, any of man's religions. Without exception, I suspect their teachings rely upon fear and fable to achieve acceptability. While I unhesitatingly acknowledge that religions are fashioned in the belief that their doctrines are for the greater good, they base their preaching on fairy tales which have little, if any, basis in truth or reality. Why then, you might ask, have the great religions survived for so long and been practised by some of the greatest intellects in our societies down the ages? I've always been bothered by that question. I believe the answer may lie in the very wisdom of those spiritual and intellectual leaders. Perhaps they truly believe that the acceptance of faith, in whatever guise, is for the greater good. Whether the faith is founded on fact or fiction is really of no concern to them. All the while God-fearing multitudes lead better lives and are better citizens, then the lesson is right. They, the leaders, live out an expediency. They set the example by being seen to worship God according to the rules of their chosen doctrine.

Having written all that, I know it's not enough. It's far too simplistic, certainly arrogant and may well be hurtful to some. It also leaves too many questions for which I do not have the answers. So many people get so much comfort because of their faith. I rejoice for them and I am not jealous. God bless them. Perhaps, at times, I may be a little envious, but there it is, I am not a believer. I am not religious and neither is Helen, which is why we were content to send Carolyn to St. Martha's Convent without fearing that she might be indoctrinated. It was also the nearest kindergarten!

Shortly thereafter, our second child was conceived. Following a late autumn holiday in Juan les Pins in 1960, my son, Adam Oliver, was born on 14 June 1961. Right from the start Adam was a mischievous baby. Whereas Carrie had been angelic and never once disturbed our night's rest, Adam took the greatest possible delight in ensuring he had a steady stream of visitors throughout the night. Not that he ever cried. I suppose it would best be described as loud baby singing, but it was clearly designed to attract attention and it most certainly achieved its objective.

Wearing as it was, Adam's bubbling good humour and happy disposition captivated us all. Rita fell in love with him. Carrie adored him. Helen and I doted upon him. So life was rosy. Business flourished and we were enjoying the rewards of that success.

On a whim, we bought ourselves a lovely week-end flat on the coast at Frinton. It was convenient to get to from Hadley Wood and was a distinctly up-market small seaside resort in North Essex. You have to drive over a level crossing to get into the town and it might have been the origin for the expression 'the other side of the tracks'. Inside the crossing gates, Frinton was a real snobby, 'posh' place with smart houses, no caravans, no buses, no pubs and the inhabitants ran credit accounts with their local shopkeepers, including 'Boots the Cash Chemists'.

I enquired, with some trepidation, as to the chances of joining the golf club. 'Delighted my dear fellow,' I was surprisingly told. It seems that only local tradesmen were barred. 'Embarrassing to partner a chap with whom you have an overdue account. What!'

We bought a boat, a sixteen-foot cabin cruiser, and kept it on the Twizzle, a lovely tidal river that, twice a day, helps drain Walton-on-the-Naze. A real Essex man, John Titchmarsh, was putting his heart, soul and life into building a marina in that beautiful but difficult environment. Today, some thirty odd years later, it's worth driving out to have a look at it. It's a joy to see how well he has succeeded. The boat added a new dimension to our happiness. What glorious fun it was to pile into that little craft on a beautiful sunny day. After whizzing round the big ships, sailing out of Harwich just across the bay, we would run up onto the beach of a tiny island in the Naze. There, just seventy miles from London, at the height of the summer season, we would have the place to ourselves. Helen and I, Rita, Carrie and Adam were the only inhabitants. We would swim, sunbathe, play ball, picnic and spend blissful hours, returning satisfyingly exhausted to our luxury apartment overlooking the greensward and the sea. We all loved Frinton. I wrote a poem during our happy years there. It's the only thing I've ever had published. Here it is.

## Essex

Old fashioned docks, much industry, some evil–smelling creeks,
   This county isn't 'county', no Royal-favoured weeks,
The many silted estuaries impede the bracken seas,
   The effluent of London, the soot-encrusted trees.

But have you on the ebbing tide found your way to Horsey Isle,
   and vanished on the sand dunes there, and lazed away a gentle while,
Then stirred and gathered samphire along the lonely shore,
   and scurried back, before the sea reclaims the road once more?

Or tripped to Southend by the sea, along the old Arterial Road,
   a fussy hour from London Town, where coaches take their eager load,
The longest pier, the golden mile, the special taste of Rossi's ice,
   where East-end kids of any age may first discover paradise?

Or wandered down a country lane, some quiet, peaceful autumn night,
   and wondered at the burning fields, and why they had been set alight,
Perhaps some fierce, marauding horde, bent on an evil path of sin?
   or farmers burning stubble, with the harvest safely in?

Or parked beyond the caravans, bespoiling Walton-on-the-Naze,
   and walked up to the headland where, in wonder, you may stand
   and gaze
At great Thames barges sailing by between the liners and the yachts,
   and merchant ships and speeding boats and dinghies laying
   lobster pots,
And on those cliffs upon whose face a million easterlies have blown,
   the fossil hunters, merrily, turn over every unturned stone.

> This portion of East Anglia,
>    this part of this great blessed plot,
> this country cockney dialect
>    this perfect English polyglot,
> this ancient prehistoric land
>    this birthplace of the free,
> this bloody earth, this muddy realm,
>    this 'Essex by the sea'.

*PZ (on the right) in the late twenties.*

*Winning Ways 1936 – admiring a cheque for £1,000 from the "Irish Sweep",
Grandma (Sarah Stodel), Grandpa (Daddy Dick), The "Old Man" (Syd Zetter),
family friend (Sophie Baruch), Mum (Esther Zetter) and front row, PZ.*

## MUSIC DURING DINNER

Selections from the following :

| March | Martial Moments | *A. Winter* |
| Anthem | Hartikvah | *Reverend* |
| Overture | Orpheus of the Underworld | *Offenbach* |
| Selection | Bitter Sweet | *S. Romberg* |
| Paraphrase | Faust | *Gounod* |
| Extract | Poem | *L. Fibich* |
| Selection | Desert Song | *S. Romberg* |
| Saxophone Solo | Ochur-Churmia | |
| | Played by Judy Jackson | |
| Medley | Let's All Sing | *Stodden* |
| Selection | Classica | *M. Ewing* |
| Popular Tunes | Old and New | Band |
| Russian | Souvenir D'Ukraine | *Ferraris* |
| Final | American Medley | *D. Somers* |

*Barnett's Orchestra*
Directed by DAVID JACKSON

*Toast Master*
**B. Bernard**

## MENU

Cocktail
———
Melon
———
Boiled Salmon, Sauce Hollandaise
Duchess Potatoes, Cucumber
———
Vermicelli Soup
———
Tomato Soup
———
Lamb Cutlets, Cauliflower
White Sauce
———
Salads
———
Benedictine Water Ice
———
Roast Chicken, French Potatoes
Green Peas
———
Cucumber, Olives, Gherkins
———
Asparagus, Sauce Vinegrette
———
Iced Peach Baskets
———
Dessert
———
Black Coffee

*Catered by*
**A. Barnett,**
43 Mossford Street,
Burdett Road, Bow. E3
ADVance 3808

**3 The Leas,**
**Westcliff-on-Sea**

*Barmitzvah Menu 1936.*

*The Old Citizens Rugby Club 1948 – PZ unusually placed in the "Front Row"
(4th from left).*

*The A.C. getting a lift to Monte Carlo (1954).*

XXIII RALLYE AUTOMOBILE DE MONTE-CARLO
ARRIVEE A MONACO

*"We made it!"*

*My beautiful Allard – two "Montes" to its credit (\*With acknowledgement to AB Nordbok, Gothenburg, Sweden).*

*The Pool Promoters (left to right) – Vernon Sangster (Vernons), Brierley Jones (Littlewoods), G. R. Kennerley (Vernons), Cecil Moores (Littlewoods), PZ.*

S.A.F. Logo – designed by Helen Zetter.

Kurt Morgenstern, PZ, Sydney Zetter at a Mansion House dinner.

A reception at "Les Ambassadeurs" (left to right) – John Mills, a lovely lady (unknown), David Nations, PZ, Eric Morecombe.

*Monte Carlo bound (1952) – Louis Brisacher, David Isaacs, PZ, Ben Ward.*

*The party to launch SAF 1977 (left to right) – Alan Weeks, PZ, Denis Howell, John Reid, Elton John.*

*Meeting H.R.H. The Duke of Edinburgh 1980 – a "Sponsors of Sport" group discussion organised by C.C.P.R.*

*Cliff Morgan, Alan Weeks, PZ, Denis Howell.*

*Sebastian Coe presenting "The Manning Award" to PZ 1982.*

*The Duke commands attention – John McDonnell, PZ, Cris Cory, Roymond Miguel, H.R.H.*

*The "Torvill & Dean" Gala at Richmond Ice Rink 1984 (front row left to right)*
*– Neil Macfarlane, Mary Glen Haig, Courtney Jones, Margaret Thatcher,*
*Denis Thatcher, Helen Zetter, PZ. (Second row centre) Jane Weeks, Alan Weeks.*

*The Mansion House SAF Dinner 1986 – guests include Her Royal Highness the*
*Princess Anne, The Lord Mayor and Lady Mayoress, Mr. & Mrs. Cecil Parkinson,*
*Mr. & Mrs. Adrian Metcalfe, Shirley Porter, Helen Zetter, and PZ.*

*Commonwealth Games 1986 – Margaret Thatcher, Helen Zetter, PZ, Carrie Zetter.*

*PZ making a point to the P.M.*

*Last days at No. 10 – PZ with Denis Thatcher in Downing Street on the day Margaret Thatcher resigned as Prime Minister.*

*The Chinese Connection – a photograph taken in Peking (no known connection).*

*Jayne Torvill and Karen Barber delighting PZ.*

*Torvill & Dean meet PZ at The Mansion House.*

*Virginia Leng & PZ 1987.*

*Maggie Hohmann (Roy Moore Award) – PZ, Malcolm Cooper receiving PZ Award 1988.*

*Karen Briggs receiving the Paul Zetter Award 1989 – admired by
H.R.H. Prince Edward.*

*Dick Jeeps informing PZ.*

*PZ, Mary Glen Haig, Sir Robin Brook.*

*PZ retires from S.A.F. (left to right) – Mary Glen Haig, Eddie Kulukundis, PZ about to embrace Shirley Porter.*

*Memories – PZ surveying a Daimler Scout Car in 1991 at a Transport Museum in Jersey.*

*California Family Group – PZ, Helen, Adam with Alex, Joni with Jake.*

# Chapter 13

# Only Pools and Horses?

Nothing stays perfect for ever. My mother died. Dearest Esther, whom everybody loved, died of lung cancer. She had smoked heavily and paid the price. I stopped smoking. There were no other dramatic consequences, but it is worth recording that she left her significant shareholding in Zetters jointly to Adam and Carrie. My father, one year later, being fearful of lonely years, remarried. That came as a complete bombshell. He rang me from home one day, which in itself was odd, as I saw him most days at the office. 'I have become engaged to marry Hannah Soester,' he blurted out on the telephone. After an interminable silence he said, 'Well, for God's sake, say something.' To his immense relief I gave them both my blessing. Hannah was a smart-looking Jewish woman about ten years his junior, whom I thought to be a distant family associate. She would, and did, make him a good wife and companion for the remainder of his days. While it is true that I was literally dumbfounded at my father's news, all in all, I was well pleased with the arrangement. Incidentally, there was no issue from the union!

During the years of my mother's illness, my father had less and less involvement in the day-to-day management of the business. Nevertheless, his knowledge of the Pools industry and his practical wisdom were invaluable. He could never really rationalise his thoughts, but it would be an unwise man who didn't take account of them. Frustrating as it so often was, my Old Man was invariably right for the wrong reasons. While it is true that, by now, I had taken hold of the Company, I leant very heavily on the advice of my father and dear Solly Littlestone, our old friend and the

101

senior partner with Littlestone & Co., the Company's accountants. 'Little-stones' had flourished alongside us and they now boasted several bright up and coming young partners. Two of them, Terry Yardley and Andreas Hadjioannou were to play important roles in the following years. It seemed that Terry had always been around. Andreas, who was, in fact, a Greek Cypriot, had come to London to study for and become a chartered accountant. He joined 'Littlestones' as a junior and Solly had virtually adopted him. Andreas was a beautiful 'Adonis' with the manners of an aristocrat, the charm of an angel and the intellect of Aristotle. I enjoyed and took great advantage of the benefit of all this brain power around me.

The Pools industry was metamorphosing. Betting duty and legislation had effectively reduced the number of Pool promoters to a respectable few. Two giants, Littlewoods and Vernons, shared about 70% of the total turnover. Shermans, a potential giant, had 15% and then the rest of us. About ten in all. It would be wrong to claim that I ever consciously made a strategic corporate plan. More accurately, one evolved as a consequence of wise counsel.

In retrospect, this was the strategy. First and most important, join the Pool Promoters Association (the PPA). Easier said than done. It was virtually a closed shop. The 'establishment' companies, those surviving the demise of the war-time Unity Pools, i.e. Littlewoods, Vernons, Copes and Murphy's, seemed intent on keeping it that way. There were chinks in their armour, however. Perhaps a little background on the Pools Industry might be helpful at this stage. After the war and the break up of Unity Pools, the nature of Pool betting changed. The hitherto popularity of the Penny Points Pools began to wane and the Treble Chance Pools to prosper. It is easy to understand why. The Points Pools consisted of a selected list of matches, generally fourteen, which the Pool promoter considered to be the most difficult. The punter had to forecast the results of them all! This used to be a formidable task. However, with the emergence of 'quality' football and improving newspaper forecasting, it was getting easier to predict results. Added to that, coupon compilers needed to go to press weeks before matches were to be played, whereas punters could forecast games just a day or so beforehand. It was a recipe for low payouts, precisely the opposite of the attraction of Pools – 'Jackpots!'

The Treble Chance, however, was a Pool of a very different nature. It was a brilliant concept which has been attributed to Thomas Strang, an early Scottish promoter. Each game result was awarded a points value. One point for a home win, two for an away and three for a draw. So, three chances for every forecast . . . hence Treble Chance. Today, with changes to the points structure, the name is now a misnomer. The punter was asked to select eight games, ideally to end as draws, from a list of over fifty matches, thus giving a target total of 24 points. The average number of drawn matches when the Pool was first introduced was about ten each week, although this average was to increase rather too rapidly as the Pool gained popularity. Finding the right eight gave us, the promoters, a return to the formula for Jackpot payouts. As the whole psyche of Pool betting was based on a simple formula 'the more difficult the Pool, the fewer winners and the bigger the dividends', the popularity of the Treble Chance was universally welcomed. Big dividends would become the norm once more. But how, then, could the smaller companies hope to compete against the bigger ones? After all, the bigger the Pool the bigger the pay out. Clever Shermans sought to redress that balance by reducing stakes (i.e. the cost of the bet). We quickly followed and so a stake war ensued, that was to rage for some years.

Companies, both in and out of the PPA, joined battle in the never-ending pursuit of new clients. In itself this was no bad thing; it coincided, however, with a new form of coupon betting called 'plans'. These were formula entries which, while consisting of a large number of lines printed in full and given a title, could be entered in a single column on the coupon thus making large bets quick and easy for the client. Together with the increase in popularity of permutations (mathematical compiled entries) and cut price stakes, the Pools were inundated with complicated coupons. Enormous checking problems ensued, in sifting winners, particularly on weeks when there was a large number of drawn matches. Of course, 'Sods Law' being what it was, there were more and more such weeks. Changing tactics in the game produced more defensive play. Defensive play produced more draws. So, with cheaper entries, easier ways to make them and a glut of winners on the Treble Chance, the industry was in disarray. Only concerted action could avert the impending catastrophy.

There were four main protagonists outside the PPA, Shermans Pools, Empire Pools, Soccer Pools and ourselves. It seemed to me that it would be a healthier industry (and a way in for us) if all the leading players could meet and agree on sensible business practices. A certain Michael Watkins was, I knew, the Secretary to the PPA. Following a highly critical article in the *Daily Mail* on the disgraceful laxity of the Pools companies, whereby thousands of their clients had needed to claim for their winnings, I took the opportunity to phone him and suggest a round table discussion on the serious problems damaging the industry. To my surprise and delight a meeting was arranged for the following week, at which all the members of the PPA attended, as did the main firms outside. That is Shermans, Empire, Soccer and us. The meeting was friendly, and productive beyond expectation. Agreements were reached on plan registrations, agents' commission and many other sensible practices. We were also all invited, and agreed, to join the PPA. The first step of my unsuspected master plan had been accomplished.

Solly Littlestone and my father were delighted. 'You have now been nationally recognised and accepted, you are making good profits, you should really think about going public,' Solly said. 'The trouble is, of course, you're a one-business business,' he added. 'You really need more than just a single source of income before the Stock Exchange will even consider you favourably.'

'What about our betting shops?' asked the Old Man.

He was referring to 'Zetters Racing' as it was called. This was an early attempt at diversification, stemming from a small, credit book-making business my father had always run. When betting shops became legal in 1949, we tried to take advantage of the new opportunities on offer. We had six ideally-sited betting shops and they never made a penny! Dave Zetter, my cousin on my father's side, was the General Manager and he employed two of his brothers in a couple of our better shops. They were all good boys, real racing fraternity graduates, who knew the game backwards. That's what the Old Man thought. Frankly, they were old-style course bookies who knew all the tricks of the trade and that was the trouble. It was neither needed nor beneficial in the modern day management of a betting shop.

As a typical example, I heard about one manager (not Dave or his brothers) who gave tips. Free tips to his favourite punters. What he did was to pick a six horse handicap and give each of six punters a different horse to back. 'Nothing for the tip,' he'd say, 'But you might like to put a quid on for me and it's a racing certainty.' . . . It was for him! There is no doubt that Dave had been promoted above his ability. A nice man, honest in his way, loyal to the Company and fiercely protective of his brothers. So tolerant! But tolerance is not a desirable attribute in racing management. So, the shops never brought in any profit. There were only two options as I saw it . . . change the management or sell the shops. I think we chose the wrong one . . . we sold! We did well, mind you. I forget the exact amount, but it was a sizeable sum which I had, in my mind, already spent on a pet project, one which satisfied Solly's prerequisite of more than one string to our bow. I had decided to go into Bingo. This, in my view, was the way forward.

Bingo had been recently legalised and was flourishing. The old 'flea pits' suddenly had a new lease of life. Those much beloved pre-war theatres-cum-cinemas, long since put out of business by the universal popularity of television, were once more playing to packed houses. This time their audiences were predominately working class ladies playing Bingo. The law required Bingo to be played in private members' clubs, so that's what the entrepreneurs made them. And didn't those dear ladies love it. Their very own club, with their very own membership card, where they could spend a happy evening while the old man was down at the pub. It took off.

It became an instant success and I wanted Zetters to be a participant in this exciting new industry. I was lucky. My friend, my best man, my Old Citizen rugby team mate, David Isaacs, was already in the business up to his eyebrows. David's father's business had gone bankrupt and ever-resourceful David had got himself a job as a Bingo caller. He worked for Laurie Marsh who had turned the defunct Classic Cinemas chain into Bingo Clubs. As they prospered, so did David, and he very soon achieved junior management level, but there he stopped. Because of the hierarchy of the company, he had, in his view, reached the pinnacle of his prospects. That's where I came in. I asked David if he could start Bingo for Zetters. I would make him Managing Director, he could write his own contract and we would make £100,000 available to a new company to be called Zetters Enterprises Limited. So it was. In 1964 Zetters Enterprises commenced trading in an unbelievably scruffy ex-dance hall, ex-boxing arena, ex-factory, ex-roller-skating rink in Birmingham. It was an immediate success. Nevertheless the Old Man was still very dubious about this latest 'nine day wonder'. Solly Littlestone had no such reservations. 'You've taken another step in the grand design, haven't you?' he queried. I'd no idea what he meant, but I was to find out by the following year.

# Chapter 14

# French Leave

Meanwhile, back at the homestead, family life was blooming. Rita, dear Rita Gassmann, returned to her real labour of love, nursing in a great Swiss hospital in Basle.

Adam joined Carrie at St. Martha's Convent School, where she fiercely protected his interests and welfare until leaving to go to 'The Mount', a girls' public school in Mill Hill. Magically the years ticked by. Before he could say ABC, Adam moved to Lochinvar House, a prep. school in Potters Bar. His stay there was unhappy and short-lived. We discovered that he was dyslexic which, as far as Lochinvar was concerned, removed them from any obligation of trying to educate him. Just before his final year, he broke a leg in a silly playground incident. As soon as he was out of plaster, we took a plane to Nice and spent two blissful weeks back at Cap Estel.

What a change it was from Frinton. An unfair comparison perhaps, but we couldn't help making it. It was a new world for Carrie and Adam, of course, and they very readily fell for the lotus charms of the French Riviera. On one expedition to Nice, we glanced into the window of an estate agent alongside the Negresco Hotel on the Promenade des Anglais. Just casually, you understand, and only to compare property prices with England. One display caught our eye. Domaine du Loup. Appartements Nouveaux. Vue de Mer. Terrasse. Piscine Privée. Parc Privé. Magasins. Club. 4 ou 5 Pièces. Près de Nice. Prix de 200,000F. Couldn't be, could it? At 13.50 francs to the pound that was less than £15,000. Roughly the value of the flat in Frinton. Couldn't be, could it? 'Let's go and have a look,' said Helen. 'It'll probably be a load of rubbish, but let's go and have a look anyway.'

André Cicurel, the estate agent, turned out to be a Jewish Egyptian emigrant living in France. The grandson of a well known and once wealthy Egyptian family, he had prudently left his doubtful inheritance and had chosen the South of France to bring up his family and earn his living. Having been educated at Repton, a fine English public school, he could boast fluency in English, as well as several other languages. Certainly, and much to our delight, his English truly was perfect. Anyway, we all piled into this charming man's car and drove just along the coast. Ten minutes beyond Nice Airport lies the small coastal resort of Cagnes-sur-Mer, and in the foothills, just above and overlooking the sea, was Domaine du Loup.

The 'Domaine', which was an almost completed development, occupied about 100 acres of breathtakingly beautiful hillside. It comprised about six well separated blocks of flats, strategically sited within a few minutes walking distance of the private Olympic-sized swimming pool, club house, tennis courts and restaurant. A smart little shopping precinct was under construction and all facilities provided ample parking spaces. There were two large artificial lakes on the estate, mature trees abounded and the landscaping, throughout the entire area, was a joy to behold. Our family requirements called for a three-bedroom apartment. We were shown the ultimate dream. Three bedrooms . . . two fully tiled bathrooms . . . a fully fitted kitchen . . . a large lounge and dining room and marble flooring throughout. An enormous tiled terrace extended around three sides of the flat. The whole thing, fully decorated to our choice, would cost us 280,000F. (£21,000).

We came, we saw, we bought it!

Now we knew the sweet life. *La vie en rose*. Of course, we sold the flat at Frinton, as being superfluous, and now, on every school holiday, down we all trooped to the South of France. Long weeks of easy living, bringing us all gastronomic and cultural delights. The fun of introducing the children to our old, well loved, haunts was enhanced by finding more and more new ones. The food market in Antibes and the enormous general market every Friday morning in Ventimiglia, just over the border into Italy. The Jacques Cousteau Museum in Monte Carlo. The Roman Amphitheatre at Arles. The wild horses in the Carmargue. The exciting back streets of Marseilles. The old town of Nice. The sensualism of St. Tropez and the spectacular aura of the Alps as the ever present backdrop. And all the time, the food! The meals we had! The choice of restaurants, from the lavish luxury of Oustan de Baumanière at Les Baux-de-Provence to the equally satisfying fare to be had at the numerous Routiers.

Then there was the sea . . . the crystal clear Mediterranean. Naturally, we bought a boat: a twenty-five foot Riva Sports Fisherman, the Rolls Royce of power boats. On Helen's inspiration we named it CHAP (Carrie, Helen, Adam, Paul). We acquired a mooring at Marina Baie des Anges, a fashionable new yacht harbour encircled on three sides by futuristic pyramid-type apartments. Being just five minutes drive away from our luxurious flat, the freedom of the hospitable seas along the Côte d'Azur lapped almost literally at our door-step. Our seagoing adventures were the highlights of every holiday. Water skiing was an early activity at which we quickly excelled. More adventurous excursions followed and those frequently took us far out of sight of land. It was commonplace on these trips for schools of porpoises to 'ride' our bow wave. Large stingrays were often encountered and occasionally, even huge whales, happily spouting and quite impervious to our presence, allowed us to get within a few yards of them. Tuna fishing, in the autumn, was exciting sport and frequently produced enough fish to supply ourselves and neighbours. On one occasion, Adam took a superfluous fish to barter with a local restaurant. Four free meals with plonk for a two-kilo tuna resulted. No bad, eh?

Sometimes our trips took us further afield. Helen wanted to go to Corsica. No great expedition, just a quick visit to give us an impression of that beautiful French island 100 miles south of Nice. One day, while waiting at Nice airport for me to arrive on the London flight, she had spotted an advert for 'Vue La Corse'. They offered a day trip every Friday, with flights to and from Nice (one hour each way) and a guided coach tour of the island, including a four course lunch with wine. All for 200F (about £16). Well, it was an offer we couldn't refuse. Punctually at 7.45 a.m. on the chosen Friday the four of us, Helen, Carrie, Adam and I, presented ourselves at the appropriate desk in the departure concourse. The smart-looking booking clerk at Vue La Corse greeted us warmly and introduced himself as Marius. 'Ah! you Engleesh are always punctual. Les Allemands, were first, of course. Now, les Hollandais and two of my French compatriots, who will be last, and then we depart.' He was right, but they arrived before 8 a.m. so we were all present and correct in time for the scheduled start. Marius shepherded the ten of us through a maze of passages and out of a back door of the terminal onto the tarmac. We threaded our way through a gaggle of parked aircraft to a shabby looking hangar where, to everybody's chagrin, was our plane. A twin engined De Havilland, with every appearance of being a survivor from the Battle of Britain. Never mind, we all crawled in, through a round hole in the belly, and occupied the ten makeshift seats. Then, the selfsame Marius came on board, donned a pilot's cap and, with a dubious looking teenager in the second pilot's seat, taxied out to a little used runway and off we went to Corsica.

It was a marvellous tour. Dear Marius produced an old charabanc at Ajaccio. He'd exchanged his pilot's cap for a beret and, throughout his circuitous drive, gave us a non-stop, multi-lingual, running commentary over the ancient public address system. Numerous Monuments de Napoléon were proudly pointed out; 'Le Générale' seemed to have slept in just about every *auberge* or hotel on the island!

We enjoyed a feast of a lunch under some olive trees in a small estaminet near Porticeiv. Feeling satiated and very contented, we were driven back to Ajaccio where we wandered through the produce market in the Caesar Compinchi Square. The olives were the size of Victoria plums and equally succulent. Fishing boats were unloading nearby in the inner harbour at the Jetée de la Citadelle, beneath La Maison Bonaparte, and the locals and hoteliers were buying fish along the quay, just as their ancestors had done before them. The time to return to the airport came all too soon. We'd really seen so little of this fascinating French island with its predominately Italian culture. I vowed to return, but sadly I haven't done so yet. The day was not to end without incident. Our general factotum, who had won the affection of us all, once more exchanged headgear and up into the blue sky we soared. Settling ourselves as comfortably as possible for the hour flight to Nice we were somewhat alarmed, a few minutes later, to note the plane descending steeply between two mountain outcrops. He landed on a grass-strip runway near Porto Vecchio on the south-eastern tip of Corsica. There, an old black American limousine, reminiscent of the gangster era of Chicago, drove out to us and handed a small parcel through a window flap on the flight deck. We took off for a second time but, ten minutes later down we went again, this time near Corte, right in the middle of the island. Yet, again, the same mysterious transaction was enacted. Twice more at Calvi and Bastia respectively, the same procedure took place. Finally, to the obvious relief of all passengers, we headed due north, over the sea, destination Nice. Notwithstanding the sinister implications of those furtive rendezvous, I couldn't resist asking Marius what those intriguing packages contained.

'Ah, monsieur, you would not understand,' he said. 'It is Friday today, oui? Tomorrow we have the football. I am an agent for the pronostique, the Football Pools, comprends? Non, I think not.'

"Oh, oui," I thought, I most certainly *did* understand, but I didn't enlighten him.

For seven years we utilised our happy, holiday home in the sun at every opportunity and then we sold it. Why? What went wrong? Well, nothing really. But using the same locale every holiday, year after year, even paradise would begin to pall. Added to which, we were getting too many visitors . . . we were hardly ever alone. The kids, too, were growing up and wanting to do other things. Then, we had a nasty burglary and that really put the kybosh on it. I put the place on the market and sold it for £80,000 tax paid. Not a bad profit after seven glorious years. A funny little incident occurred during the sale. André Cicurel most ably conducted the transaction. When the price had been agreed he confidentially informed me that I would receive 50% of the money in cash in order to avoid Capital Gains Tax. 'Quite normal,' he explained, 'everybody does it'.

'Not me,' I told him.

'But, Paul,' he protested, 'You must, otherwise you will set an unacceptable precedent.'

'So what?' I replied with gross insensitivity.

'So you will cause a sensation, that's what,' André replied somewhat huffily, quite surprising for such a mild mannered man. 'By French law,' he explained, 'property gains tax income in the Provence Region has to be published. Every year it's zero, but this year your payment will be recorded. It will be the only one. You could be lynched.'

I wasn't.

# Chapter 15

# Who's looking after the Shop?

During those seven years of glorious gluttony, commercial life went on and I was still most actively engaged in it. I commuted regularly between London and Nice and could justifiably claim to have been an early 'jet setter' (or 'Jet Zetter' as Helen put it).

The Pools Promoters Association commanded the greater part of my thinking time, for it was to play an ever-increasing importance in my undefined corporate plan. The rapport that existed between promoters had its real origins in the appalling winter of 1963. A short one-and-a-half years after we'd all first got together as PPA at the Mayfair Hotel, we were hit by the worst winter weather in anyone's experience. Week after week, dozens of games were snowed-off and the Pools cancelled. On the Monday, following the third abortive Saturday, an emergency meeting was called to see if anyone had any bright ideas which would enable us to run a Pool. The situation really was very serious. All operating expenses, e.g. staff, printing, post, advertising and a myriad of other costs, still had to be met, but there was nothing coming in. To make matters worse, the long-range weather forecast predicted a continuance of the bad weather with no let-up in sight.

The meeting took place at the Grosvenor House Hotel in Park Lane, where Cecil Moores had his permanent suite. It was scheduled to start at 11 a.m. thus giving time for the Liverpool contingent (i.e. Littlewoods and Vernons) to catch the first train out of Lime Street to Euston on the Monday morning. Owing to the dreadful weather, the train was delayed by over four hours, so the meeting eventually got under way at 3 p.m. It went

111

on, with just a midnight to 8 a.m. break, for thirty-two hours. At the end of that time, we had agreed to consider a proposal from Mr Jim Ledwith, the rough-diamond Managing Director of Empire Pools of Blackpool. He had suggested that we put together a panel of well known, well respected experts on football, who would adjudicate on those cancelled Saturday football matches and award a result which would stand for the pool bet. It was the most far-fetched, outrageous idea any of us had ever heard, but it was about the only one on the table. The arguments raged over all those long hours. Finally two things were agreed:

1. We should get a legal opinion.
2. We should meet again immediately an opinion was available.

Three days later, on the Friday morning, we were summoned back to Grosvenor House. The opinion was ready. As I remember, it came from Sam Stamler, an eminent barrister destined to become an even more eminent QC. Like all legal opinions it was equivocal. Basically, he admitted that he didn't know, since there was neither specific legislation nor, of course, any case law. He was definite that it wasn't a lottery, in that the findings of a panel of experts clearly were as a result of their expertise. On balance, he gave a favourable judgement, but added a caveat. Should the police decide to challenge the operation of a Football Pool where the results were decided by a Pools Panel and the court judgement went against us, we would be subject to a fine not exceeding £100 . . . clearly, no cause for concern. There was, however, a further penalty which could be imposed. Our licence to operate Pools could also be withdrawn. Stamler pointed out that, in his opinion, the chances of a prosecution were extremely unlikely. In any case, even if there were to be one and the court, against all probability, found against us, there wasn't a magistrate in the land who would impose the severest penalty and take away our Promoter's licence. Certainly not in Liverpool, where literally tens of thousands of people were employed by Littlewoods and Vernons and unemployment in the area already exceeded the national average. We all agreed that this was an acceptable commercial risk. All except Cecil Moores, that is. We cajoled, pleaded, argued, yelled, we tried every known persuasion to get Cecil to change his mind. No way! Notwithstanding the almost certain fact that most Pool Companies represented at that meeting that day, would be wiped out if the bad weather continued, Cecil would not risk even the remotest possibility of Littlewoods losing their licence. We were all bloody livid, but I don't think anyone, in their heart of hearts, blamed him. Finally, with everybody feeling utterly frustrated, I asked our association lawyer, Michael Watkins, a fairly simple question, 'Which authority is empowered to bring a prosecution against any of us?'

'The police in the local area where your bookmaker's licence is issued,' he replied.

'Well, as far as Littlewoods are concerned that must be the Chief Constable of Liverpool,' I said.

'Yes,' was his response.

I turned to Cecil Moores, 'So ask him, Cecil. Ask him whether he'd bring a prosecution against Littlewoods. If he confirms that he would or even if he prevaricates, well, that's an end of it. But if he says no, there's nothing to stop you, or Vernons come to that, proceeding. I'm damned sure the rest of us would follow suit.' Nobody said a word. Cecil pondered judgematically. 'I'll sleep on it,' he said at last. The meeting broke up and we all went back, through the Arctic weather, to our respective homes.

The next day was a Saturday. I listened to the 1 o'clock BBC news. The weather was as bad as ever. The whole country was in the grip of the worst winter in living memory. Ice and snow were causing chaotic conditions everywhere. Every race meeting was off and practically every football match postponed. Pools were again cancelled, of course, and the long-range weather forecast continued to prophesy no relief for the foreseeable future. On Sunday morning, I received a telephone call at my home in Hadley Wood. To my utter astonishment it was from Arthur George, the dynamic General Manager of Littlewoods Pools. He told me that Mr Moores had spoken to the Chief Constable of Liverpool, explaining the dilemma facing the Pools industry and of the inevitable and massive job losses that would result should the bad weather persist and the Pools continue to be cancelled. He had described the Pools Panel proposal and the favourable legal opinion we had received.

I have no idea of the identity of the Chief Constable of Liverpool in 1963. Suffice to say that his assurances to Cecil Moores enabled the establishment of the Pools Panel. The first members were Arthur Ellis, well known and respected international referee and four very famous retired footballers . . . Tommy Lawton, Tom Finney, George Young and Ted Drake. Initially the Chairmen were changed almost weekly. Lord Brabazon was an early appointment, as was the wartime hero, Douglas Bader.

As expected, this amazing innovation was greeted with universal scorn and derision by the media. Not so the general public. The vast majority instinctively accepted what was seen to be a common sense solution to a difficult problem. Had that not been the case, the Pools industry would have been decimated. The bad weather lasted all the way through January, February and well into March. The Panel adjudicated every week and we were able to run the Pools.

The Pools Panel started out as a device to enable the promoters to avoid cancelled Pools with the inevitable enforced redundancies and huge losses to the Exchequer and the Pools Companies. Almost thirty years later, that original purpose still holds good. The perception of the Panel has, however, changed. It has now gained universal respect for its absolute fairness and integrity. It is part and parcel of our industry. Adjudication by the Panel, on every Saturday match that is postponed due to bad weather, has now become accepted practice. Indeed, public opinion now demands its use, because it is seen that Panel results give punters a fair run for their money.

The success of the Pools Panel and the ready co-operation of all members in helping to put it together, firmly cemented relationships within the PPA. Getting to know, like and trust our competitors was certainly a key factor in the future of Zetters.

I quickly became aware of the character, strengths and defects of the different promoters. It was all too easy to befriend and all too flattering to be befriended by those moguls. Not that they all were, of course. Moguls I mean. Much nearer to my mark for instance were the Berry brothers and their formidable father, Harry Berry. Well respected bookies from Leicester, they ran a very well organised football pool called Soccer Pools.

Then there was Empire Pools from Blackpool. A superb little company, run with great flair and efficiency by the Edwards, a solid sensible Lancashire family. Their Managing Director was Jim Ledwith of 'Pools Panel' fame. Jim was a real working class lad with a potato-sized chip on his shoulder.

Copes Pools were a fair bit bigger. Alfred Cope was the proprietor and he was almost certainly a tycoon. He'd had some serious family problems, so he retired to Switzerland and left the running of the business to Leslie Payne. Leslie should have been a civil servant. That's how he ran Copes. One quickly discovered the frustration of Alf's son-in-law, Cyril Easterman, and his grandson, Steven Easterman. They took the view that their entrepreneurial skills, especially Steven's, were constantly being thwarted by Leslie Payne.

Shermans Pools – the third largest in the industry – had, by then, been taken over by Littlewoods which, together with Vernons, made up the full complement of the PPA membership.

Vernons were big. Not like Littlewoods, of course, but still big. Three major players represented Vernons. The founder was Mr Vernon Sangster. Butter wouldn't melt in his mouth, but his reputation belied it. Anyway, he was charm itself as far as I was concerned. It was he who instigated a change in the character of the PPA Christmas gathering from a small private party to a grander and more formal affair.

Nowadays we, the representatives of the industry, just before Christmas every year, entertain Ministers (and ex-Ministers) of the Crown, the more 'sporty' Members of both Houses of Parliament, a wide variety of senior Civil Servants, the top members of both the English and Scottish Football Associations and Football Leagues, the Chairman and Trustees of the Football Trust and other current football and sporting personalities. It has become a most prestigious event and fulfils an excellent image-making and Public Relations function.

In those earlier days, young Robert Sangster, the Chairman of Vernons, was always around, although it soon became clear that his interest lay in the horse racing game and blood stock. George R. Kennerley was the Vernons Managing Director and was one of the most charismatic characters I've ever met. He ran Vernons with panache, skill and enterprise. His wit was renowned and cutting. He once told his advertising manager, who had proposed an absurdly low budget for a promotion, that 'You can't dung a field with a fart.' He was never a respecter of persons and if you were the butt for his humour, you could only laugh or suffer. Fortunately most of us laughed.

Finally, Littlewoods and the great Cecil Moores. Cecil always appeared to be in the shadow of his older brother, John, who was the clever one and the originator of Littlewoods. John was the master-mind behind almost everything that was Littlewoods but, perhaps, the cleverest thing he did, was to appoint his younger brother, Cecil, to run the Pools business. Cecil was a Pools man through and through, a giant in a giant industry. He knew his business backwards and ran it with a rod of iron. In two words Cecil was 'The Boss'. I make no secret of the fact that I went out of my way to befriend him. I had first met Cecil Moores at the momentous meeting in the Mayfair Hotel in 1961. I very quickly came to admire and respect him. I thought a fondness had developed between us and I felt that we had a special relationship. Indeed, when his elder son Nigel died in a car crash in France, I shared his grief. I knew Nigel well. His was a sad loss to the industry, but a most tragic loss to his parents, from which Cecil never really recovered. Yes, Cecil was a great man. He was only wrong in one of his strongly held opinions . . . he was *not* in the shadow of his brother, for he was a man of stature in his own right. I attended his funeral in 1989 and remember saying to one of his colleagues, 'I hope somebody is writing his biography.'

It is, perhaps, appropriate at this time to give a little more background to the infrastructure of the PPA. The secretariat was, and still is, under the control of a firm of North Country solicitors by the name of Cuff, Roberts (formerly North Kirk & Co.). In the immediate post-war years, Michael

Watkins was a junior partner in the company. He was our in-house legal adviser having, as he did, a comprehensive knowledge of gambling law and the case history pertaining to it. His boss, the senior partner, was a certain Mr Holland Hughes. Holland Hughes, or 'Duchy', the name by which everybody knew him, was an almost mystical figure, with an aura of profundity and elegance. A 'true gent' to his manicured fingertips, he looked more like a Hollywood version of the British aristocracy than a Lancashire lawyer. He had long been associated with John and Cecil and had become a close friend of the Moores family.

Holland Hughes, until his premature death at about fifty years of age, played the role of Chairman of the PPA. I discovered that it was he who supplied the intelligence to the Home Office for the drafting of the legislation governing the operation of football pools, i.e. The Pool Betting Act 1954. Every aspect of Pools, from distribution and return of coupons, declaration of dividends, types of entries, permutations, payments to winners, advertising restrictions etc. etc., were governed by this Act. The subsequent legislation resulted in the fact that nobody could get into the Pools business. Many tried, including such giants as William Hill, but the odds were stacked against them. To this day nobody has succeeded.

In a souvenir brochure, issued by Littlewoods to commemorate their Golden Jubiliee, this is what they said:

> The first Pool Betting Act of 1954 was wholeheartedly welcomed by Littlewoods, as its provisions were exactly in harmony with the company's own philosophy of safeguarding the interests of clients. Indeed, this 'charter' for investors incorporated many of the principles on which Littlewoods already based their own rules and regulations.

Prior to 1954 there were some dozens of football Pools. Littlewoods was always the biggest with approximately 50% of the market and an annual turnover of around £30M. Today only three companies of any substance remain, Littlewoods, Vernons and Zetters. Littlewoods now enjoy 77% of the market and have a turnover of over £500M . . . They have, indeed, done well!

Frequent PPA meetings were now commonplace and the effervescent George Kennerley of Vernons emerged as the leading personality. While Littlewoods dominated, Vernons, as a consequence of 'Ken', were always taking innovative initiatives. One such was the industry's abortive attempt to run a National Lottery. At a specially convened meeting, Ken described to us his latest proposition: 'Lucky Numbers' it was to be called and was almost an exact copy of the German 'LOTTO', a new game sweeping West Germany which had decimated their hitherto popular Football Pool 'TOTO'. The 'Lucky Numbers' punter had simply to choose seven numbers from thirty-six numbers. The promoters 'drew' the seven winning numbers each week and published them.

Successful entrants with all seven correct won the Jackpot, whilst those with six and five correct, won minor prizes. With 8,347,680 combinations of seven different numbers, we were unanimous in our view that Ken's proposal would make a viable competition. By this time the PPA had dwindled to just six members: Littlewoods, Vernons, Copes, Empire, Soccer and ourselves. Littlewoods and Vernons had clearly been discussing some kind of joint venture. I have no idea who decided to include the rest of us, but it was tremendously exciting for all the smaller companies. For the first time, a partnership with the 'Big Boys', in a major commercial undertaking, was in the offing! Everything was ready for the grand launch when, out of the blue, representatives of each of the companies in the Association were invited to attend a meeting at the Home Office. Officialdom had clearly got wind of our scheme and intended to scotch it before it became a *fait accompli*. We were desperately disappointed, but there was no way we could fly in the face of Government disapproval. Never mind, the precedent for a joint PPA business activity had been set.

It wasn't then surprising that, within a short space of time, another proposition was on the table. Again, it came from Vernons – a horse racing Pool which they had named 'Roll up'.

'Roll up' required the punter to place the first six horses, in the correct order of finishing, from a sixteen horse race. Despite tremendous co-operation from the Tote, it proved impossible to guarantee all sixteen listed horses actually running on the Saturday. Furthermore, as the bulk of coupons were picked up on Thursday evenings by the collectors, information on 'the going', up-to-date 'form' and the betting was not readily available to the punter. Then with a preponderance of favourites and fancied horses always in the frame, the projected High Odds competition was not achieved. 'Roll up' broke a golden rule . . . it seemed difficult to win and it wasn't! So, with forecasting difficulties and poor dividends, 'Roll up' was doomed and died after a few weeks.

Two down and one to go, maybe third time lucky. Number three, 'Spotting-the-Ball', came from Littlewoods. Long established as a newspaper game, 'Spotting-the-Ball' required the entrant to find the ball, by marking a cross on an action photograph of a football match from which the actual ball had been artificially removed. The newspapers seemed to be attracting growing support for the game, with cash prizes getting bigger and bigger. Bookmakers – and, particularly, Ladbrokes – saw the opportunity to run a game which might just grow big enough to challenge the Pools. Littlewoods certainly weren't going to sit back and let that happen – hence their invitation to the PPA to join them in a partnership to run 'Spotting-the-Ball'.

We took legal advice – of course! – and although, inevitably, it was punctuated with prevarications, generally it gave a favourable opinion, emphasising that it was essential for the punter to exercise skill in finding the position of the ball. Unbelievably, the legal opinion was that it was much more skilful to determine where a panel of experts 'placed' the ball.

We all agreed, at first, that the law truly was a ass, but the more one thought about it, the more one could understand the logic. If acknowledged experts chose the position of the ball by the exercise of *their* skill, then it must take skill on the part of the punter to find it. This was the kind of logic we all wanted to hear giving, as it did, a legal virtue to a commercial necessity. A little daring, perhaps, but we needed a win, so we went with it.

A partnership agreement was drawn whereby shares were allocated on the basis of the current market proportion of the members of the PPA. This meant that Littlewoods retained 65% of the shareholding, Vernons 26% and the remaining 9% was equally apportioned between Copes, Empire and ourselves. (In the interval between the failure of 'Roll up' and the introduction of 'Spotting-the-Ball', we had acquired Soccer Pools of Leicester . . . a story I will tell, in more detail, later.) The STB partnership was an important policy decision. It ensured that no member would compete against another by running their own STB which until then had been a real possibility. Indeed, we at Zetters had, until recently, been involved with *The Winner*, a well respected weekly sporting newspaper, in jointly running a similar competition.

STB got off to a most encouraging start. Since the bulk of Littlewoods' Pools business was received through their Collector Service, it was sensible that STB would be promoted only through collectors, even though this virtually precluded the smaller companies from playing any active role, as their collector service was too small (less than 10% of the whole) and their varying collection times were deemed to make it neither workable nor worthwhile. The consequence was that the whole operation, apart from Vernons collectors, was handled by Littlewoods. They accounted the entries, they organised the panel of experts, they checked the coupons (to an amazing degree of accuracy by using an extremely sophisticated image projector) and paid the winners. They, too, determined the policy. The only task for the other partners was to pay in a dividend cheque twice a year! It seemed an ideal arrangement.

Only later did we perceive that there was a down side . . . two, in fact. Firstly, our own collectors bitterly complained that Littlewoods and Vernons collectors were able to earn extra commission as a consequence of carrying the STB coupon alongside the Pools coupon. This was a serious complaint, because it was difficult enough for the small companies to get collectors. It now became almost impossible, owing to the added inducements available to Littlewoods and Vernons collectors brought about by STB. Somewhat later, the second problem emerged . . . the prizes being paid to STB winners began to match – and, ultimately, to exceed – the Treble Chance prizes being paid by the smaller companies. To this day, neither of these problems has been redressed. Consequently, any expansion of the Pool business became unattainable. Not for Littlewoods with their mammoth million pound plus dividends, but certainly for all of us and, to a lesser degree, even for Vernons. Over the years, we have received a considerable return for our modest investment in STB and it would be carping to be either negative or begrudging about it. I do not believe that the decision to invite the smaller companies into the STB coalition was a 'Machiavellian' plot to limit their growth in the Pool business. Nonetheless, there has been, and still is, a harmful effect on the turnover of every Pools company except Littlewoods. Perhaps we didn't spot the dangers because we were too busy laughing on our way to the bank. I don't think we've been raped, but if we have, we've certainly enjoyed it.

# Chapter 16

## Growing Pleasures

After some reluctance by every member of the family, Carolyn moved to a boarding school. The first attempt was a disaster. We'd found a very attractive private school called Tortington Park, near Arundel in Sussex. It had a good academic reputation, lovely grounds, a delightful headmistress and a truly homely atmosphere. On top of all that two of Carrie's best friends were joining at the same time.

I'd made some enquiries from Gabbitas Thring, the private school specialists, and although they spoke highly of the school, they did hint, confidentially of course, that there were rumours of financial problems. Although clearly cause for some concern, this was quickly set aside. It turned out that the grandfather of one of the girls, with whom Carrie was joining, was a school governor. He was quite positive in his assurances that the school was in a very sound financial position. 'Absolutely no problems at all,' he declared . . . and he should know, shouldn't he? So, in September 1967, with a few initial tears and an expensive new wardrobe, our ten-year-old daughter left home. In November, we received a letter from the school governors stating that 'owing to unforeseen financial pressures the School, very regretfully, would not be reopening after the Christmas break.'!!

An urgent search for a new school followed. One of the only places we could find, able to take her at such short notice, was Croft House, a truly lovely place in a tiny village called Shillingstone, near Blandford Forum in Dorset. It was an early indication of Carolyn's strength of character that she easily and quickly re-adapted to the enforced move at the beginning of 1968. It was here that Carrie was to receive her basic education and where she met many good chums, some of whom are still close nearly twenty years later. It was a good school and Carrie was happy there.

The success of Croft, coupled with our disaffection with Lochinvar, prompted us to consider a boarding school for Adam. We found an excellent prep/boarder at Abingdon, near Oxford called Millbrook House (not to be confused with Millfield, the well known independent high school). Adam spent two enjoyable years there; so that, too, was a great success. They understood the problems caused by dyslexia and were able, with skill and kindness, to prepare young boys for further education. Adam enjoyed his stay as seemingly did Viscount David Linley, a fellow pupil. Adam graduated from Millbrook to Bryanston, a fine Public School, also near Blandford Forum.

Helen and I were overjoyed at this development, not only because of the school itself, but because it was just a few miles from Carrie at Shillingstone. The long journey to Dorset, almost every other weekend, enabled us to see both our children at the one visit. Nevertheless, it was still a bind driving well over a hundred miles each way. We were also country-starved, having moved by stages from Hadley Wood into a flat in Central London, so we discussed finding a cottage somewhere *en route*. It was then that one of those happy chances, which have punctuated my life, occurred.

One morning, at the office, David Isaacs was updating me on the latest position of our Bingo business. He reported that Ian Pontin, his live wire field manager, had just negotiated the purchase of a small Bingo club in Devizes in Wiltshire mentioning, in passing, that we were buying it from a Mr Lance Barrett who happened to be the Mayor of Andover. Almost flippantly, I asked David to see if Barrett knew of any small property in the locality, that might be on the market. Ever resourceful, Ian Pontin came back to me within two days. Lance Barrett had told him of a cottage in Goodworth Clatford, a village a few miles from Andover. Apparently, it was derelict and had had a demolition order on it to make room for a road widening scheme. The scheme had been dropped, as the Council had run out of funds, so the cottage was back on the market. It didn't sound very exciting, even though it was just off the A303, our road to Blandford Forum. I was very busy at the time, so I'd virtually dismissed the place as not being worthy of further investigation.

A week or so later, David told me that Lance Barrett was coming to the office to exchange contracts on the Devizes Bingo Club and they were then going on to lunch. I promised to join them if I possibly could, but felt it was very unlikely. In the event, I finished a meeting earlier than anticipated, so I wandered round to where they were eating.

Lance proved to be a pleasant young man, hard working, wily and clearly going places. He asked me if I was still interested in the cottage that he'd mentioned to Ian Pontin.

'I don't think so,' I said, 'It sounds a mess and I don't want to buy a load of problems.'

'It's true', he said. 'It's in an awful condition. It has no mains water; no sewerage, no electricity and the walls and roof are falling down. But it's in a pretty Hampshire village, it's going for a song and the outlook along the river is spectacular. Why don't you buy it, pull it down and build yourself a smart new cottage?'

My antenna went to full alert. 'River! What river?' I asked.

'Well, it's only a stream really,' said Lance. 'The Anton. It's a chalk stream and it runs into the River Test a mile or so below the cottage. You would have about two hundred yards of fly fishing with full riparian rights in your own garden.'

Fishing! Dry fly fishing! The Test! I cannot describe what those words meant to me. They represented the summit of my desire. Even that doesn't begin to explain the emotional impact of this news.

Perhaps the following old chestnut will give you a better conception of my feelings. 'God had granted a keen fly fisherman any three wishes as a reward for some great good deed he'd performed. His wishes were: Chalk stream. Chalk stream Chalk stream.'

You may now understand why I was almost breathless with excitement. 'When can I see it?' I stammered.

'Well, any time you like. The place is open to the elements. You can just walk in,' answered Lance.

I dropped everything, picked up Helen, and we motored down, there and then. It was perfect. Not the cottage, of course, but the river and its setting. Two days later I drove down again, this time with Jim Clarke, and met the owner, a Mr Jamie Thomson, on site.

Mr Thomson lived near Goodworth Clatford and gave me the impression of being the local squire. I also formed the view, however, that he was not as well heeled as he would have liked me to believe and was fairly desperate to sell the cottage. For all that, he was clearly intent upon ensuring that the 'city slicker' was not going to get the better of an honest-to-God country gentleman of immaculate breeding. I was suitably impressed by his social superiority, but indicated that I was an unlikely buyer, who might take the ruin off his hands providing the price was right. Little did he know that I'd have sold my business, my wife, my children and my very soul for the place. I bought it for £15,000!

It's true, of course, that it was then necessary to spend a great deal more to make it habitable. A local architect (recommended by Lance Barnett) strongly urged us to demolish it and start again but, very fortunately, Helen and I resisted that suggestion. We had the shell of a seventeenth century cottage which, with sympathetic treatment, would emerge as a real gem and of which we and the whole village could be proud . . . and so it was!

We were extremely lucky to find the right builder, Ken Butcher, a shrewd local lad running his own business, K.W. Butcher Ltd. Ken was a Hampshire man who quickly understood what we wanted and possessed the skills to be able to give it to us. It cost another £15,000 by the time he'd finished and I suppose, over the fifteen or so years we lovingly lived there, I must have spent another £20,000 on it. This included adding a studio for Helen and buying about an acre of land opposite to give me double-bank fishing! Not only did the additional ground ensure our privacy, but it was almost essential, because it also belonged to Jamie Thomson who again – or still – needed to top up his coffers. I dreaded even the remote possibility of any development on the site. So, all in all, the place stood me in for approximately £50,000 over a fifteen year period of delightful use. We sold it in 1987 when Adam and Carrie had long since departed the fold and we were using it less and less. On advice, we put it up for auction and it went for £360,000. Not a bad investment, notwithstanding Capital Gains Tax! I think poor Jamie Thomson was less than amused.

However, back to 1975 and the cottage. We were soon well ensconced and I like to think that we were not the archetypal town dweller with a country pad. In fact, we spent more time there than at our new London home, a beautiful flat we had recently acquired in Chelsea. Commuting was easy. The very good A30 and A303 were minutes away and the M3 was nearing completion. Travelling time between Chelsea and Goodworth Clatford was just over an hour by road. The train journey to Andover (only ten minutes from the cottage) from Waterloo was only about forty-five minutes. Blandford Forum was only forty miles away, thus enabling both Carrie and Adam easy access to our new country home. Carrie, in fact, was soon to leave Shillingstone, in order to round off her education. She went to the Coaching Inn, a 6th form crammer in Sussex. Nevertheless, she still managed many a week-end with us. Not as much as Adam, of course. It was even possible for him to come home on his free Sundays in time for one of his mother's massive lunches . . . and some fishing!

The fishing was too good to be true. One soon became blasé at the ease with which two pounders could be tempted to rise to a well presented fly.

Helen hand-fed her favourite 'leviathan', a huge rainbow trout of at least five pounds which, naturally, then qualified for protected status. We also introduced a 'catch and return' policy for the others, unless one was needed for the pot. I started trout breeding with qualified success. It was certainly a demanding and fascinating hobby, calling for the input of considerable time and energy which, in the main, had to suffice as its own reward. Mind you, I like to think there may still be some healthy fish in the Anton, and even the Test, which are there as a result of my efforts (with a little aid from mum and dad trout, of course).

We all loved the 'Fishing Cottage' as it was named. Not by us, that was its name long before we four Zetters had ever existed. It had, in fact, been the home of the water bailiffs of that catchment area for centuries. During our occupation, I excavated an area to create a small lake, on the extra land I had bought, to use in my trout breeding programme. It became known locally as Zetters Pool. I do hope the name survives. Each one of us derived much pleasure and what I would describe as bountiful benefit from this our latest acquisition. I had my fish breeding programme. Helen resumed painting and produced more and better work than she had ever done before. Working in 'tempora', her country scenes commanded widespread and deserved praise. I still own and treasure several of them. Even though Carrie was not nearby, she still came frequently and adored the place. Undoubtedly, it confirmed her love of the English countryside and its life style. I believe it set the pattern for her future, for, eventually, she acquired her own home in the country. Adam scored most. It filled his early teenage years with an abundance of joy. He brought his friends to stay. He, too, learned to love the countryside. He grew up in lovely surroundings and a happy home but, above all, he discovered fly fishing! Virtually self-taught, he became one of the most skilful exponents of this gentle art I have ever seen. Whereas our apartment in France had been a holiday destination, Goodworth Clatford was much more like our real home and, in many ways, the better for it. One obvious advantage was that we now went to faraway places, mostly in winter, for exciting new holiday venues.

Barbados was joyously visited, but better still was discovering Africa and, particularly, Kenya. Certainly to know it, in those years, was to love it. We returned year after year for several years and we, all four of us, shared the delight of going. The magical mystery of Africa never waned. Story upon story, incident upon incident always attended those trips. Adam and I loved the deep sea fishing expeditions into the Indian Ocean which are so easily available along the Kenyan coastline. Just along from Mombasa there is a creek, a safe mooring, where a Mr and Mrs McConnell, a Scottish-named

French couple living in Kenya, kept a 32 ft. deep-sea fishing cruiser. Joining them for a day's game fishing was always one of the highlights of our holiday.

On the first visit, we arrived to find Tom, a young black boy, preparing the boat and tackle. Bright of eye and brimming with youthful energy and intelligence, I asked him if he thought we'd chosen a good day for our trip.

'Jes' perfect, baas,' he replied.

'What chance of a marlin?' I queried.

'Pretty good, baas,' was the happy response, 'Could get a good one today.'

'And the sea,' I enquired, 'Not too rough, I hope?'

'Like a lit'l pond, baas,' he assured us.

Well, Adam and I were really chuffed. That is, until Mr McConnell came down and introduced himself.

'Sorry you haven't chosen a better day, Mr Zetter,' he said.

'How's that?' said I, feeling puzzled.

'Well m'sieur, we've a nasty on-shore wind, which will give us a very uncomfortable sea. The big fish, marlin and the like, will have gone deep and won't take a bait. All in all, I can't promise you a good day's fishing.'

Adam and I were astounded. 'But, Tom here has just given us an entirely different story,' I said.

McConnell laughed, 'Tom is a sweet-natured Samburu . . . the best natives in Kenya. He'll tell you what he thinks you want to hear. Ask him if he thinks you'll catch some Scottish smoked salmon out there and he'll say "Sure thing, baas".' McConnell was absolutely right, of course, we caught nothing in that rough sea. It didn't put us off. We returned many times, always enjoyed it and became friends with both Tom and McConnell.

Which is why, a year later, we were most distressed to see Tom looking pale (for a black man), listless and clearly quite ill. The reason was transparently obvious . . . he had the most frightful festering eight inch leg wound. I quizzed McConnell about it.

'How did he get that and why don't you send him to a doctor and get some penicillin into him?'

'He got it in a friendly spear fight and he won't take white man's medicine,' McConnell replied.

'But he'll lose his leg or his life,' I protested.

'I keep telling him that, but he tells me, in the politest possible way, to mind my own white business. He has faith only in his tribal medicine man,' said McConnell.

A year later, we returned and there was Tom, two-legged, hardly a scar and as bright as a pin.

'I see you got him to see sense and get some penicillin into him,' I said.

'No way, m'sieur,' replied McConnell, 'His witch doctor cleared it up in a couple of weeks.'

Maybe he used leaf mould!

We enjoyed Africa so much. This was a time when tourism was in its infancy. Sightseeing meant that you really were able to see sights that were new and exciting. Needless to say, we went on safari, a photo safari of course, and were so lucky to be in the Serengeti during the migration. The sight of the lemming-like intensity of purpose by countless millions of wildebeest, will always remain in my memory. We arranged a visit to a Masai village where twelve-year-old Adam was propositioned by a beautiful young negress. She carried a tiny baby on her back and asked, quite earnestly, in pidgin English, if Adam would join her in her mud hut, to help make another baby. I suspect Adam may have been willing, but his mother didn't think we had the time! We visited the Ngorongoro Crater, a spectacular self-contained lost world, in which all the wild life of Africa can be seen within a few hundred square miles of splendid isolation. It was in this crater that poor Carrie suddenly developed the most ghastly diarrhoea. There we were, the four of us plus Sammy our native driver, in the jeep when Carrie was suddenly taken ill.

'Stop,' she screamed, 'I must get out!'

'Sorry missie, can't stop here,' replied Sammy, 'Too many lions.'

'But I must,' pleaded poor Carrie, 'I need to go NOW.'

'Stockade near here, we go quickly,' said Sammy with real concern and consideration.

A few minutes later we came to the stockade. It was a fantastic circle of tall tree trunks in a fifty-foot clearing in the bush. So much did it resemble a Wild West film set, that we almost expected Red Indians to start shooting arrows at us as we approached. Sammy drove the jeep up to the crude but effective double doors, removed the bar and in we drove. In the middle was a small wooden 'privy'. As the jeep stopped Carrie jumped out and ran to it.

'Be careful, missie,' cried Sammy, 'Sometimes snakes in there.'

'Well, they're going to be very unlucky snakes!' Carrie yelled back over her shoulder.

Of all the continents of the world I have visited, Africa is, without question, my most beloved. The climate, the terrain, the variety, the mystery, the flora and, of course, the fauna but, most of all, the people. Yet there is another side to this pretty picture. The poverty, the disease, the squalor, the desolation and, again the people. They, the people, remind me of a little ditty I used to read to my children when they were young. It went . . .

> There was a little girl,
> who had a little curl
> right in the middle of her for'h'd.
> When she was good
> she was very, very good,
> but when she was bad,
> she was horrid.

Of course, to talk about the people of Africa is like talking about 'liquorice allsorts'. There are so many different tribes, races and colours, that one cannot generalise, but generally speaking when I think of Africa, I think of Black Africa. I suspect, in my heart of hearts, that Equatorial Africa is the very cradle of civilisation.

# Chapter 17

# See a Pin

I have always believed that luck plays an important part in our destiny. Most of us have our fair share of it, both good and bad. Success is achieved by spotting a good opportunity, and making the most of it . . . and keeping your head down during a bad spell, and making the best of it. Belief in this philosophy has dictated the pattern of my behaviour for most of my life.

Whatever the yardstick used to measure achievement, the seventies would surely qualify as my best decade. The components for success were assembled during the fifties and gathered pace during the sixties. A good marriage and two wonderful children is the perfect foundation for any budding career . . . it certainly was for mine. Being a director of a family business, the very nature of which was beginning to bring the name of Zetter to public awareness totally disproportionate to our size, was also very significant. Last, but most, was the fantastic good fortune of finding that Jim Clarke, my old army colleague, had proved to be an inspirational choice of partner. His many qualities, ability, sound common sense, wisdom, work ethic, etc. were to assume untold value and assistance to me which became pre-eminently manifest during the seventies.

However, in 1961 I very nearly lost it. I nearly lost Jim Clarke, my greatest asset. This is how it happened. During the early post-war years Zetters, in common with several of our competitors, boasted a very healthy overseas turnover. Many former colonies were involved, but by far and away the biggest was Nigeria. It may seem astonishing that this third world West African state should 'play the Pools' but, indeed, they did with an almost fanatical fervour. The popularity was such that, at its peak in 1961, over 20% of our global turnover came from this one source. Zetters so dominated business in that part of the world that we were known, in the trade, as the Littlewoods of Lagos. There were several reasons for this success. The low stake on our Treble Chance Pool was clearly a major contributory factor, but of greatest importance was the appointment of one Albert Ogunnubi, as our area concessionaire. Albert was an outstanding local character. I have no idea how we had recruited him, he'd probably recruited us, but he was terrific. His method of distribution was unrivalled. He utilised Mammy Wagons, a nationwide truck-cum-bus service, run by a kind of female 'mafia'. These formidable ladies carried the virgin coupons to a network of field agents each week, bringing back the staked coupons to Lagos on the return trip. He then processed and despatched them by air cargo to London every Thursday, in ample time to be included into the Pool each Saturday.

There were, understandably, a few problems in handling something like 50,000 weekly coupons from this source. Illiteracy caused some difficulties, although in the main, when a client was unable to fill in a coupon, the village scribe obliged, charging a modest fee for his literary and forecasting skills. A whole new service industry developed in the African bush as a consequence of Pool betting. The incidence of incorrect claims, by clients who thought they had won but hadn't, was appreciably above the average in the UK. Fraudulent attempts at winning also reached epidemic proportions. All manner of means were tried and, as far as I know, failed. I will not go into details. These minor ailments didn't cause too many headaches, although one major concern required urgent attention. The poor quality of the coupon, not only the paper on which it was printed, but the legibility of the printing itself, left much to be desired. Sequential numbering of the coupons was also considered an urgent necessity, owing to the illegibility of the client's name and obscure address. To have them printed in London and air-freighted out was fearfully expensive. If there was a printer in Nigeria, reliable enough to produce an accurate coupon each week working to a tight time schedule, the problem would be solved . . . But did one exist? Jim Clarke went to find out.

He quickly and easily accomplished that task and then put his energy and time to other requirements. He met with Albert Ogunnubi and, with him, visited many main agents. A press conference was conducted in the biggest hotel in Lagos and, by all accounts, was one hell of a hooley. An advertising campaign was arranged, together with a speedy dividend publication service and all-in-all, a good business was transformed into a spectacular one. The trip was clearly an outstanding success, and on his departure, Jim Clarke invited Albert to visit us in England.

A few months later, Albert descended upon an unsuspecting London. Now Albert wasn't just big, he was enormous. He was certainly well over six feet tall, probably nearer seven, and half as wide as one of his Mammy Wagons. He wore tribal dress throughout his stay and that, in London in the early sixties, attracted considerable attention. At our first meeting in the Strand, he prostrated his entire length along the pavement, much to the amusement of passing pedestrians and the total embarrassment of Helen. We took him to the Derby, where he could easily have been mistaken for Prince Monolulu (still around). An evening at the Palladium went well, although we had to restrain him from joining the chorus girls on the stage. He assured us that he only wanted to compliment them on their performance! He made a visit to the London Zoo where, to our amazement, this true, black African gent saw his very first elephant and lion. Helen and I invited him home for dinner, delighting in his company and enjoying a super evening. Then my mother and father did the same and that proved to be a riot. We laughed our way through a lavish Jewish meal; after dinner my father poured him a good measure of brandy into a traditional brandy bowl. Albert started laughing, and it was so infectious that we were soon all roaring our heads off without knowing the reason. After some breathless minutes, my mother was able to ask him what the joke was about. 'Such a big glass for such a little drink,' rumbled Albert. So we all collapsed with laughter again! He stayed about a week and all who met him loved him. Everybody had fun just being in his presence and were sad and somewhat deflated when he went home.

The trip enhanced an already thriving association and the whole Pools business in Nigeria began to assume a considerable importance. And there's the rub!

The outflow of currency began to alarm the Nigerian Government, so they set about looking into the possibility of running their own National Pool. Quite honestly, who could blame them? The trouble was how to do it. A Mr Trecerri then appeared on the scene. Trecerri was a South American millionaire who had influential connections with the Nigerian Government. With their approval, he set out headhunting in England, to put together a team of British Pools experts who would be based in Lagos and run the Nigerian State Pool. He advertised for top personnel and visited most of the companies in the PPA. It's flattering, but not surprising in view of Jim's reputation, that he offered the top job to Jim Clarke.

Jim, to his great credit, immediately reported the offer to my father, telling him, of course, of the very lucrative inducements that went with the position. Very sadly, my father blew his top and told Jim if he wanted the job he could go. I have always felt that I should have stepped in at that stage and made the Old Man see reason. Jim had a wife, a young child and a widowed mother to keep. His position with the Company had not been firmly established and his income was distinctly modest. Certainly he had prospects, but they were nebulous and, in any case, some way off. I wanted to say to my father that if we could be a little more positive and generous I was certain he would stay with us. I didn't do it. I like to think I had good motives. Whatever we might have been able to do, we could never match the lucrative and virtually tax free income he would earn out there. In any case, they had offered him a five year contract. I felt certain he'd be back with enhanced knowledge and ability. I was sure of our friendship. I banked on him coming back to Zetters. He did. We kept in touch during his absence and we met up on his every trip to the UK. After the third year, he told me that he wanted to come home and having established the Nigerian State Pool, Trecerri would, albeit reluctantly, release him from his contract. Against some fierce in-house opposition, Jim Clarke rejoined Zetters in 1964, as General Manager. So all the ingredients were now back in place. In 1965, with the sale of Zetters Racing all but complete, Zetters became a Public Company. The actual launch could not be described as an outstanding success. It is true to say the issue was oversubscribed – just. Some judicious share applications ensured that the embarrassment of requiring the underwriters to take up a quota, was avoided. I'm not sure if this behaviour would be acceptable practice today, but twenty-six years ago it meant that, when trading began on 1 July 1965, Zetters were quoted on the London Stock Exchange at two shillings and one halfpenny. A ha'penny premium! It was during this episode that Terry Yardley, the young accountant with Solly Littlestone, distinguished himself in my eyes with his keen insight and shrewd advice to my father and me.

   The company now ran two successful businesses, Pools and Bingo. Both to do with 'soft' betting. Both good cash flow generators. Both having similar working class customers. Jim Clarke ran the Pool and David Isaacs the Bingo. Nobody has ever been luckier than me in the quality, honesty and loyalty of their senior management. I'd known Jim for years of course. After all, we were old wartime army chums. We were like brothers. But David was a new boy. How would he fit in? How would it work? Well, it was the dream ticket. It was superb. David worked for me for twenty-three years. In that time he built up a company running over thirty Bingo Clubs and other ancilliary activities. This was achieved without recourse to any gearing (borrowing money). It was partly self-funding, the pump having been primed by Zetters Pools. They provided further capital for new acquisitions as and when it became necessary. In 1987 Zetters Enterprises floated as an independent Public Company and in 1988 was sold to Corals (Bass) for over £22M, a financial triumph for me, my family and, indeed, all our shareholders. David Isaacs, at 62 years old, retired moderately well off. I often think he could and should have written himself a different contract or looked after his own interest with greater avarice. It wasn't his way. He did fairly well for himself, but as his last school report might have said . . . 'he could have done better'.

The family fortune was notably improved and my own status in the PPA and elsewhere, clearly enhanced. There can be no doubt, for example, that it was an important element in my developing relationship with Cecil Moores who was now looking on me and Zetters with keener interest than hitherto. Perhaps, as a result, he accepted my dinner invitation one evening before a PPA meeting that was scheduled for the following day. He was staying at the Grosvenor House Hotel of course so we dined in their Grill Room. I was enjoying the occasion even though troubled by a painful attack of gout. An amusing ailment to all who have never suffered it.

Being the first time I had played host to Cecil, I wanted to do it in the grand manner. 'What will you drink now?' I asked him at the end of what had been a splendid and very liquid meal.

'I'll take a glass of port, thank you, Paul,' he responded. 'Taylors '42 please.'

The wine waiter first showed me the wine list and whispered discreetly that they only sold it by the bottle. I noted, to my horror, the price . . . twenty-six pounds! This liquid gold was duly decanted before our very eyes. Cecil had one glass but, because of my gout, with the greatest reluctance, I resisted the temptation to join him. The full decanter of wine was left on the table when we departed. Can you imagine the glee of the wine-waiter?

The same old problems were plaguing our industry yet again. Too many drawn matches causing too many winners causing too few jackpots. It must have been as a result of changes in the pattern of football. Defensive play was producing a dearth of goals and, week on week, there were numerous games where neither side scored. All drawn matches, including the ubiquitous nil-nil result, were awarded 3 points, an away win scored 2 points and a home win 1 point. With so many games every week scoring the maximum 3 points, winning had become too easy. The solution seemed so patently obvious that it is hard to believe that it took the industry several painful years before they adopted it.

My father first bounced the idea off me following a particularly poor season, during which nobody had won a 'Jackpot', or even a really worthwhile dividend. 'Why don't we devalue the points allocated to scoreless draws?' he said. Like all great ideas it was so simple. Jim Clarke and I worked on a viable new structure and came up with two possibilities. The first was as easy as 3, 2, 1 . . . 3 points for a draw where goals were scored, 2 points for a scoreless draw, and 1 point for any other result. Very desirable, in that it eliminated any use of unpopular half-points and it recognised the Treble Chance for what it really was, a Pool whereby 'drawn matches' gained the greatest reward. All very fine in theory but, in practice, we felt sure that awarding equal value to any other result would lead to the frequent loss of minor dividends.

Our second – and preferred – proposal introduced four values for results, rather than the original three from which the Treble Chance had derived its name. We made the Score Draw pre-eminent followed by the No-Score Draw, followed by the Away Win and finishing with the Home Win being of least value. Nothing like as attractive as three values but, technically, far superior and certainly protective of minor dividends. Both Jim and I were delighted with our research, but having produced a winning formula, or so we believed, what were we to do with it? Start using it, you might say, but it would be either a brave or a crazy promoter who would ask his clients to accept the principle of a nil-nil draw being of less value to them than a draw where goals were scored, when our competitors required no such qualification. Well, we were neither brave nor crazy, so we took our brilliant brainwave to the PPA with a view to getting the whole industry to adopt the scheme, repeating the similar action we had taken some years earlier, when we had brought in Shermans Pools to help the launch of Pools on Australian football. They rejected it! They turned it down flat! This was in 1966, when the impact of poor dividends had not yet seriously damaged the bigger companies and our proposal was seen as far too dramatic to remedy a passing ill.

By 1968, however, the ache had become a real pain and the patient deteriorated. Even the fittest and fattest started to worry. A series of meetings ensued, with just one item on the agenda: 'the decline of our industry and what to do to arrest it'. Over and over again, Jim and I argued in favour of our 'Score Draw' proposal. Over and over again we were told that such a fundamental change to the Treble Chance would be unacceptable to the general public and a less radical solution must be found. G. R. Kennerley of Vernons broke the log jam. He had satisfied himself that a drastic problem needed a drastic cure and the Zetters option was the only worthwhile one on the table. His authority and persuasiveness tipped the scales. Every member of the PPA agreed to adopt the Score Draw principle and introduce 'New Deal', as we decided to call it. Although Jim and I were feeling rather self-satisfied, there was still a vexing little irritation we were forced to endure. The PPA – against our advice – opted for the three category points allocation (3, 2, 1) instead of our much preferred four category (3, 2, $1\frac{1}{2}$ ,1) proposal. Argue as we would, we could not convince them of the merits of our case. Always suspicious to the point of paranoia, the two giants seemed convinced that, in some obscure way, the four category scheme would give the smaller firms an edge. Annoying, as it was, we finally yielded for we had, after all, won the main issue . . . the scoreless draw was devalued. 'New Deal' was introduced in August 1969 and the Pool betting public accepted it without demur.

The top dividend payout improved overnight as, indeed, it was bound to do with far fewer selections qualifying for 3 points on the Treble Chance. As we had predicted, business started to pick up, even though there were frequent cancellations of minor dividends. I still find it remarkable that the formidable surfeit of high powered statisticians within the Littlewoods and Vernons organisations were so blinkered as to prefer an inferior formula. I can only believe it was as a result of protectionist attitudes. Never mind, justice was to prevail in the end, albeit surreptitiously. In the late spring of 1970, Arthur George, the Managing Director of Littlewoods, telephoned me from his home. He told me that they had discussed changing the points structure on the Treble Chance, in order to reduce the frequency of cancelled minor dividends. The decision was that they would adopt a four category version of 'New Deal' (3pts, 2pts, $1\frac{1}{2}$pts, 1pt) from the start of the new Season. All the small companies would, of course, be formally advised of the change, but he thought I should be the first to know. With this news, our original version of 'New Deal' had now been fully adopted by the Pools Companies and its success is best illustrated by the following table of Total Stakes of the Pools Industry over a six year period from 1966 to 1971:

1966 – 67  £114M.
1967 – 68  £110M.
1968 – 69    £94M.
1969 – 70    £97M. ('New Deal' Score Draws introduced August 1969)
1970 – 71  £125M. ('New Deal' four categories introduced August 1970)
1971 – 72  £168M.

The Jackpot payout was back and the turn around was dramatic, immediate and ongoing.

It would be pleasing to report that Zetters were the main beneficiaries of a scheme for which they were wholly responsible . . . I cannot. In the way of these things, it was the biggest who gained the most from an idea which, self-evidently, had pulled the industry back from the most serious decline it had ever known. Of course, we shall never know what would have happened had we gone 'New Deal' on our own. I think we would have failed and there is some evidence to support that assertion. Some years later, 1990 in fact, the same old problems were besetting the industry, i.e. too many draws (yes, even Score Draws were now too numerous), too many winners, not enough Jackpot payouts. We, at Zetters, tried an experiment further to qualify the Score Draw by favouring high scoring draws. Neither Littlewoods nor Vernons agreed to join us, so we went alone. It achieved only moderate success, but also attracted too many letters from disgruntled clients who complained that our Treble Chance was more difficult than that of our competitors. Consequently, for the moment, we have dropped the idea. A pity really, for the industry again has the identical, unresolved problem. As before, it is not yet as damaging to Littlewoods and Vernons, but history has a funny habit of repeating itself. In the meantime, we must accept that we need them more than they need us. So what's new?

# Chapter 18

# Three Little Fishes

Confidence, bordering on conceit, was a by-product of our 'New Deal' triumph. Anything seemed possible and a passing comment by Arthur George had stuck in my mind. It was during one of our convivial lunch sessions at a full PPA meeting at Grosvenor House. 'Within ten years,' he said, 'the Pools market will only be able to sustain three companies, Littlewoods, Vernons and A.N. Other.' I was vain enough to think that he looked at me when he said it. There were still the four 'little' ones . . . Copes, Empire, Soccer and ourselves, in that order of size. The three of them would have to go. What temerity! Or what *chutzpah*, as my mother would have said. Did you ever hear of a roach tackling three pike?

Now although the seventies started in fine fettle for the industry as a whole, there were clear indications that all was not as well as it should have been with Soccer Pools in Leicester. The main problem stemmed from the power-house, old man Berry. The years were taking their toll of his energies and his commitment to the pool business was flagging. In any case, his real interest lay in his own local betting shop. It gave him a greater day-to-day stimulus and was far less demanding. His two sons, Leslie and Harry, were left to run the Pool. Harry was bothered by ill health and Leslie was finding it burdensome to run the show alone. It was, undoubtedly, as a consequence of the excellent relationship which Jim and I had established with the family that we, alone, were privy to all of this knowledge. We concluded that a serious and fair offer of take-over would be timely. In 1971, Soccer Pools of Leicester ceased to exist and Zetters had absorbed their entire business. We could not be certain, however, that all Soccer clients would switch to us, so our delight was enhanced when they, in fact, did so. At a stroke, Zetters had overtaken their immediate competitor, Empire, to become the fourth biggest football pool behind Copes.

In retrospect, we really took too long to press home our advantage. However, both Copes and Empire were powerful companies, each under the most effective management, or so we believed. It wasn't so. The more we got to know them, the more dissent we discovered. Alfred Cope, the dynamic proprietor, following a family tragedy, had long since retired to Switzerland. His son-in-law, Cyril Easterman, was left to run the business alongside Leslie Payne. Leslie was hard working, loyal, trustworthy and efficient. But he lacked flair and entrepreneurial skills. It was clearly frustrating for Cyril and even more so for Steven, Cyril's son and Alfred's grandson. In any case, Cyril was keen to retire and Steven was thought to be too young to be given the responsibility of top management. Once again, the rapport which we had cultivated, put us into the unbelievable position of being the only suitors when Copes decided to sell. It came about in 1976, and was even more successful than the Soccer take-over. Cyril Easterman retired to Switzerland. Leslie Payne retired to St. James, S.W.1 and the youthful Steven Easterman joined the Board of Zetters.

Only Empire Pools of Blackpool stood between us and the prediction of Arthur George. Empire, however, were an entirely different 'kettle of fish'. Far from suffering management problems, they enjoyed the most vigorous and youthful administration of any member of the PPA. The business was owned by the well respected Edwards family and two young brothers, Michael and Alan Edwards – nephews of the founder – ran it with the very considerable assistance of Jim Ledwith, their streetwise Managing Director. They were a good team and, with the perfect mixture of executive skill, marketing flair and very low outgoings through being based in Blackpool, were almost impregnable . . . but not quite! Their position in the industry had suffered as a consequence of our acquisition of Copes. They were certainly finding it harder to compete against us and while I never thought their situation was untenable, they did. I have no wish to be flippant, but with their father and uncle, the founders of Empire Pools, having both died from coronary thrombosis, neither Michael nor Alan had the heart for a battle.

We opened discussions within months of the completion of the Copes transaction and by early 1977 it appeared that an early and easy conquest would be concluded. It was not to be. With the inherent commercial common sense of true Lancastrians, Michael and Alan put themselves into the hands of Deloitte, Haskins and Sells, a firm of top accountants. The advice they received led them to the door of Vernons. Now, while it is true that the turnover of Empire was of insignificant value to Vernons, G.R. Kennerley, sharp as a scalpel, saw a different game plan. Rather than absorb Empire into Vernons, he would run them as a separate entity. With the muscle of Vernons collector network plus the utilisation of Vernons technology, Empire would aim to capture the low-stake sector of the market. They would certainly present a formidable challenge to Zetters and undoubtedly win over much of our hard-bought and hard-won clientele. Clearly, we had a battle on our hands. Happily, Jim and I had a close affinity with Michael and Alan . . . we liked them and they liked us. I do not believe anyone at Vernons enjoyed the same kind of rapport. It was later that I learned that G.R.K. had conducted negotiations himself and had been absent in Australia when our latest bid went in and was accepted. That lovely Lady Luck had smiled upon me again.

# Chapter 19

# Nations to Win

I was first introduced to David Nations in the early seventies. The consequences of that meeting were to have so profound an effect on the rest of my life as to have been unimagined at the time.

It all came about because David used the same accountants, Littlestone & Co, as did we. Terry Yardley, now a senior partner in the firm, brought David along to my office one day for an informal chat – or so I thought. David appeared to be a typical, well heeled, 'rag trade' Jewish boy, about forty years of age. At least, that was my immediate impression. I soon discovered that there was far more to this man than I first thought. For over an hour, I listened to a lecture, a veritable diatribe, on British Sport and its many imperfections.

'Why me?' I managed to ask during a pause in the verbal onslaught, 'What has all this to do with me?'

He was outraged, but not speechless, that I should even ask such a question! 'Did I not realise that my whole commercial life was to do with Sport . . . that I earned my living as a consequence of Sport . . . that Sport was the very ethic, the ethos of life . . . that I owed it to my country, my business and myself to recognise that truth and become involved?'

So it went on. Throughout my life I have met many brilliant exponents of causes, but David Nations surpassed and outclassed anyone I had previously experienced. He was, without doubt, the greatest 'name dropper' of all times. He unashamedly bandied about the names of well known personalities to such an extent as to make me feel certain that here was a con man up to his tricks. That is, until he delivered. He *did* know them all and what's more they all knew him! He *could* ring up film stars, Ministers of the Crown, even Buckingham Palace. He could . . . and he did.

What it came to in the end was moral blackmail. David, you see, was a member of the Central Council for Physical Recreation. Now this was the first time I'd ever heard of this pre-war organisation with its Soviet-like title – abbreviation CCPR – and you will forgive me if I take a few paragraphs to sketch in some detail of this important sporting body. The Central Council of Recreative Physical Training was started by a certain Miss P.C. Colson in 1935, to encourage the adult population to participate in recreative physical training to keep fit. The name of this body was changed in 1944 when its main function was that of training volunteers as recreation physical training leaders. As time went on, the CCPR concentrated more on helping its member organisations, the governing bodies of sport, outdoor pursuits and movement and dance, to run courses for coaches and to stage events to popularise their activities.

In 1957 a CCPR-sponsored 'Sport Enquiry' under the Chairmanship of Lord Wolfenden – The Wolfenden Committee – recommended that Government should provide substantial sums for sports development and facility provisions and that an independent Sports Council should be appointed to allocate these funds. These recommendations had not been acted upon by 1963 when Walter Winterbottom succeeded Miss Colson as Secretary of the CCPR. The Conservative Government, however, gave Lord Hailsham the responsibility for Government funding of Sport, so the CCPR and sports bodies received increased grant aid towards facilities (national and local) and towards costs of administration and coaching, as well as international events overseas.

When the Labour Government came to power in 1964, Denis Howell* was appointed as a Junior Minister for Sport. He did proceed to act on the Wolfenden Report by setting up a Sports Council. He was unable to get approval for an independent executive Sports Council so, instead, set up an Advisory Sports Council, with himself as Chairman, responsible to the Department of Education and Science, and with Walter Winterbottom as the Director.

When the Conservative Government again took office in 1970, they decided to set up Executive Sports Councils in England, Scotland and Wales and suggested that CCPR and SCPR (the Scots) staff should administer them. This newly styled CCPR received a substantial, annual grant from the Sports Council in order to carry out its functions. This has been a source of

---

* He covers this subject at length in his own autobiography – *Made in B'ham* (Queen Anne Press), Chapter 10 'The Fortunes of War'.

some controversy since, it is claimed by detractors, it made CCPR a semi-quango. Finance was still a problem, for the grant was never enough and, for a body wishing to be seen as independent, was only grudgingly acceptable. So CCPR set about raising funds for itself and that is where David Nations came in.

David's lively mind and commercial flair had already brought him wealth and personal success. I never discovered what caused him to turn his considerable abilities to helping British sport. Whatever, he shrewdly identified the immense fund-raising potential that vanity generates, by creating an élite club which he entitled 'Sponsors of Sport'. Top business men were selected for membership with the promise of unimaginable kudos. To become a 'Sponsor of Sport' would cost £1,000 per annum. Not an insignificant sum in those days, but eminently affordable to far-sighted Chairmen of Public Companies, who thought it a small price to pay for the privilege of meeting a Royal or a Minister of the Crown once or twice a year! 'Now, everybody knows how far-sighted you are,' David said to me. 'You must become a Sponsor of Sport.' The ear bending had been so complete, so all consuming, that I knew I had been brainwashed and meekly agreed to cough up the thousand pounds, just to be rid of him. I had no conception of what I'd let myself in for, or of where that single concession was to take me.

Within weeks, I found myself on a round of receptions and parties, the like of which I wouldn't have believed possible. David Nations certainly delivered. As one of his conquests, I was introduced to top sports personalities, TV presenters, Members of Parliament, Government Ministers and the *coup de grace*, Royalty itself in the person of His Royal Highness, the Duke of Edinburgh. David was very well known to Prince Philip and it was through that association that I thus met my very first Royal. Thereafter, I visited Buckingham Palace on numerous occasions and, on one very memorable day, even stayed to lunch.

Inevitably, David Nations knew Peter Moores and it is strange that I should have first met the Littlewoods heir as a consequence of joining 'Sponsors of Sport'. Peter was the son of John Moores (founder of Littlewoods) and at that time was not directly involved with the Pools business. This was to change with the passage of time and some years later events within the industry led us to establish a closer working relationship. Peter was very much his father's son, profound, clever and at an intellectual and cultural level several degrees above any other of my immediate contemporaries. While undoubtedly kind and considerate, he was, nevertheless, a difficult man with whom to establish a rapport but I hope and believe I may have done so. Peter was an enigma. His patronage and love of opera and the visual arts appeared to be so all-consuming that one was constantly surprised at his considerable commercial abilities and his amazingly detailed knowledge of the huge Littlewoods empire. Meeting Peter Moores was, in my view, at least one tangible result of joining 'Sponsors of Sport'.

I was particularly delighted to meet another close friend of David's, the Minister, Denis Howell, himself. As a consequence of this introduction, over a time, I developed a good relationship with Denis Howell which was to prove to be fortuitous.

I was also immensely flattered and clearly prey to the fund-raising aspirations of my new-found celebrated associates. Consequently, Zetters soon began supporting certain sporting and leisure activities, modestly enough, at first, and all exceptionally worthy. Then, at a VIP dinner one evening, I found myself on the top table, sitting next to the Minister, Denis Howell, who very quickly got around to telling me of the desperate circumstances attending the forthcoming Hastings Chess Tournament. The only international chess tournament held in Great Britain and it was about to founder through lack of funds. It seemed that at the very last moment their sponsor had, through circumstances beyond their control, dropped out leaving a shortfall of £5,000. If that sum couldn't be found within the next few days, the tournament would have to be cancelled. 'Prince Philip is distraught,' explained Denis. 'You see, Hastings would put us in line to achieve the first ever British "Grand Master", something very close to His Royal Highness's heart.' Just five 'grand' for one Grand Master! Who could resist such a bargain? Zetters sponsored the Hastings Chess Tournament. I don't know what the Company got out of it, but a young British chess genius, by the name of Tony Miles, became the first British Grand Master. So he was, naturally, well pleased. The Prince, I was told, was well pleased. Denis Howell, who was credited with saving the Tournament, was well pleased. David Nations, having me his protegé 'come good', was well pleased and I gained a reputation with which I was, at that time, very well pleased.

Little did I know where it would lead.

# Chapter 20

# Tragedy to Triumph

On 2 January 1972 a Scottish Cup match between Rangers and Celtic at Ibrox Park seemed certain to end with neither side having scored. Then, with just seconds to go before the final whistle, Johnson of Celtic scored what everybody believed must be the winning goal. As large numbers of spectators began to leave the ground, Colin Stein of Rangers with the last kick of the match, equalised. The roar that went up from the crowd remaining caused those leaving, to turn back to see what had happened. The resulting clash on a narrow stairway serving one of the terraces caused a major sports ground disaster which resulted in 66 supporters being killed. The Conservatives were in power when the Ibrox disaster occurred.

It took several years, a nationwide study of sports grounds by a Government operated group led by Walter Winterbottom, a committee of enquiry chaired by the Rt. Hon. Lord Justice Clerk Baron John Wheatley, a change of Government and Denis Howell, once more in place as Minister for Sport, to produce legislation in the form of a Bill known as 'The Safety of Sports Grounds Act'. This Bill set out the standards and procedures with which clubs were to comply. Statutory powers were soon enacted whereby sports grounds with a capacity of more than 10,000 spectators, were required to obtain a safety certificate from their Local Authority. To qualify for this certificate, the stadia had to meet the stringent safety requirements laid down in the Act. All very fine, of course, but these regulations affected most of the clubs in the Football League and they didn't have the funds to carry out this essential work. Now, as it just so happened, at about this time, the PPA 'Spotting-the-Ball' Competition was taking a fair amount of 'flak' from the media. Criticism abounded and, in the nature of things, there was inevitably talk of Government intervention, to challenge its legality.

Cecil Moores, with vision and profound common sense, took the initiative. He invited Alan Hardaker, the tough, well-respected Yorkshire Secretary of the Football League and personal friend of Denis Howell, to join him in putting together a 'Football Trust'. Properly constituted, with independent Trustees and a prestigious Chairman, the Trust would be fully funded by the PPA Spotting-the-Ball Competition. Its primary aim would be to produce the revenue so desperately needed by those soccer clubs caught in the net of the Minister's Sports Ground Bill.

Consultation with Denis Howell and Denis Healey, the Chancellor of the Exchequer, took place and the first steps were taken to form what was to become known as 'The Football Grounds Improvement Trust'. Everything seemed to be proceeding according to plan when an unhappy incident occurred. The BBC ran a witch-hunt programme on television, wherein they absolutely castigated STB and all those connected with it. Furthermore, they were specifically critical of the Moores Millionaires, especially Cecil and Nigel. Needless to say, Cecil was devastated. His honour and integrity and, indeed, that of the whole family, were of paramount importance to him. His action was predictable. He suspended all discussions with the Government and, although I cannot be certain, I understood that he was seriously considering withdrawing Littlewoods' participation in STB. All the other members of the PPA were sure it was both an incorrect and emotional reaction. Nonetheless, when Cecil Moores was adamant, who was there to convince him otherwise?

Argument aplenty, in favour of STB, was paraded . . . It was a long established game . . . It was much enjoyed by many players . . . It was only a modest wager . . . It was run with a professionalism and integrity for which the PPA were justly renowned. Added to all that, we were making a healthy profit! Even if these considerations were to be set aside, what about the new element that had entered the equation? What about the Football Grounds Improvement Trust and the promise to Denis Howell?

Alan Hardaker was quickly at pains to point out that the Football League and the whole structure of football would face enormous problems unless sufficient income was forthcoming to carry out the statutory safety requirements. Therefore, should the Trust be still-born because of an ill informed, unfair TV programme? Cecil never saw it in those stark terms. He had been badly hurt and wasn't about to change his mind. Nobody seemed to be able to persuade him. I certainly couldn't . . . but I knew a man who could! The one man with more to lose from the failure of STB than even its promoters, was Denis Howell. Its successful continuation was virtually the only chance of saving his Safety of Sports Grounds Bill.

That is how I reasoned – and I knew Denis Howell, didn't I? By this time, I had began to develop a good relationship with him and had also come to know the ministerial advisers in his department. Consequently, I rang Jerry Rendell, a senior civil servant and Denis's private secretary, to explain the unfortunate dilemma that the BBC had caused with their programme. 'If the Minister wants the revenue, he will have to convince Cecil Moores that STB has Government approval and public acceptability,' I ventured. Jerry, who had apparently been nonplussed that negotiations had seemed to have stalled, now understood the reasons and was grateful to me for pointing them out. I have no idea what transpired between Denis and Cecil, but shortly thereafter agreement was reached. The appropriately named Football Grounds Improvement Trust was created and Sir Norman Chester appointed the first Chairman. The sole source of income for the Trust was 10% of STB turnover. Ambitious objectives were set, over and above the immediate work required to improve ground safety. All seater stadia . . . measures against hooligans . . . additional police presence . . . video cameras for monitoring crowds . . . and many others. As time has gone by, many of these aims have been achieved, so everybody won – Denis's Bill (and bacon) were saved – football had an ongoing revenue – the Pools, with many thousands of staff and collectors, preserved a lucrative element of their business. Even the Treasury won as they imposed VAT (then at $7\frac{1}{2}$%, but soon to be increased to 15%) on the STB Competition. I cannot think STB would have perished and the Trust been still-born had I not made the right 'phone call, to the right man, at the right time. I will not pretend that my intervention was critical, but I like to think I played my part in what turned out to be a very happy outcome for all concerned.

# Chapter 21

# Blue-eyed Boy

I could do no wrong, least of all with Denis Howell. On two occasions now, with the Chess Tournament and the Football Trust, I had been instrumental in playing him on-side. He invited me to lunch with him on the terrace of the House of Commons. I was delighted to accept, expecting nothing more than a good meal, at an exciting venue, purely as a 'thank-you' gesture. I was wrong on both counts. I'd had better meals at Lyons Corner House before the war and Denis wasn't saying 'thank you', he was propositioning me.

Two other guests were at that lunch, David Nations, with whom I had now become quite friendly, and Walter Winterbottom, this man of many parts, all of them sporting and noteworthy. As the Director of the Sports Council, he had attended the 1972 Munich Olympics (the tragedy games), and had brought back with him the story of '*Sporthilfe*' (Sport-help). This was a West German organisation dedicated to raising funds, from private sources, to help their athletes to train and prepare for international competition. *Sporthilfe* had caught the imagination of the West German commerce and industry, as well as large sections of the general public. Working in reasonable harmony with their establishment bodies of sport, such as their Olympic Association and the equivalent of their Sports Council, they had become a major influence for the furtherment of West German sporting excellence by raising and distributing huge revenues with renowned West German efficiency.

Walter wanted Britain to adopt a similar fund-raising scheme to help individual Olympic participants. The British Olympic Association had turned down the offer, because it was felt that the new scheme would clash with its own well established fund-raising activities. The difference was, however, that *Sporthilfe* funds were being used to grant aid to individuals towards the cost of personal equipment, travel and coaching preparation for all international sporting events, whereas BOA funds were used for the expenses involved in taking a British Olympic squad to the Games and housing and feeding them. I have heard BOA described as 'a glorified travel agent'.

The Sports Council arranged a meeting with officials of the BOA, the CCPR and representatives of governing bodies in the Olympic movement and got them all to agree to the formation of a national Sports Aid Foundation. Naturally, in order not to breach regulations on amateur status, the governing bodies were to have control by nominating the individuals and administering the grants. It was agreed also that the Chairmen of the Sports Council, the BOA and the CCPR should serve on the Committee of Governors of the Foundation.

Denis Howell warmly welcomed the scheme and set out to find a suitable chairman and other influential members of the public, to serve as Governors to the Foundation. The Minister met Peter Cadbury, a member of the well known Cadbury family, and persuaded him to take the chair. Mr Cadbury had not joined the famous family chocolate business, preferring to create his own brilliant success in a number of spectacular ventures. He had been a test pilot for the Ministry of Aircraft Production during the war. Called to the Bar in 1946, he practised until 1954, when he then turned his skills to commerce. He became Chairman of Keith Prowse, Alfred Hays Ltd. and Air Westward Ltd. and executive Chairman of Westward Television Ltd. He was also a Director of Independent Television News Ltd. along with other activities too numerous to mention. His sporting pursuits included golf, tennis and sailing. At a youthful fifty-seven years of age, he was now ready to take on a major role in public life and was seen as the perfect candidate to bring SAF onto the British scene and lead it to glory.

There had been one tiny snag. When first approached, just over a year earlier, he was setting out, for the second time, on the road to a dissolution of his marriage. Everyone agreed that it would be better out of the way and waited the year for it to happen. Now they were all ready to go.

This, then, was the story that emerged during our lunch on the Terrace.

'All very interesting,' I said, 'But what has it to do with me?'

'The Minister would like you, along with David Nations here, to become Governors on Peter Cadbury's new board,' replied Walter Winterbottom.

Well, I didn't say yes and I didn't say no. Between David's outpouring of enthusiastic verbage, I hadn't even managed to find out what it entailed. Nevertheless I did agree to meet Peter Cadbury and the other prospective Governors.

The meeting took place in the Minister's office at the Department of the Environment in Marsham Street, just behind Westminster Abbey. They were all there, all those Godly persons I'd heard so much about. The Minister, Denis Howell, acting as host, introduced us to each other. Lord Rupert Neville, Sir Robin Brook, Mrs Mary Glen Haig, David Nations, a young chap called Tony Stratton-Smith and the great man himself, Peter Cadbury. He was tall, good-looking and distinctly upper crust but appeared to be slightly nervous and apprehensive. Together, we were to be the nucleus of this splendid new sporting body, entrusted with the role of transforming British sporting achievement. We broke up shortly after the introduction and speeches and agreed to have another meeting at Peter's offices, at Marble Arch, a few days later. My head was in a whirl. What on earth was I letting myself in for? What time would all this stuff take? What did I know about sport, anyway, and as to fund raising, well, I hadn't a clue.

David Nations was, as ever, reassuringly enthusiastic and persuasive. 'Give it a trial, Paul,' he said. 'It will be good for you, it will create new horizons and broaden your perspective of life and, if you don't like it, well, you can resign after a few months.'

So it was that on 27 November 1975 I attended the first formal meeting of SAF. It was held in Peter Cadbury's offices and he, of course, assumed his role as Chairman. At the end of a slightly fraught discussion, at which everyone seemed to be very defensive, Peter took me to one side and asked if I could possibly join him for dinner that evening. He had something important to talk to me about. I phoned Helen who was at the cottage in Hampshire.

'Where will you eat?' she asked inconsequentially.

'He mentioned Scotts or The Mirabelle,' I replied. 'I'll get a late train from Waterloo and tell you all about it tonight.'

In the event, we went to The Mirabelle in Curzon Street and Peter astonished me by asking if I would become his Vice Chairman.

'The three quango bosses Rupert Neville, Robin Brooke and the Glen Haig woman are a total waste of time as far as fund raising goes,' he said. 'Nations might be useful if he ever stops talking, although I doubt it. Stratton-Smith is a nonentity and I shall lose him with some rapidity and that leaves you. I would like you to be my Vice Chairman,' he concluded.

Well, in those days flattery, even backhanded flattery like that, got anyone anywhere. So I was now the Vice Chairman of SAF! After a magnificent meal, he gave me a lift to Waterloo in his Rolls Royce. I had wanted to 'phone Helen from the restaurant to tell her what train I was catching. 'You can 'phone from the car, Paul,' he told me. 'Phone from the car already! Wow, was I impressed! I wasn't prepared, however, for Helen's reaction.

'Where are you? How are you? Are you in hospital?' she screamed down the 'phone.

'What on earth's the matter?' I asked.

'Were you at Scotts?' she screamed again.

That very evening, while we were dining in splendid luxury at the Mirabelle, an IRA bomb had gone off in Scotts, killing two diners and badly injuring twenty-three others. Helen had seen the pictures on the 9 o'clock BBC news.

Everybody seemed pleased enough to learn of my appointment as Vice Chairman, but the general atmosphere, at the next couple of meetings, left much to be desired. Peter was clearly incensed at being hedged in by the disciplines applying to fund raising for amateur sports persons. He was irritated beyond belief at what he saw as the undisguised delight, particularly by BOA, at the many frustrations we would be facing. 'You can't use the names of well known athletes in "Brand" advertising. It's against Rule 23 of the International Olympic Committee,' BOA affirmed with some glee. 'There are serious tax implications in giving grants to individuals' was the message from the Sports Council. 'The Governing Bodies of Sport will have to be consulted as to disbursements,' said the CCPR. Peter was certain they were trying to sabotage the whole idea before it got off the ground. He 'phoned me one evening with dramatic news.

'I have told the Minister that I cannot accept a number of his appointees on my Board,' he told me. 'You are excluded, of course, but most of the others must go. The Minister has called us all to a meeting at his office tomorrow.'

I was flabbergasted, but too uncertain of my ground to argue with him. However, I did venture the view that it was hardly fair to have agreed to the composition of the Board and then, effectively, to disband it within two weeks. He either didn't listen to me or didn't want to hear what I said. So it would have to be thrashed out at the Minister's office on the morrow.

We all assembled at the given time, all except Peter that is; he arrived half-an-hour late! He eventually came in and almost immediately, made a forthright and uncompromising statement to the effect that SAF, as a consequence of the members foisted on him, was a 'busted flush'. Unless he was given free rein to form his own Board – and not to be tied to the 'pettifogging constraints' imposed by 'anachronistic establishment figures' – he would resign forthwith. The Minister responded without hesitation.

'Mr Cadbury,' he said, 'I am not going to seek the resignation of eminent people whom I have just appointed to the committee. Further, I have no power whatsoever to remove those members sitting in a representative capacity and nominated by organisations such as the Sports Council, the CCPR and the BOA.' He went on to say that, in the circumstances, 'you had better reconsider your position'.

'I have made my position quite clear,' Peter said.

'Then I accept your resignation,' said Denis Howell. Peter got up and left without a further word.

After a few moments of tense silence Denis spoke. 'There could hardly have been a more unfortunate start to an organisation which we, all of us, hoped would play a notable and leading role in British Sport. It has, as you know, taken three years to put together, two of which were spent in finding a suitable Chairman. It would be devastating to see it fail, untested, within three weeks. I don't think it has need to, but it's up to you. There are six of you, members of the Board, Governors of the Sports Aid Foundation. You have a Vice Chairman, Paul Zetter, who now automatically becomes acting Chairman. I must call a press conference tomorrow to explain Cadbury's resignation. I hope, at the same time, I can tell them that you will all continue to serve and strive to achieve success for SAF. Please let me know, as soon as you've had a chance to talk it over, but, in any case, no later than tomorrow morning. Thank you.'

With that he left the room and half-a-dozen speechless witnesses to a sensational happening. But not for long. Inevitably, David Nations spoke first. 'Naturally we go on. It's worth doing isn't it?' he said rhetorically. 'So we do it. That's it.' They all agreed, Lord Rupert, Sir Robin, Mary Glen Haig and Tony Stratton-Smith.

I have never been more unsure of myself. Suddenly, I was in the deepest end of totally unknown waters. My instinct told me to let them get on with it. After all, it was their scene, not mine. What did I know about it? Anyway, I had other responsibilities . . . a wife, two children and a thriving business, all needing my time. While I knew little enough about this new foundation, I was damn sure of two things – it would take time and money, my time and my money! All this was surging through my mind when I noticed they were all looking at me. Sir Robin Brook then spoke. 'As acting Chairman, Paul, it is your job to keep the team together until a full

Chairman is appointed. We shall do that as quickly as possible. But I fear that if you reject the interim responsibility and the Minister cannot announce our continuity tomorrow, then SAF will cease to exist before it even started. I hope you agree – and needless to say, we shall all give you our unstinted support.'

I looked around and they were all nodding enthusiastically.

'It's nearly Christmas, Sir Robin,' I said, 'If I take it on, say until next Easter (1976), what target figure, how much money, would you expect the Foundation to raise by then?'

He considered for a moment. 'If you raise £20,000 by Easter, I'll kiss your boots.'

'O.K.' I said, 'Let's go and tell the Minister SAF is up and running.'

(It is difficult to be entirely accurate after sixteen years, but I truly believe this is an almost verbatim report of those momentous days).

# Chapter 22

# 'Giving Britons a Better Sporting Chance'

Following the Christmas break, I set about putting together the nuts and bolts of SAF. There was a pump-priming grant of a couple of thousand pounds from the Sports Council with which I opened a bank account. We then advertised for a full time Director. From some dozens of applications, Alan Weeks, the well-known television commentator, was appointed. It was our first major decision and what a wise one it turned out to be.

With an office the size of a telephone box and a secretary, both cadged from the Sports Council, we set up our stall in Brompton Road. They were heady times, those early days of 1976. I quickly learned that the hasty judgement Cadbury had made about the Governors who had been foisted upon him was, at the very least, grossly ill-considered. The various advice I received, of how best to handle delicate situations prevalent in the politics of sport, was invaluable. That most kindly man, Lord Rupert Neville, befriended me. Regular meetings at Buckingham Palace with him, Alan Weeks and me eased our acceptance by BOA and clearly led to an ongoing rapport which developed between our two organisations. Both Sir Robin Brook and Mary Glen Haig were enthusiastic and helpful Governors and, I'm happy to say, still are to this day. Of even greater significance, however, was the input from David Nations and Tony Stratton-Smith. Those two were the early fund-raisers and they set about their task with a dynamism that seemed certain to bring success. Early donations came from the Tobacco Industry, the Pools Promoters and from an Elton John Pop Concert, in every case without strings. With the approach of Easter, I reviewed our situation. BOA had accepted 'the new kid on the block' as long as he didn't fish in their

152

waters. We had established a Committee of Advisers (later to be the Grants Committee) under the Chairmanship of Bill Slater, a highly respected, ex-Wolves and ex-England soccer international, and the famous David Coleman, BBC Sports commentator exceptionel, as his Vice Chairman. Their role was to liaise with the governing bodies of sport, in order to identify individuals suitable for consideration for grant aid. The governing bodies would then be sent the sums agreed and administer them, on our behalf. So, at a stroke, we had won friends and support in practically every sport in the land; we had avoided any tax liability, for grants were handled by responsible bodies and only handed over for legitimate training expenses. Moreover, we had raised income without recourse to linkage with any branded products. Our bank balance exceeded the £20,000 set by Sir Robin and our pattern for grant-aiding sports people was now established, a fact which had not gone unnoticed by the media.

During those weeks I regularly visited Sir Robin and Walter Winterbottom as well as Denis Howell. Amongst other discussions, they assured me that the search for a Chairman was well in hand. Some splendid names were pulled out of the air, considered and jettisoned . . . Lord George Brown . . . had other pre-occupations! Chris Chataway . . . too busy! Dr Roger Bannister, Ex-Chairman of Sports Council . . . not appropriate! These and many others were bandied about, but there always seemed to be some snag. Anyway, with Easter approaching I didn't believe it would be my problem for much longer. Then, just before Good Friday, I was called to an unscheduled meeting with Denis Howell. Upon being ushered in, I was surprised to find Sir Robin Brook with the Minister. Denis greeted me warmly and said, without preamble:

'Paul, Sir Robin and all of the Governors would like you to cease being acting Chairman of SAF and become its fully fledged Chairman. I have to say that I fully endorse their views.'

I said yes. Not there and then, you understand. I requested a few days to consider my position. I now understood the ramifications of the task I was being asked to undertake, so I wanted to seek the views of those near and dear to me. Helen and the children. My father, Jim Clarke and David Isaacs and last, but certainly not least, Andreas Hadjioannou and Terry Yardley. Without exception, I was told to go for it, so I did. On 8 April 1976 the Sports Aid Foundation was incorporated as a limited liability company and I became its first Chairman. I often ponder the reasons why I changed from being a reluctant semi-conscript to a willing volunteer. It may have had to do with what I believed were my achievements as acting Chairman. I was almost certainly influenced by the authority my new position had given me and the respect which that authority commanded. It was also immensely rewarding to see the instant results and benefits which SAF was achieving. In short . . . I loved it. I quickly established rapport with Alan Weeks and it soon became apparent that his appointment as our first full time Director was an inspired one. Alan knew everyone in sport and everyone knew and loved Alan. Any lingering question as to our acceptability quickly evaporated so the political in-fighting, that the pundits feared, just never happened.

# Chapter 23

# Celebrity Cause

The geraniums that I have just planted in the window boxes on the terrace of my superb apartment in Chelsea remind me that we are once more in the merry month of May. I know the year is palindromic (1991) because that's the kind of unimportant detail which I enjoy. I've called it an apartment rather than a flat, for the description more suitably befits the status I have achieved.

What with one thing and another it is, at least, two months since I have managed to put pencil to paper. I seem to have been much too busy and frankly, at my age, that must be plain daft. I love writing these memoirs and wallow in the nostalgia they induce. Consequently, I become irritated when I am unable to find the time to indulge myself. On top of that, I get out of the routine of writing and find it difficult to re-start. It's also fair to say that I'm now becoming a little nervous. I've reached the time when, of necessity, I am writing about recent events, current occurrences and contemporary people. Inevitably, I must include in my story a few well known – some even famous – people, who are alive and well and living all around me. I have already relished a certain amount of name-dropping and there are many more still to be dropped . . . and that is why I am slightly worried. I don't want to be controversial and I certainly don't want to be hurtful to anyone, particularly the famous. I've been advised to tell it as it is and to hell with the consequences . . . 'He who hesitates is not published', so they say. Well, so be it. To paraphrase a fashionable comment, I shall be economical with my controversy. What I shall do is send a draft of any particular passages to those mentioned within them. Thus, not only will that enable them to

155

comment, it will also help me to be as accurate as possible with my account of events.

So here we go again, back to 1976 with Alan Weeks sitting in his spacious 'telephone box' in the Sports Aid Foundation office in the Brompton Road. When Alan became SAF's first Director, it was agreed that he would still be able to undertake some work for the BBC. His SAF contract permitted him twenty-two days leave of absence per year, thus enabling him to cover all major international swimming and ice skating events. These, of course, included his specialist sporting commentaries for the Beeb. It was considered, quite rightly in my view, that Alan's high TV profile was advantageous to SAF by association. His name was synonymous with ice skating . . . mention Alan Weeks and a Double Salchow or Triple Lutz automatically sprang to mind. But there was another, even greater, name in ice skating in 1976. It was the incomparable John Curry, who achieved the Triple Crown of figure skating by winning the European, the Olympic and the World Championships all in the same year . . . and Alan Weeks was the BBC TV commentator for all three events. As SAF was not in being when John was in training, he never benefited from a SAF grant, so Alan's broadcasts of his triumph could not – and did not – advance the cause of SAF. Nonetheless, I learned much about the psyche of the job I'd set out to do as a result of John Curry's three victories. I discovered that time, dedication and money are the basic essentials for anyone engaged at that level of sporting competition. I witnessed, for the first time, the adulation bestowed upon sporting heroes by their adoring public. I understood the passionate patriotism generated by victorious compatriots. I grasped then what SAF was all about and what was needed to put more Britons on the rostrum.*

I suppose it is true to say that the teething years of SAF were the most demanding and the most fun. The founder Governors neatly divided into two very distinct groups. The sages consisted of Sir Robin Brooke, Lord Rupert Neville and Mary Glen Haig. These three wise counsellors managed to keep us other three – David Nations, Tony Stratton-Smith and me – on a reasonably straight and very narrow path. David and Tony were the money men, the fund raisers. They it was, who were going to convince the great British public – along with the moguls of British industry and commerce – that if they wanted to cheer British sporting victories they had to put their money where their cheer was. David Coleman, while still doing sterling service on the Committee of Advisors, soon joined our executive cartel and I

---

* This appraisal led in fact to the SAF logo. Helen, my ever-supportive wife, designed the logo which is in use to this day.

believe we made a formidable nucleus. It started well enough. David Nations pulled in substantial cash from the tobacco industry, particularly BATS who were especially helpful. Tony, along with David, convinced Elton John to run a pop concert at Earls Court on our behalf. It was a colossal success and brought us £20,000, a truly magnificent sum in 1976. It also brought us to the public notice. Hardly surprising really, the very sound generated from that Earls Court stage probably shattered Waterford Crystal in Harrods some three miles away. It certainly was a memorable night. I venture to bet there has never been such a gathering at such an occasion. The Minister, dear Denis Howell, was, of course, my guest of honour. VIPs. from Government and industry, all looking somewhat shellshocked, were there in abundance. A host of famous sporting personalities were pulled in by David Coleman and many show biz stars, including the lovely Shirley MacLaine, graced the occasion. The world's funniest comedian Eric Morecambe, with whom I became very friendly, honoured us, along with many, many others, I also met David Nations' wife, Elaine, for the first time. She was then – and is to this day – one of the loveliest woman I have ever met. As if that were not enough, she is blessed with an abundance of wit, charm and wisdom. I wonder how many poor old buffers on first meeting her feel as Charlie Chaplin felt when, at eighty-seven years of age he first met Sophia Loren and said to her, 'I wish I'd met you five years ago.'

It had always been considered that SAF would quite easily raise the necessary cash to fund its operation. The great British public would fall over themselves in their eagerness to cough up the 'readies', in order to see their heroes win fame and acclaim. It just wasn't so. In fact, there was even a significant resistance barrier to our efforts. A number of our citizens took the view that they were not about to part with their hard-earned, highly taxed 'shekels' to support élite young men and women on world-wide jaunts to sunny climes. Hardly a fair appraisal, but who said life was fair? What we did attract were celebrities. In all shapes and sizes, from every walk of life, they flocked to our cause. The beautiful people of show business doted upon us as if we were an agent with a handful of contracts. The media, in all their guises, saw us as good news. Politicians, of whatever hue, clearly thought we were worth embracing. They took to their hearts an organisation dedicated to helping British sports people win and I tried to use this unexpected bonus to our best possible advantage. It seemed that there was no one out there, particularly in show biz, too glamorous to cleave to the objectives of SAF. Elton John had, of course, been the first. None of the others were quite so supportive, but they turned up in their droves to all of our functions. I loved it, mingling with the mighty.

At that time, I had been invited to become an honorary life member of the famous Les Ambassadeurs Club in Park Lane. David Nations, of course, knew the proprietor John Mills – the Polish one, not the English one and, in many ways, almost as well known. John became a Governor of SAF and put 'Les A.' at our disposal over and over again. It was at this venue that we were to meet, entertain and describe our virtues to our glamorous supporters.

'How,' you might well ask, 'did all this help SAF?' Well, quite apart from providing me with a well loved ego trip, not a lot, I'm bound to say. It was still true that fund raising was terribly difficult and the 'beautiful people' made little material contribution. They did, however enhance SAF social occasions such as dinners, balls, concerts and the like. More importantly, they were providing us with a public image. As a result SAF acquired, within a few short years, a public recognition on a par with many longer established bodies such as the CCPR, BOA and others. Did it help? Well, I don't know, but it was fun and it sure didn't do us any harm!

# Chapter 24

# Scotland the Brave

In the meantime, the more mundane activities of SAF occupied a great deal of time. Alan Weeks and I were travelling the country in order to spread the gospel. Through the good offices of the Sports Council we visited the nine English regions which effectively run and control sport in the UK. In every case, we set up regional arms, each with their own chairman, governors and administration but all coming under the auspices of SAF Head Office in London. Scotland chose to go a slightly more independent route but, nevertheless, formed the Scottish SAF as a sister company. Even that had a most difficult birth . . . it is a story worth recounting.

In June 1976, I had arranged with the Scottish Sports Council to address a number of eminent Scottish persons with a view to describing SAF and hopefully seeing the formation of a Scottish SAF. Peter Heatley, Chairman of their Sports Council, along with his Director, Ken Hutchinson, had invited a number of Scottish VIPs, including His Grace the Duke of Hamilton. Helen, my son Adam and I had taken advantage of this trip to have a short fishing holiday near Inverness, just before the Edinburgh meeting. At the end of a pleasant few days, we left our hotel early for the long drive south in order to be in Edinburgh for the 2 p.m. start. This was comfortably accomplished and Adam and Helen went off sightseeing while I joined the meeting.

I cannot say that I was warmly received. I described SAF, its purpose and its functions and tried to enthuse my listeners to patriotic fervour. Well, I was new to the job and clearly not very good at it. After two hours or so, just about the only reaction was from His Grace, the Duke, who was deeply concerned at the possibility of ballroom dancing being one of the beneficiaries of any funds raised. On that account, he would not wish to be supportive. Just when I was feeling a little tired and rather depressed, Peter Heatley's secretary, whom I had previously required to confirm my car train and sleeper booking to London, came into the room.

'I'm sorry to tell you, Mr. Zetter,' she said quietly to me, 'All the trains have been cancelled due to a lightning rail strike. Oh, and by the way, your wife and son are waiting in the outer office.' I was devastated. Adam had to be back in College in Eastbourne the next day, whilst I was scheduled to make a speech at a SAF South West inaugural dinner. There was only one thing for it, I'd have to wrap up this abortive meeting and start driving from Edinburgh to London as quickly as possible.

The Scots were still talking about the insoluble problems of raising money for Scottish athletes when, largely out of frustration and eagerness to get away, I interrupted. 'I understand your difficulties,' I said, 'However, please do not concern yourselves. Scottish sports-people are some of the finest in the British Isles but, like their English counterparts, they need financial help for their preparation and training. So if you will advise us, in London, of those you consider qualify, I guarantee that every one of them will get grant aid.' Well, it was like a red rag to a bull! They were not about to let this cockney sassenach pick up their tab. Scottish pride overrode all their instinctive frugalities. Without a single dissenting voice, agreement was reached on the formation of a Scottish SAF. It has run with tremendous flair and constant cash flow ever since.

We drove to London, arriving at about three o'clock the next morning. At 6 a.m. my bedside telephone rang. It was Hannah, my stepmother, to tell me that my father was unwell and could I come to their home in Hove right away. I drove down in a hurry, only to find my father sitting up in bed, as perky as you please, having just got over a mild bilious attack. I then drove from Hove to Bristol, not the easiest of journeys, to arrive in time to save Helen, who had herself driven directly from London, from having to read my speech to the SAF inaugural dinner. I'm told it went well but, truly, I recall nothing of it.

# Chapter 25

# Lucky Chance

Just as we were too early to play any part in the 1976 Winter Olympics neither were we involved with the Summer Games in Montreal . . . with one very notable exception, that is.

During one of his BBC breaks, Alan Weeks had been sent to Miami to interview a young British swimmer by the name of David Wilkie who was based at the University of Miami. Now David, it seems, was a fine Olympic prospect, hence the BBC's interest. Upon his return Alan reported that, with three months to go to the start of the Games, David Wilkie's funds had run out and unless he could raise the wherewithal, he would have to leave the University, with the consequent break in his training schedule. Well, with the flexibility that independence brings, we acted without delay and David Wilkie was one of the very first recipients of a SAF grant. There could hardly have been a more 'fairy tale' start. As we all now know, David Wilkie won the gold medal for the 200 metres breast stroke. He won it in style with a world record-breaking swim and he won with the support of a SAF grant. Wilkie was voted 1976 'Sports Personality of the Year' on that popular, annual BBC programme. During his live interview by David Coleman, he acknowledged, to some sixteen million viewers, the great help SAF had been to him and that he would be joining them in their fund raising and public relations activities. So he did and for a few years visited large factories and other work places on our behalf on a 'sponsored appearance' arrangement. I'm very happy we were able to help David Wilkie, I'm even happier that he helped us.

It was an exciting time and it would have been very easy to have allowed

the glamour to obscure the realities of the task we had set out upon. I had
always been taught to 'keep my eye on the target' and basically 'the target'
was easily defined . . . Money!! But how much money? Well, at a modest
estimate, in order to give a modest number of modest grants and run an
organisation on very modest expenses, we would need an income of
something like £200,000 per annum . . . putting it modestly! You sit down
with a blank sheet of paper and end up with £200,000. The prospect was
daunting, to say the least. Oh, I had a good team all right, but a one-off pop
concert or donation, welcome as they were, were not enough. We needed,
we had to have, a reliable, continuing source of income. Remember the
constraints under which we were attempting to operate . . . no brand-name
linkage with athletes! . . . debarred from using the Olympic Rings! . . . a
veto-like restriction on which companies we could approach! The obstacles
seemed insurmountable and I nearly despaired. I had, however, forgotten
my greatest ally. That one feminine abstract without which I would
probably have still been plying my wares in Bethnal Green. I refer of course,
to 'Lady Luck'. Just when I feared that my ventures were exceeding my
abilities, there she was again, reliable as ever.

How did she manifest herself this time? Through four words and a year.
Lotteries and Amusements Act 1976. How poetic. How sublime! 'Why?' you
may ask, 'What are you getting so excited about?'

Let me tell you by quoting from the introductory paragraph of a
government consultative document on this most blessed Act. 'The Lotteries
and Amusements Act 1976 authorises the promotion of public lotteries on
behalf of societies, established for charitable athletic or cultural purposes, or
for non-commercial purposes, and by local authorities as defined in the
Act.' That's it. Therein lies the magic. Sports Aid Foundation were a
'society established for athletic purposes' weren't we? It couldn't just be
fortuitous coincidence. My 'lady friend' must have had a pact with divine
providence (or the Labour Party). There I was, a Pools Promoter, with the
know-how of agent networks, distribution and collection structure and
management, dated-material handling, prize-winner publicity etc., etc., and
this new golden opportunity falls into my lap. Talk about the right man in
the right place at the right time!

Well, of course, I jumped at it. It wasn't that easy, but then, nothing ever
is. In those early days, everybody tried to climb on the band-wagon.
Commercial interests attempted to capitalize on a venture which was never
intended for that purpose. All failed. Hundreds of 'cowboy' operations
came and were soon gone with the wind. Many laudable societies 'set up'
shop but, lacking the necessary skills to maintain viability, very soon 'shut

up' shop. In every case, they lacked the one essential ingredient required to make the operation successful – low cost outlets. In other words, suitable sites, frequented regularly by members of the public in large numbers. I knew this problem had to be solved if our lottery was to save SAF. I knew I had to find a giant nationwide retailer, such as, say, a supermarket chain, who would let us in. Well, I had another 'right man in the right place' etc., my stalwart colleague David Nations. David was said to know everybody, but did David know any supermarket bosses? Don't be silly . . . 'You want to see Jack Cohen or Leslie Porter of Tesco? . . . So when do you want to see them?' It's true. Just like that, he set up a meeting with Leslie Porter, Chairman of Tesco, the result of which undoubtedly secured the future of SAF. Within a few days of my initial enquiry, David and I were warmly received by Leslie Porter and his dynamic wife Shirley, in their breathtaking penthouse near Hyde Park. Shortly thereafter, I followed up with a further meeting at the Tesco Head Office in Waltham Cross. Alan Weeks and I joined the senior Tesco management in creating the blueprint for the lottery operation through their stores. The co-operation we received was outstanding, particularly on learning of their decision to seek neither commission on sales nor kiosk rents.

Fifteen years later, this partnership continues and I don't exaggerate when I claim that many millions of pounds have gone to British competitors as a result. You can imagine, therefore, the delight with which I welcomed the award, some years later, of a Knighthood to Leslie Porter and, some time after that, the Dame Knight's Cross to Shirley. An amusing incident occurred on that first visit to join the main board Directors for lunch, following our morning discussions. During that very happy meal, Sir Jack Cohen appeared unexpectedly. He blinked with surprise to see a busy Directors' dining room and two visitors. 'What is this?' he queried, 'A *barmitzvah* party and nobody invited me?'

Chapter 26

# Lake Placid

The Labour Party had been defeated in 1979 and I was sad that SAF had lost its powerful friend and mentor Denis Howell. I need not have worried. Hector Munro became the Minister for Sport in Margaret Thatcher's administration and we were speedily welcomed to the kindly affection of this quite delightful new man. I had, as a matter of routine, met Hector when he had been responsible for sport in Margaret Thatcher's Shadow Cabinet, and had every good reason to be pleased that I had.

In 1980 Helen and I decided to go to the Winter Olympic Games at Lake Placid in Upper New York State. Actually, Helen made the decision because she loves ice skating, while I was willing enough, because SAF were funding a brilliant young skater by the name of Robin Cousins. I wanted to see how we were spending SAF's money. It was our first major, international sporting event and we were completely naive as to the street-wise necessity for using whatever influences could be mustered in order to enjoy the Games. I learned very quickly, in Lake Placid, that if you are a nobody, then stay at home and watch it on the 'telly'.

The first warning came when, in the late autumn of 1979, I tried to book an hotel in Lake Placid. The official Olympic travel agent recovered from his incredulity and then enjoyed pointing out to me that, unless I was 'accredited', the best he could do was a room in a farmhouse nine miles from Lake Placid and I'd better grab it, because it was available only due to a cancellation that very morning. He had an aura of authenticity about him, that chap, so I put down a deposit there and then and booked our flight to Montreal. We went a couple of days before the start of the Games, hired a car and drove the hundred or so miles south from Canada into the USA. We found our farm and were enormously cheered by the warm welcome and hospitality heaped upon us by our American hosts, the farmer and his wife.

The next day, we decided to drive in to look around Lake Placid. Shock and horror. Two miles out of town, there was a police barrier through which no one without 'accreditation' was allowed to pass, except by public transport. 'That's the second time I've heard this word "accreditation",' I said to Helen. 'What on earth does it mean?' I was soon to find out. Officials, competitors, part-time helpers, VIPs, and their guests were given a kind of passport with different degrees of importance according to status. With the highest qualification, you were a notch or two above the rank of King, Emperor or President. Without 'accreditation' you were one of the great unwashed.

Every morning, we waited 'in line' for public transport. It was there that I heard, for the first time, of the 'Wind-Chill Factor' . . . and I learned it the hard way. Queueing for a bus for two or three hours, in temperatures of fifteen degrees below freezing, minus 10° or so for the WCF, was very educational. Anyway, I certainly learned my lesson. Hell is cold! Never again would I submit myself and Helen to such discomfort. Helen, in fact, caused quite a stir. A local journalist, canvassing our bus line for a good story, asked her where she was from and if she was enjoying the Games. Helen can be very lucid on occasion. She gave him her opinion of the American transport system. She told him that the only event tickets on sale to the general public were going, at inflated rates, in a barber shop in Lake Placid, what we in England would call the black market. She explained the impossibility of getting from one event to another in the time between competitions. She described the catering in less than flattering terms and wondered if Americans had ever heard of plates, knives and forks. Then she told him that we were waiting to see our chap, Robin Cousins, skate tomorrow night and win his Olympic Gold medal. After that, we would not be staying for the rest of the Games and would be on the first flight back to England. She willingly supplied our full names and hoped he would publish her comments. He did, next morning, front page in the most widely read local paper.

We shall never know whether it was as a result of that publicity, but that afternoon, while watching some practice skating, John Disley, Vice Chairman of our British Sports Council, spotted us in the crowd and came over. 'The Minister, Hector Monro, regretted that he had not been advised of our presence in Lake Placid. Could we be his guests at a reception that evening?

Yes, he could supply passes equivalent to temporary accreditation.' Well, the whole scene changed from that moment. We attended a round of parties and receptions. Transport between venues was by courtesy of the BOA Land Rover. We were given 'guest-tickets' to see Robin Cousins spectacularly win the most prestigious event of the Games . . . the Gold Medal for the Men's Figure Skating. Another SAF-backed winner and, yet again, the commentary by Alan Weeks. Robin's four-minute programme was scheduled for about 9 p.m. local Eastern time USA, that being 2 a.m. in Great Britain. The BBC bravely televised it 'live', but with some understandable trepidation about viewing figures. In the event, it was estimated that some twenty-four million people huddled around their sets, in the early winter hours, to watch Robin win the only British Gold of the Winter Olympics. To be there, to see it actually happen, to see a Briton atop the rostrum and to sing our National Anthem, made up to Helen and me for every discomfort we had earlier suffered. But, afterwards, to join Robin, his parents Fred and Jo Cousins, the Minister Hector Munro and all the British team for the tremendous celebration party in the Olympic Village, transformed what had been a dreadful trip into a truly wonderful experience.

I have another happy memory of that day. During the Ice Dancing earlier that afternoon, I had watched a young British couple skate their programme. They certainly were not medal prospects and they only gained polite applause and moderate marks from the judges. Nevertheless, I thought they were a stunning-looking couple who skated with such harmony, that they reminded me of Fred Astaire and Ginger Rogers at their best. He, though, was better looking – tall, blonde, handsome – and she, petite and quite lovely. This opinion was confirmed when I was introduced to them at the party. Their names were Jayne Torvill and Christopher Dean! Robin Cousins failed, by a whisker, to repeat John Currie's earlier grand slam, coming second to Jan Hoffman of the German Democratic Republic in the World Championships later that year. Although disappointed, Robin told me that there was a compensation. It seems that Hoffman's brilliance as a skater had, by order of the State, obliged him to perform for his country until such time as he either won a major championship or was over the top. This edict had kept Jan from his true love, studying medicine. After his World Championship success, he was allowed to resume his studies and, I believe, shortly thereafter became a doctor. Robin went on to great things, but he always remembered – and publicly acknowledged – the help he had received from SAF '. . . without which, none of this would have been possible. . .' A generous quote, not strictly true, but it put another feather in our SAF cap.

Chapter 27

# The Prince's Trust

On 10 June 1980 the Duke of Edinburgh celebrated his fifty-ninth birthday. I can be accurate with that information because I was privileged to wish His Royal Highness many happy returns of the day, personally, in his study in Buckingham Palace.

What happened was that Alan Weeks, quite unbeknown to me, had asked Lord Rupert Neville, a Governor of SAF and aide to Prince Philip, if he could arrange to have an audience with HRH in order to tell him about SAF and all its good works. He believed, did Alan, that the Duke knew of us through Peter Lawson, Director General of the CCPR, his ears and eyes on the world of sport. Either in spite of, or perhaps because of advice from Lawson, HRH was not enamoured about our role . . . or so rumour had it. Paul Zetter would soon straighten him out . . . so thought Alan Weeks.

Now as it happened, on the date granted to us, I was due to start a short holiday in Switzerland with Helen so, naturally, we called it off so that I could attend this important event. Helen was not best pleased! I'd met His Royal Highness previously on a number of occasions, but never on a one-to-one basis and I was very, very nervous.

Alan and I were ushered into his room where formal bowing and greetings occurred. It was 10 a.m. and the Prince, clearly preoccupied with his birthday celebrations, did not appear to be enthusiastic about hearing a report on SAF by Paul Zetter. In fact, he sat stony-faced, unmoving and unmoved in his chair as I stammered and stuttered my way through our story. For a half-an-hour I suffered the personal indignity of my own inarticulate meandering. With a dry mouth and sweating forehead I stumbled on, trying to paint a word picture of our laudable aims and efforts. And he just sat there. He didn't murmur or nod or shake his head or smile or frown. He might have been cut from marble. It was the most desperately uncomfortable thirty minutes of my life . . . and I finally ran out of words. I was on the edge of my chair, silent and feeling utterly drained. Alan Weeks, just beside me, was fidgeting and clearly ill at ease.

After what seemed to be an eternity of silence His Royal Highness turned his head slowly, looked at me and said, 'And what has all that to do with me?' I was flabbergasted, absolutely astonished but, much more to the point, I was furious. I had cancelled a holiday, just to see this man. His unreceptive attitude had caused me agonies for the last half-an-hour and that was all he could say! Well, I was angry and I wanted him to be aware of that anger.

'I thought, Sir,' I said, 'that you were interested in British Sport. If I have been misinformed I must apologise for wasting your time.'

His head came up and his eyes opened wide . . . and he smiled disarmingly.

'Mr Zetter,' he said, almost with warmth, 'I am well aware of the role of SAF. I understand what you wish to do, but I must tell you that I do not applaud the "win at all costs" attitude in sport. It smacks of the East German philosophy and I would deplore it in this country.'

Although that's roughly what he said, it was the way he said it that changed everything for me. Suddenly, he was responsive . . . he was kind . . . he was clearly now interested in discussion and that's precisely what happened. Although describing SAF as a 'self-perpetuating oligarchy' – a not wholly inaccurate description – nevertheless, he seemed to ease his position. I dared to suggest that 'oligarchies are not all bad; indeed some of our best institutions are oligarchal'. I took up his critique on East Germany and suggested that it added a good dimension to life by uplifting pride in an otherwise depressed nation. His Royal Highness gave better than he got. He asked if I had played rugby in my younger years and if 'winning at all costs' was the team objective. I quoted David Coleman's neat comment that 'the British gained their reputation for being good losers at the time when they were always winning'. 'Better by far had we retained that earlier accolade,' quoth the Prince and so it went. For the best part of a further three-quarters of an hour we enjoyed good-humoured debate.

I wouldn't say he changed his views, but he was more tolerant of ours and has certainly acknowledged the role of SAF ever since. I came away from Buckingham Palace in a far better mood than I had thought likely. In fact, at one time during the audience, I had visions of The Tower. I have met His Royal Highness on a number of occasions since that unforgettable day. He has always been most courteous towards me and I have the utmost respect for this quite exceptional man.

# Chapter 28

# Have Sport, Will Travel

The Lake Placid experience should have been the greatest disincentive to being a camp-follower. It wasn't! For most of the following decade, everywhere the British sporting fraternity went, so did I. Summer or winter, snowskiing or waterskiing, running or rowing, whatever the games, the two little, rotund figures of Helen and Paul Zetter were ever-present. With our Tweedledum and Tweedledee image, we were soon affectionately adopted by all the important establishment figures in sport, including those honourable gentlemen (no girls!) of the media representing TV and Press. Commonwealth Games . . . Olympic Games . . . European Games . . . World Championships . . . European Championships crowded my diary like a Cooks Tour. This is Helsinki . . . it must be 'The Worlds'. Friendly Brisbane . . . 'The Commonwealth' of course! Beautiful down-town Los Angeles . . . it's got to be 'The Olympics'. Hideous traffic jams and those ugly towers? . . . Oh God! Crystal Palace.

We loved it all, the parties, the excitement, the VIP treatment – with accreditation, of course! But, most of all, the competition and the competitors. I honestly don't know if our world travels were a necessary part of SAF or even the Chairman's role within it. I do know that we established a worthwhile image among sports people and I believe we earned their trust. We always paid our own way and always managed to host some kind of SAF party where competitors could relax between events and meet officials who, perhaps, became less forbidding over some 'Gluwein and Donuts'. There were some truly memorable venues where the results of the efforts of so many people, came to successful fruition. The older I get the less jingoistic I become, perhaps because I am aware of the short step from National Pride to the sinister dangers of Nationalism. I may be aware of it, but who is there who doesn't thrill to 'one of ours' beating 'one of theirs' in the arena of international competition? And if you actually know them, if you have helped them, if you can dine with them in your favourite restaurant and glow in their reflected glory . . . oh! my! your cup most surely runneth over.

We'd had a taste of it with Robin Cousins and David Wilkie. So many more were to follow. Sarajevo for the 1984 Winter Olympics where those two sweet young skaters whom, you will remember, I first met in Lake Placid, were representing Great Britain . . . Jayne Torvill and Christopher Dean. Their brilliance outshone everyone who has ever graced the ice. Even today, their very names are still musical magic. We were there, Helen and I, along with all the British team. With top officials of the British Olympic Association, including their Chairman, Charles Palmer and their splendid Director, Dick Palmer: both marvellous chaps. Dick Palmer, the gentle Welshman from the Valleys, the best administrator in sport, loved by all and with a rare wisdom that serves BOA and British Sport so well. On the big night, the Minister, Neil Macfarlane, very sadly had to return to obey a threeline whip, but he left his stalwart right-hand – David Teasdale – to witness the Torvill and Dean 'Gold' performance. Her Royal Highness Princess Anne was there, in her own right, as a member of the BOA and that is where we were first privileged to meet and, indeed, to establish the most rewarding rapport, which stood us and SAF in good stead on numerous subsequent occasions. Actually, the first contact we made was not entirely auspicious. At the party following the great victory, Helen stepped smartly aside to avoid one of the many champagne corks whizzing around the small room. Unfortunately still clad in ski-boots, she trod very heavily on the Royal toe within its Royal court shoe. A gracious, if somewhat tight-lipped, smile acknowledged Helen's abject apology, but all was soon forgotten and forgiven in the jollity of the occasion.

The triumphant *Bolero* is, of course, familiar history as is the one hundred per cent marks never before, or since, achieved. I am sure I will be forgiven for revealing a little cameo story, told to me by that great British champion skater, that man of inestimable delight and an eminent ice-skating judge, Courtney Jones.

On the evening before the great finale, an Eastern European judge had called Courtney to one side. In the friendliest of ways he had told Courtney that, although *Bolero* stretched the disciplines required to the limit, he, being a man of taste and vision, totally accepted its artistic licence, except, that is, for one particular movement which exceeded his tolerance barrier and he, very sadly you understand, would be marking down the British skaters. He would also make his views known to all the other judges and remind them of their duties.

Courtney was dismayed; this could cost Jayne and Chris the Gold Medal, for whilst they were so superior and well ahead of all their competitors, including the Russian couple lying in second place, they were not necessarily unassailable. This one judge's attitude could, if implemented, at the very least diminish Torvill's and Dean's accomplishment and clearly take the gilt off the gingerbread and lose the coveted Gold Medal they deserved. He called the young couple together and told them of the problem.

'We'll put it right,' said Jayne. 'It's only a small adjustment, we'll practise all night and get it right.'

'You're crazy!' said Chris, 'We've worked on that routine ten hours a day, seven days a week, including Christmas, for a year. Change one thing, one tiny movement, and we could blow the lot.'

'We must and we can and we will,' said the ever-determined little Jayne.

And they did!

Didn't they just! Every judge gave maximum marks for their skating of Ravel's *Bolero* which must rank as one of the greatest performances of all time. Yet again, it was Alan Weeks who described the triumph to millions of viewers back home. 'Another Gold for Alan,' said the wits. 'If you want to win a gold medal, ensure Alan Weeks is doing the commentary.'

One sad omission from our worldwide itinerary was the Moscow Olympics . . . the 'boycott' Games. You will remember that the United States of America refused to send a squad, in order to demonstrate their disapproval of the Russian invasion of Afghanistan. Many other Western nations followed suit but we, in Great Britain, adopted what, I believe, was a more democratic attitude. Basically, what our Government said was, 'We disapprove of the Games and we don't want a British team to go, but we are a free country and we will not impose a boycott.' All very laudable – and I'm not being sarcastic – but they tried every possible means of persuasion, short of an actual boycott. Almost unacceptable pressure was put on team officials and competitors. Numerous meetings with the hierarchy of British sport took place, culminating in what was a confrontation at No. 10 Downing Street. Notwithstanding all their powers of influence being brought to bear, the man of the moment, Sir Denis Follows, the Chairman of the British Olympic Association, stuck to his guns. His reaction was absolutely predictable and absolutely right. 'The members of BOA have opted to send a team to compete in Moscow. I am their servant and, as such, must obey their command. So, I must take the team or resign as Chairman. I shall take the team.' Of course he disapproved of the Russian action in Afghanistan. But he had a job to do, an obligation. He would not go for the pleasure of it, he would go to fulfil a duty.

I was involved in the periphery of all these events. Helen and I listened to and joined in the debate. We both agreed that Sir Denis was right, but how did it affect us? We were all set to go. We had our flight tickets, our accreditation (highest category!), seats for the Bolshoi, a high-level, fully organised trip to Leningrad – the whole thing! It was going to be a wonderful experience. We were going for pleasure . . . well, we just couldn't! Oh, I suppose one could claim that it was the responsibility of the SAF Chairman to see how his 'investment' in 'grant-aid' worked out; but who do you think you're kidding? So we cancelled the lot. Not without the greatest of regrets, for it would have been our first Summer Olympics. Fresh-faced youngsters were competing whom I had come to know and like. Then and later, many of them were to distinguish themselves on the track and in the field. New stars would be born. I knew them and I wanted to see their triumph. Sebastian Coe . . . Steve Ovett . . . Daley Thompson . . . Alan Wells . . . Duncan Goodhew . . . and many more. Nearly all of these young gladiators, whose names were to become legends, had each received substantial financial assistance from SAF. Most of them were grateful and acknowledged their gratitude. Seb Coe wrote a book entitled *Running Free* . . . I have it in my bookcase. In it he has written 'To Paul – With every best wish – thank you for helping to make much of the story possible!!' It is a warm and generous comment from a warm and generous man. I like to think it is not just kindness which prompted those most rewarding words.

We won a number of medals at the Moscow Olympics, but there were losers, too. Dear gentle Hector Munro was too gentle, in fact, to defend the Government's stance at the Despatch Box in the House of Commons. He was required to relinquish the task to the 'Iron Lady' herself! She unmercifully swept aside any opposition while, alongside, her Minister for Sport sat in silence. Moscow was Hector's Waterloo and shortly thereafter – with a not inadequate reward of a Knighthood – Sir Hector left his office to the youthful, dynamic, Neil Macfarlane.

Chapter 29

# Buck House Revisited

The letter came on May Day 1981.

The envelope bore a Coat of Arms; it was from 10 Downing Street and it was addressed to me. I won't quote the contents verbatim, just in case it breaks the Official Secrets Act (which I had signed over fifty years ago), but it asked me if I would like to become a Commander of the British Empire.

I have no idea whether my reaction was normal. I felt slightly light-headed and just a little sick. I could not eat breakfast, but downed two cups of strong coffee. The letter told me not to tell anyone, prior to the publication of the Queen's Birthday Honours List on 13 July. I told Helen. Well, there are some things that you can keep from your spouse, but this certainly wasn't one of them. Mind you, I could hardly enunciate the message, so I showed her the letter. We were both overwhelmed and overjoyed. It was an emotional experience which lives with me to this day. I was required to let them know if I would accept it. Would I accept it? What an extraordinary question! That anyone could turn down an Honour offered by the Royal Head of State on the recommendation of your own peers and approved by the Prime Minister of Her Majesty's Government, was absolutely unthinkable. And yet, later in life, I have met and have reason to know, several distinguished persons who did that very thing. No such concern occurred to me that day. I returned my acceptance letter with such alacrity that I spent the next two-and-a-half months in an agony of suspense, wondering if I had put my 'X' in the right box! Had I said 'yes' or, in my haste, inadvertently 'no'?

I have never waited for the morning papers with such eagerness. Not being able to tell anyone was awful. I truly was in the most dreadful quandary of self-doubt about whether I had returned the acceptance form correctly. It could also have been lost in the post, couldn't it? After all, according to disgruntled punters, thousands of 'winning coupons' get lost in the post all the time, don't they? To make matters worse, there was no acknowledgement either from Buckingham Palace or, indeed, anywhere else. There was nothing to reassure me. There was no communication of any kind. It was as though nothing had ever happened.

I was certain something must have gone wrong. Should I ring one of my high-powered friends to find out? Perish the thought. Wouldn't I have looked a twit? No, I would just have to suffer in silence. I couldn't even tell my children or my father, Jim Clarke or, indeed, anybody. Helen and I faithfully kept the secret until the day before the Queen's Official Birthday. On the morning of 12 July, I decided to tell Carrie, Adam, my father and Kurt Morgenstern, as well as Jim Clarke and David Isaacs. For all of my unsubstantiated doubts, I wanted those closest to me to hear the good tidings if, in fact, there were good tidings, directly from me, not read about it in the papers. I think it is superfluous to record their reactions. In many ways, the joy that award brought to me was multiplied beyond reckoning by the warmth of affectionate response from so many loved-ones, friends and associates.

Adam was esconced at his photographic institute in California, so Carrie came with Helen and me to the Investiture at Buckingham Palace. Being in a trance throughout, I don't remember too much about it. We were shepherded through the procedure with a military precision reminiscent of the Trooping the Colours. The recipients were parted from their loved ones, who were then seated in the Throne Room to await eventual reunification with their heroes, bedecked and adorned with their newly acquired 'gong'. Meanwhile, we 'Honourees' were formed into long lines, Knights in the vanguard (of course) then CBEs (that's me!) then the 'Os' and finally the 'Ms'. I do remember one thought, on catching a glimpse of that great gallery filling with relatives and friends there to witness the ceremony. I thought of the Queen and what her feeling must be to come out onto that lonely dais and see a multitude of faces just staring at her. Knowing, too, of the hundreds of hands she would have to shake and the dictionary full of trite comment in which she must engage, before she could go quietly back to her drawing room for a rewarding cup of coffee. Not that we got any coffee, nor anything else come to that. It occurred to me (and not for the first time) that Royal hospitality was a mite sparse. Never mind, we had our photo taken in the courtyard of Buck House, resplendent in all our finery and then went on to celebrate the momentous day with a spectacular lunch at Les Ambassadeurs.

Chapter 30

# VIGs (Very Important Governors)

Neil Macfarlane, if anything, was an even greater supporter of SAF and we very quickly became firm friends. He recognised the valuable contribution SAF was making to the quality of sporting life and set out, purposefully, to further our ways and means. It was through Neil that I first met Denis Thatcher or, more properly I should say, Denis Thatcher met me. Knowing of Mr Thatcher's great love of sport, Neil had told him about the Sports Aid Foundation. His enthusiastic reception of our story led me to meeting the great man. It was not long before he became one of our most prestigious Governors and, to my great joy, a personal friend.

It is almost certainly superfluous to describe the boost to my ego that this association brought to me. I am sure, by now, you are well aware of this aspect of my character. In the event, I think I was far more impressed with my self esteem than were my colleagues and friends. Nonetheless, to be able to call regularly at Downing Street and have morning coffee, afternoon tea or, perhaps, something a little stronger in the top flat – with the occasional chance of having the Prime Minister pour for you – is a bit special. Visits to Chequers, culminating in Helen, my daughter Carrie and I joining the entire Thatcher family for Christmas Day lunch, were undreamed of rewards for the tremendous rapport I had established with Denis. I make no secret of – nor do I apologise for – the fact that I exalted in our association . . . and still do to this day. It was, and is, a privilege which I shall treasure all my days. Denis Thatcher was a noteworthy addition to the Board of SAF. He, too, added the dimension of prestige which was the hallmark of our early years. There were others.

177

There was the man who gave money to British Athletes. His motives were simple enough; he wanted them to win, so he gave them money to help with their costs of training. His name was Eddie Kulukundis. Now it may seem obvious from that name that he was not the archetypal 'Brit' but, then, you could be excused from making the same mistake about Paul Zetter. The fact of the matter is that we are both as British as Roast Beef and Yorkshire Pudding. That he has a Greek name, is neither here nor there . . . Eddie wanted the 'Brits' to win, which is why he was funding them. Here was someone I had to meet, for we both had the same purpose. Mine was structured, his was not – but the aims were the same.

Eddie was a splendid fellow. A very big man in every way. He was clearly delighted to accept the invitation to become one of the earliest Governors of SAF. Undoubtedly very wealthy, his kindness and generosity attracted many worthy – and some not so worthy – appeals for help. His overwhelming love of sport, particularly athletics, made him an absolute 'natural' for the SAF Board and he very quickly took us to his abundant heart. With a disarmingly innocent manner, he soon told me that he saw SAF as a true labour of great love and personal ambition. With his proclaimed philosophy, he would, he explained, endeavour to advance his cause in the time-honoured way of the Greeks.

I responded modestly enough to the many tempting invitations that followed. There was one lovely occasion, however, when I succumbed to his proffered hospitality. Helen and I were collected from our Chelsea home by Eddie and his girlfriend Karen, in a chauffeur-driven Rolls Royce, which took all four of us to a multi-star restaurant on the banks of the Thames. Following the champagne, we were served a truly sumptuous meal with what was, undoubtedly, the finest wine I had ever tasted. So exceptional, in fact, that I commented repeatedly upon it, much to Eddie's surprise . . . that is, until the bill was presented to him at the end of our meal! He was visibly taken aback at the total which, even by their high standards, was quite outrageous. Demanding a detailed breakdown, he quickly learned that the bottle of wine alone came to £100, and that was in the late 1970s! Eddie asked for the wine list in order to confirm that the wine he had chosen, a very fine 1978 Château Lynch-Bages, was listed at £18. 'Ah! non, monsieur,' responded the wine waiter, 'You chose the one below and that's what you drank, a Château Latour 1955. The empty bottle is still on your table, you can see the label. That wine, Monsieur, is priced at £100.' And so it was. Of course, Eddie was astonished at his apparent error, but was gracious enough to accept it. Indeed, he congratulated me on the perception of my palate. I would have thought no more of the matter, had it not been for an incident which occurred some weeks later. I was having lunch in the City with Alan Weeks and Michael Parkinson whom I told of our famous bottle of wine. Instead of being amused, he became quite annoyed. 'I eat there frequently,' he told us, 'Several times I have seen the wine bill questioned by other diners and, on each occasion, it seems they were served a wine considerably more expensive than the one they thought they had chosen.' It was a long time ago, I'm sure it doesn't happen now.

When Eddie married the lovely Susan Hampshire a few years later, she supported his involvement with SAF as enthusiastically as Helen had done for me. Susan was – and still is – one of the loveliest women I've ever met. I believe she was one of Patrick Lichfield's 'Hundred Most Beautiful Women'. For my money she would qualify in the Top Ten. More importantly, she is so nice . . . not only beautiful . . . not only talented, but nice. What rare and wonderful qualities! Actually, she is a gifted singer too. Some years later, in order, I believe, to recoup some desperately unlucky losses as a Name at Lloyds, she played the leading role of Anna in 'The King and I'. Her performance was rightly acclaimed and the show enjoyed a long and successful run. Eddie eventually became the Chairman of SAF, but more of that later.

I often look back in wonderment at the quality of Governors we attracted. The other Parkinson, Cecil, joined us following his resignation from Government and Sara Keyes. He spoke quite freely about it, but I won't tell you what he said. There were those who suggested Cecil saw SAF as a way back into public favour. I don't accept it. Cecil had no ulterior motive. He wanted to help British sport and saw SAF as the way to do it. So he did and he was right.

We also attracted Adrian Metcalfe. Adrian chaired one of our regions – London and South-East – with flair and ability, of course. It was he and Norman Jacobs, one of his more talented Governors and a senior partner with Slaughter & May, who initiated the move which resulted in the creation of the Sports Aid Trust; a vital furtherment of our aims because of the valuable charity status thereby acquired. Adrian soon joined the main Board and notably enlivened our proceedings. There is a story about Adrian Metcalfe. I don't know if it's true, but this is how it goes. At the time he was a student at Oxford, Adrian was a world class 400-metre runner with every prospect of achieving Olympic glory. At the peak – and on the strength – of his athletic career, he received an offer of a place at some obscure American mid-west university. 'Thank you for your offer,' he responded (or so the story goes), 'But I am at an educational establishment

which was in existence when your forefathers were hanging from the trees.'
How rude! How Adrian Metcalfe! How marvellously funny!

The Governors of the Sports Aid Foundation *are* the Sports Aid
Foundation. They, all of them, are important to its success and survival. I
have highlighted but a few. I could go into chapter and verse on many more.
Major General Ian Graeme, for example . . . the Grants Committee would
have been hard put to function without his unbelievable contribution.
Dickie Jeeps, whose very name conjures magical memories of rugby glory
and who went on to become Chairman of the Sports Council: the stories I
could tell of that young man . . . but I won't. David Coleman . . . he is
mentioned elsewhere and I won't compete with other publications in writing
about this remarkable character. Similarly for Sir Arthur Gold, Anita
Lonsborough, Charles Palmer, etc. etc. I must stop; this is not an accolade
for those I admire. I must get on with my story.

Chapter 31

# A Change of Life

The emergence of Sports Aid Foundation in the eighties, as an important new force in British Sport, was increasingly evident. It had clearly changed the life and style of many people, not least my own. It's odd really, that the reputation it gained was far greater than its achievement, which is precisely what could be said of my company, Zetters Group PLC. Zetters must be one of the smallest quoted companies, yet we are far better known than many Corporations which dwarf us. In both cases, SAF and Zetters, status exceeded standing.

The fortunes of Zetters PLC were not adversely affected during my ten year sabbatical with SAF. At any rate, not in my view. After all, the top management was sound – Jim Clarke running the Pools Company and David Isaacs, the Bingo Company. So they were looking after 'the shop' and I thought all was well with our commercial world. However, Andreas Hadjioannou, the now senior partner with Littlestone, our accountants, saw things differently. Solomon-wise Andreas, supported by solid, sensible, Terry Yardley – the other main partner – were not happy. They said, in effect, 'You have two main core businesses both doing well, both running efficiently, but they lack leadership and policy. It's been fine up to now, but you cannot let them drift. The time has come when you must make a choice. Putting it bluntly . . . SAF or Zetters.'

The year was 1984. I'd been deeply involved with SAF for the best part of ten years. Had I really neglected my own business during that time? Probably! There wasn't really a choice open to me; I must resign as Chairman of SAF. It would be heart-wrenching, but it had to be done. In any case, as Ted Heath (not the band leader) once said, 'No one should have a freehold on any job.' SAF was in good order. The kindergarten years were over; perhaps the puberty years needed a new man with the vision to go on to bigger and better things. Alan Weeks, SAF's first and 'golden' Director had, in fact, already retired. His place had been superbly filled by one Noel Nagle. Noel (born on Christmas Day . . . what else?) was a youthfully retired Brigadier (Gunners). SAF was growing, new Governors were being appointed, the time had come for me to move on.

I informed the Executive Committee of my decision and, after their most flattering protestations, the very real problem of my successor was broached. Following considerable heart-searching, it was decided that we should seek a Chairman who, loving sport, would have the time and the infrastructure to lead SAF into the future. By common consent, Ian MacLaurin, the youthful and dynamic Deputy Chairman to Leslie Porter of Tesco, was the one chosen. I agreed to sound him out. The following story is the one truly sad episode of my entire career with SAF. Sad, because a very unhappy consequence was as a result of my own serious error of judgement. This is what happened.

I had decided to elicit the support and assistance of the Minister, Neil Macfarlane, taking the view that both he and Ian would be pleased to be involved. The three of us lunched in the River Room at The Savoy on 10 April 1984. Ian was charming and seemingly flattered at the approach and Neil promised both his and the Government's support to Ian and SAF. Before we broke from lunch, Ian agreed to accept the Chairmanship, provided only that the appointment could, for personal and business reasons, be delayed for one year. At a subsequent Executive Meeting, I agreed to soldier on for a further year and, on that basis, to the Committee's huge delight, everything was tidily and beautifully in place.

A week or two later I received a bombshell. It took the form of a letter from Leslie Porter. I won't quote it verbatim (although I still have it on file) but, in essence, this is what he wrote. 'Delighted to hear of the appointment of Ian to succeed you as Chairman of SAF. However, sadly, he will not be able to take the appointment for about three years. He is my Deputy, at the moment, but will become Chairman next year. Consequently, he will be totally committed to Tesco for, at least, his first two years in the Chair and will not have any time for outside interests. Shirley [Leslie's wife] shares this view.'

What a body blow! Straight from Ian's boss, the Chairman, and the largest shareholders of Tesco. As the Tesco Stores were still SAF's main contributor, through the lottery outlets, it posed one huge dilemma. It was then that I made my great fundamental mistake. I went to see Leslie Porter, without telling Ian MacLaurin. My idea was to talk Leslie round . . . I failed. There is absolutely no doubt that Leslie wanted Ian to lead SAF. He was positively enthusiastic about it, but not for, at least, three years. 'You can surely go on for that bit more, Paul,' he said to me. 'After all, you've agreed to do one more year, make it three and everyone will be happy.' I was tempted. I would have loved to have done it, but then I thought of Andreas and the business and my duty and so on and so on, so I resisted the temptation.

Just as I was about to leave I had, what I thought was, one of my inspirations. 'What are you going to do with yourself next year, Leslie, when you retire?' I asked a little breathlessly.

'Not a lot,' he replied. 'Play a bit of golf, do some charity work, have fun.'

'Great!' I exclaimed. 'Then why don't you take the Chairmanship of SAF for a couple of years. Keep the chair warm for Ian?'

He was flabbergasted. 'What do I know about sport?' he queried.

'About as much as I did ten years ago,' I replied, 'And, in any case, you would have the most sophisticated Board of sports buffs and Noel Nagle, their splendid new Director. They would see you through any sporting problems. All you would have to do is Chair the meetings, go to fantastic sporting venues as a VIP, meet marvellous people and have fun.'

He mused for a while and asked if I thought he would be acceptable to my colleagues. Despite my reassurances, he said that he would only agree if, after consultation, I could confirm the Board's approval. More importantly, it would be strictly on the understanding that he became what he called 'the interregnum Chairman' for Ian MacLaurin.

'Be in no doubt, Paul,' he said, 'This is Ian's job, not mine, but I'll keep it warm for him.' I was overjoyed as were my Board and Neil Macfarlane when I 'phoned them later that day. I then had to tell Ian MacLaurin. A tiny niggle of doubt crossed my mind when I 'phoned him. Should I, perhaps, have spoken to him before I did any of this? Bloody right I should!

Ian did not approve of the arrangements I had made. He thought that SAF ran the risk of being considered a 'Tesco take-over – with one Tesco Chairman as SAF Chairman and the next Tesco Chairman already lined up to succeed two years later.' It was certainly a point I had not considered. To my very great regret and sadness, Ian resigned as a Governor of SAF. To his enormous credit, he still supported us to the hilt particularly when, the following year, he was appointed as Chairman of Tesco. A few years later I asked him if he would consider rejoining SAF as a Governor. I was very pleased that he did so and it went some way to alleviating my distress at what had been a very unhappy episode.

Chapter 32

# Life goes on

In 1985, just ten years after that momentous lunch on the terrace of the House of Commons when Denis Howell had first told me about SAF, I retired as Chairman. They gave me a marvellous retirement party and a beautiful cut glass champagne bucket as a parting gift. Leslie Porter became the new Chairman; he inherited a very worthwhile organisation, a great Board of Governors and an absolutely splendid Director, Noel Nagle, to run the show. I was made an Honorary Vice-President for life for which I was both delighted and grateful.

It was difficult readjusting to normality at first and I clearly missed the high profile life style to which I had become accustomed. Not that I gave up all sporting activities . . . far from it. In fact, the very good relationship I had already established with Noel Nagle flourished. Both he and, indeed, Leslie Porter were kind enough to consult me on numerous occasions, seeking my views on SAF affairs and I enjoyed still being part of 'the family'.

I had also accepted an invitation to become a full member of the Sports Council and, shortly thereafter, Chairman of its Southern Region. Although fairly interesting, it was in no way as demanding as SAF and, of course, very different. I cannot pretend I enjoyed my new roles too much. The Sports Council, and its regional arms, are wonderful bodies doing an incomparable job for Sport in Great Britain. They are, however, quangos – public bodies funded by Central Government. This is right and proper, but it does mean that the Chairmen, particularly the Regional Chairmen, are little more than figure-heads. While it is true that they play an important part in establishing good relationships with Local Authorities, whose role in sports and sports facilities is so vital – and, in the main, so excellent – one gets a shade tired of being asked to do little more than open a new swimming pool or an all-weather bowling green. I suppose that's not entirely fair, because we were regularly consulted on policy matters by the new Minister for Sport, Dick Tracy. All very fine, of course, but not the same as establishing policy, which I had been doing for the last ten years. Dick Tracy was the unknown and wholly surprising choice to replace Neil Macfarlane.

To welcome the new Minister to his appointment, I invited him to lunch at the River Room of the Savoy. During our very pleasant meal, he commented that he knew only one other person with enough clout to get a window table at the Savoy; a west country gentleman farmer, by the name of Wallace. A real hunting, shooting and fishing character, as he described him. Although it was a fairly common name, the description rang a bell with me and, on further enquiry, I found that it was, undoubtedly, my old recce platoon officer Captain 'Nellie' Wallace from those Royal Gloucestershire Hussar army days. I established contact with him and we lunched together at the Savoy with Jim Clarke, who, you will remember, I first met as 'Nobby' Clarke in the RGH. We enjoyed our reminiscences, although I came away with the clear impression that Jim and I had undergone an experience of *noblesse oblige*. Incidentally, it was one occasion when I didn't manage a window table!

In many ways it was a time for readjustment and, indeed, for an appraisal of what had happened in the real world during the last decade. There were sad things. My dear father, the 'Old Man', had died. Peacefully enough, at the good age of eighty-six years. I was with him an hour or so before the end, and almost the last question he asked me was, 'How many draws were there last Saturday?' Everybody loved my dad and a multitude turned out, on one of the coldest days of the year, to pay their respects at his funeral. He left a widow, Hannah. I had promised him that I would take care of her and I have done so. My father-in-law died, also peacefully, in his bed at night. Kurt Morgenstern had been a difficult man, but we became close and he certainly mellowed as he grew older. He had lived an unfortunate life, having grown up in Nazi Germany, only escaping with a loving wife and a lovely seven-year-old daughter (Helen) a few short months before the outbreak of hostilities in 1939. A few years after the end of a fearful war he suffered the loss of his dear wife Hilda. He was never a lucky man and his comparatively early demise – just when life was being kinder to him – seemed a little unfair. David Nations, volatile, loquacious David Nations, the man who'd got me into the whole sporting scene, died. So, too, did Tony Stratton-Smith. Dear Tony, who never quite 'delivered', but you loved him anyway. Beautiful Andreas Hajioannou had married a lovely Athenian and returned to their homeland to become a Greek shipowner ... I sorely missed him. Those were the sad things, but to be expected over a ten years timespan.

There were good things, too. Very, very good. My children had grown up. My son, Adam, was now twenty-four years old and at a technical institute of photography in Santa Barbara, California. Helen and I missed him with a passion, but he was clearly happy there and doing very well. America suited him for all manner of reasons including their quick recognition of talent and the numerous outlets available to develop that talent. He loved their easy-going way of living and the comparative absence of any class barrier. He delighted in not having his surname readily recognised with the sometimes unacceptable consequences. Lastly, but by no means least, it was no great hardship living in California ... and the weather ain't bad either! Carrie, lovely daughter Carrie, was achieving many things. Flying was the love of her life. She had gained her private pilot's licence at a very early age (eighteen years old, I believe) and that was the start of a far greater involvement in flying. Just to be 'up there', she took a job as an air-stewardess with Dan Air. Shortly thereafter, she saw an advertisement in *Pilot* for a 'Pilot Assistant' with Air UK. The prospect excited her imagination so, on the Saturday morning of publication, she telephoned the number shown in the advertisement, to be given an appointment for the following Friday in Exeter. Impatiently, she took the first train to Exeter on Monday morning and presented herself at the office of Air UK. Noting that she had jumped the queue she, nevertheless, got her interview. She was told that, though eminently suitable, she lacked one vital requirement. The job involved flying twin-engined Bandoranti's and she did not have a twin-rating. With great charm and enthusiasm, she elicited a promise that the job would be kept open for her for four weeks, providing she could get the necessary rating in that time. I suspect they thought it an impossible task for, being autumn, daylight hours were too short to get enough flying time. They had reckoned without Carrie's determination. Two days later she was at a flying school in Florida. Three weeks after that she obtained her twin-rating and four weeks later she started work with Air UK. Just to round off the story, after one year she left the job. She had flown twice a day, five days a week, from Southampton to Amsterdam and back. 'I knew every bloody cloud in both directions,' she explained. She went on to become a Pilot Instructor; she obtained her helicopter pilot's licence; she even flew in various air races – such as the King's Cup and the Schneider Trophy – but all the time kept her feet well on the ground. Boy friends there were aplenty, but none of them seemed to be Mr Right.

So both my children were making good lives for themselves. We were still such a close family and it brought Helen and me great joy that this was so, notwithstanding the passage of time, the inconvenience of distance and the merit of their independence. We were – and are – lucky and proud parents. Jim Clarke and David Isaacs seemed pleased to be seeing more of me at the office and I enjoyed my greater involvement in the day-to-day business activities. As I have said, I still kept a foot in the sporting arena and still attended major sporting events. The Commonwealth Games in Edinburgh in 1986 drew Helen and me and it was a great pleasure to be so warmly welcomed to that beautiful city by all the sporting fraternity. We had enormous fun up there. Elaine Nations joined us and lots of friends were in town, including the delightful David Teasdale, the man from the Ministry. We had become close friends, having rubbed shoulders with him at the Sarajevo Winter Olympics and Los Angeles Summer Olympics, when he had been Neil Macfarlane's advisor. In Edinburgh, he was looking after the Prime Minister's visit and other matters of protocol. There was one uproarious incident that I shall tell of him. One of his duties was to arrange the motorcade, for the Prime Minister and her large entourage, between venues. He accomplished this with his usual efficient flair and profes- sionalism only to find that, as the last official car departed the stadium, he'd neglected to arrange for his own transport to an important meeting at which his presence was also required. Ever resourceful, David commandeered a car and driver. He actually stopped a car in the street, explained that he was 'on Prime Minister's business' and 'please take me to Stormont at all speed'. What a *chutzpah*!

I managed to pull off a nice one during those Games. I ran my usual party for competitors and was absolutely thrilled and delighted when Princess Anne, the Princess Royal, and the Prime Minister both agreed to be my guests. It was a tremendous occasion and quite unique, I believe, in having both a top Royal and a top politician together at the same function.

In many ways this was an eventful and happy time. I had opted out of major responsibility with SAF but still enjoyed my involvement. My other sporting duties were fairly painless and I was back in full harness at Zetters. It really seemed I was having my cake and eating it. And yet, in an odd sort of way, I was unsettled and experienced a distinctly anticlimatic feeling. The climax was nigh.

# Chapter 33

# Not having the Heart for it

Just three weeks after the Commonwealth Games in Edinburgh, the European Athletics Championships were taking place in Stuttgart. Well, we had to go, didn't we? I'd arranged to leave a few days before the Opening Ceremony, drive across Northern France to Zurich where we would spend a short time with Shula, Helen's Israeli aunt, and then on to Stuttgart.

On Tuesday, 19 August 1986 I drove myself to the office, having arranged for Liam, my driver, to take in the Rover for a quick service before leaving the next day for the Continent. I had my usual coffee, at my desk, as I opened my morning mail and then went downstairs to David Isaacs to discuss current events in Bingo and to see his chart figures etc. Back in my own office just before 11 a.m. I was about to call in Jim Clarke for a 'Pools' discussion, when I had a sudden spasm of indigestion. I sucked a Rennie, to dispel what was really a most unpleasant heartburn across my chest and shoulders, but it didn't seem to work too well. At that moment, Jim came in. He took one look at me and said, 'Are you all right?' Half-an-hour later I was in the Humana Hospital in Wellington Road, St. John's Wood, having had a heart attack. Jim, ever reliable Jim, had got me there by way of my own doctor, whose consulting rooms happened to be *en route*. Actually his locum was on duty and, decent fellow that he was, he came out to the car, having been pre-warned by telephone. Failing to find my pulse, he speeded us on our way to the hospital. Liam was driving and wasn't sure where to go, so I had to direct him. Jim was in the back, looking far worse than I and I wouldn't have been surprised if the emergency crew, awaiting us with wheeled stretcher at the hospital entrance, hadn't plonked him on it

189

by mistake. Anyway, I enjoyed a cup of hot, sweet tea followed by an injection and then, watched by a gorgeous-looking nurse, dozed off into a long, deep sleep. I can remember hoping, quite calmly and rationally just before nodding off, that I would wake up again. I did, some hours later, feeling absolutely marvellous and overjoyed to see Helen and Carrie anxiously peering at me. What a delight it was to see the relief flooding their faces.

The next few days were a bit of a hoot really. The Humana is almost like a five-star hotel. I was being waited on hand and foot. The food was plentiful, rich and outstanding. I had a telly, a private bathroom, of course; a terrace in the sun and I felt fine, rather as President Reagan explained after surviving an assassin's bullet, 'Euphoric and great to be alive.' I even began to wonder if they'd got their diagnosis right. So I started nagging them to let me go home . . . not a lot, to be honest, because I was enjoying the experience, even though I felt a bit of a fraud. By this time, my own doctor, Donald Rau, was back and produced a heart specialist by the name of Dr Spurrel, who was reassuring, calm and very British. He was quite certain that I'd had a mild heart attack and wanted me to have a complete rest in the hospital for just a few more days. Then, next week, they'd carry out a few simple tests, after which he'd decide on whatever treatment was required and I could go home.

Well, that seemed fair enough, so I settled down to enjoy my enforced leisure. That enjoyment was enhanced when Adam, my wonderful, loving son, flew over from California, because he was worried about his dad. The days passed pleasantly enough for me. The nursing staff were as wonderful as are all nursing staff, and it really was no hardship being waited on by lovely people in luxurious surroundings. I was sorry for the *sclapp* that Helen had, twice a day, to come and see me. She absolutely refused to miss a visit, I suspect she was a little uneasy about all those pretty nurses fussing around my bed! On the ninth day of my incarceration, Dr Spurrel told me I was to have an 'angiogram'.

'What we shall do,' he explained, 'is to insert a probe into a vein in either one of your legs or arms. We shall then guide it along the length of the vein until it reaches your heart. Then we'll take a video of what damage, if any, has occurred and then decide what, if anything, needs to be done about it.'

'That sounds a bit hairy,' I suggested.

'Well, sometimes the patient experiences a degree of discomfort,' he responded, 'But I certainly would not perform it, if I didn't think it advisable. The whole procedure will only take about half-an-hour. You will be fully conscious all the time, we will have the results immediately and you will be able to go home tomorrow.'

All very reassuring so down I went, feeling confident and interested in what was about to happen to me. There was a cheerful team of nurses and doctors in attendance – and piped music – as I was bundled onto an operating table, surrounded by what looked like 'Doctor Who' equipment.

'Are you comfortable?' I was asked.

'Well, I wouldn't put it quite that way,' I replied, 'And I'd prefer the Beatles to Wagner, if that could be arranged.'

They all fell about laughing, then slit open my arm and went about their business. I did not enjoy the experience one bit and was pleased to be back in my room with tea, biscuits and Helen. Dr Spurrel came in after a few minutes, to tell me there was good news and bad news. 'The good news is very good and the bad news isn't too bad,' he quickly added. It seems the heart attack had not seriously damaged the heart . . . good! The arteries leading to the heart, however, were badly clogged-up and I would need a by-pass operation . . . bad! I was sent home the next day to rest, recuperate and prepare myself for major surgery in six weeks' time.

Those six weeks were, far and away, the worst spell of that whole unfortunate incident and, probably, the worst sustained period of my life. Never mind, like all things, good and bad, it soon came to an end. The operation went like a dream, I had a 'quad' by-pass, which is a better score than most achieve. I was nursed with loving care by a lovely staff, supervised by Sister Anne Clarke from Dublin . . . and what a girl she was! My surgeon was a bubbling, effervescent, fun–loving Welshman by the name of Gareth Rees. He was hugely delighted at the way my body had responded to his skills. So was I! He gave me one bit of advice on leaving the Humana two weeks later.

'Don't you go rushing back into sexual activity now,' he admonished, 'And when you do, keep with your own wife for the moment, I don't want you getting too excited.'

He needn't have worried. In fact, it took four months of convalescence for me to be able to resume a normal life style. I returned to my office in January 1987, a fitter, healthier and – who knows? – perhaps, wiser man.

# Chapter 34

# Three Score Years and Eight

If the passage of time has not affected my limited mathematical abilities, I conclude that the year is 1991. In other words, right now. So this is going to be the last chapter . . . of the book I mean!

It is five years since my heart attack and I am fit, well and active. Much has happened during that time. One of the first post–operative events was one of the best. You may remember that my parents had scrimped and saved to send me to the City of London School on the Victoria Embankment. If so, you will know that I can hardly claim to have distinguished myself at that most progressive establishment of teaching and learning. Nevertheless, I made lifelong friends and acquired a wealth of practical knowledge and common sense which, I believe, have been invaluable to me. I have already written warmly of those post–war years, when the Old Citizens Rugby Club played such a vital role in my re-introduction to normal life, after five years of army service. You can imagine, therefore, my overwhelming delight when, in 1987, I was elected to be President of the John Carpenter Club, the Old Boys Association of the School (named after the founder of The City of London School). It was an honour to equal any that I had previously been privileged enough to receive. One simple statistic alone made me both proud and humble . . . of something like one thousand pupils at CLS, only one Old Citizen can become President each year. I made my speech at the Mansion House, before the Lord Mayor, his Sheriffs, several Peers of the Realm and many distinguished guests. They were, I believe, all genuinely amused by my funny stories and were warm and generous in their applause. I treasure the memory. Actually, my election was an honour postponed. I'd been 'in the frame' for the previous year, but hadn't the heart for it at the time. Another good reason for having survived.

My presidential year went quickly and enjoyably. I don't think the Committee of the JCC achieves very much, other than to be there as a link for boys leaving the school and sometimes to extend a helping hand. Fortunately, the latter was not often needed but, nevertheless, comforting for it to be known to be there. During my term, I was somewhat disturbed to discover that the great sporting tradition of my Old School had been sorely neglected. It seemed that successive post-war headmasters, with the misguided belief that the pursuit of academic achievement is total and paramount, had relegated school sport to a very minor role. In an attempt to change attitudes I was able, with the help of my influential friends in the sporting world and the enthusiastic support of fellow Old Citizens – particularly Peter Jones, Basil Jackson and Brian Landers – to create an Old Citizens Sports Trust. The happy and encouraging news is that the Trust has been well received by the new Headmaster, his staff and the School Governors and is already benefiting appropriate pupils.

I am also pleased to think I am still able to play a part in the affairs of the Sports Aid Foundation and they are kind enough to let me think it. Eddie Kulukunidis became Chairman, as he inevitably would. Denis Thatcher still periodically threatens resignation but, so far, I've managed to talk him out of it. I had lunch with him on 22 November 1990 but not, on that occasion, to talk about the SAF. The circumstances leading to and attending the lunch are, however, worth the telling.

The date was originally fixed for 19 November and the venue was Mosimanns, a swell, private dining club in Belgravia. Now, although it's true that I regularly dined with Denis, there was a particular reason for me to see him at this time. A couple of weeks earlier, I had been at a high level fund-raising seminar for the Conservative Party. About thirty 'Captains of Industry' were present and we were to be addressed by the Prime Minister, Margaret Thatcher. Just before she arrived, the Chairman of one of the country's biggest companies gave us an introductory preamble. This man, a Knight of the Realm, explained the need to raise sufficient funds to fight the next General Election. He rounded off his five minute peroration by saying that '. . .we must keep that man Kinnock out of Number 10. He's a socialist, and even worse, he's a Welshman.' This incredible comment was received in astonished silence by his mixed audience of Protestants, Catholics, Jews, Irish, Scots and almost certainly some Welsh. Fortunately, Margaret turned up on schedule and for an hour or more dazzled us with her expert knowledge of any and every subject. Whatever question of whatever complexity was asked of her, she answered without notes or reference. It was a masterly performance, delivered with charm, and I felt honoured to have been present.

Anyway, that's not the point. I wanted to see Denis to tell him of the awful insensitivity of one of their top fund-raisers and to urge him to tell the Prime Minister of the poor quality of her support in the run-up to the next General Election. With a temerity that even I found astonishing, it had been my intention to give him my view that their campaign, so far, lacked professionalism and co-ordination. However well meaning, the team whose job it was to prepare for a fourth term had just not started out very well. I was going to add that I would have brought back Jeffrey Archer to run the show. Here was a man of charisma and proven ability. Totally loyal to the Prime Minister, he was the man to put the Tories back on the road to victory. With all humility, I honestly felt that these words might possibly have some influence on great affairs because of my personal friendship with Denis. That was the reason I had arranged that particular lunch date. It was not to be. Oh! I told him all right but, by then, we had been overtaken by events.

Early in November 1991, Geoffrey Howe had resigned from the Cabinet. Almost immediately thereafter, Michael Heseltine wrote an open letter to the Chairman of his constituency party in which he was highly critical of the Prime Minister and her style of leadership. A few days later in the House of Commons, Geoffrey Howe delivered the most scathing and damaging attack on the Prime Minister. He effectively blamed her for all the woes of the Government, with particular reference to her antagonistic European stance. He was vitriolic and vindictive and, in the event, damaged her position beyond repair. There was uproar, of course, during which Michael Heseltine, setting aside his oft-repeated proclamations to the contrary, challenged Margaret Thatcher for the leadership of the Tory Party. Such challenge is, by their own rules, permitted annually and invariably in November. The poll, of Conservative MPs, was to be held on 21 November, two days before I was to have had lunch with Denis. I was not, therefore, altogether surprised when Joye Robbilliard, Denis's secretary at No. 10, telephoned to ask if I could postpone it until 22 November, the day after the poll. This was fine with me; I thought we would be able to celebrate Margaret's victory in an appropriate manner. One little snag occurred. The 22nd was American Thanksgiving Day. Mosimanns were having a party and were booked solid. So Sylvia, my secretary, got us a table at one of our more favoured venues, the Grill Room at the Savoy.

The poll result is history. Michael Heseltine gathered 152 votes to Margaret Thatcher's 204. There were 16 abstentions. So, because of archaic and ill-considered rules, the margin was insufficient to gain her outright victory at the first ballot. After some prevarication, as we all now know, she announced her decision not to contest the second ballot, but to resign as Prime Minister. This happened on the morning of 22 November. I expected Denis to cry off. He didn't. I waited at the Savoy with his favourite tipple, a Dry Martini, ready to greet him. He arrived looking composed and immaculate as ever. Indeed, I was far more emotional than he. I shall never forget that meal. It seemed the world beat a path to our table. Diners, be they friends or strangers, all wanting to offer him their sympathy and their regret at the going, and the manner of it, of one of the greatest Prime Ministers this country of ours has ever known. During this extraordinary and staggered meal the head waiter approached us and apologised for the many interruptions. He further explained that the BBC had got wind of our presence. They had sent a camera team and a reporter who had enquired whether he could please come in and ask Mr Thatcher a few questions. 'What shall I tell him?' queried the concerned waiter. 'Tell him to f--- off,' said Denis without hesitation. Denis Thatcher is one of the most principled gentlemen I have ever been privileged to know. His immaculate good manners and dignity are rightly renowned, but he would not suffer fools, tolerate bad manners nor mince his words.

Normal conversation, at that extraordinary lunch, was clearly extremely difficult. There was, however, one thing he said to me which borders on tragedy. I had been talking about the recent Conservative Party Conference in Bournemouth, which Helen and I had attended. Denis shook his head sadly and this is what he said.

'I hated that Conference. I'd come back from a business visit to the States and went straight to Bournemouth. I was tired and I told Margaret that I was getting too old for all this stuff and that I was dreading the next General Election, whenever it might come. "All right, Denis," she said to me, "We've had a good run. We'll see Christmas and New Year out at Chequers and I will resign as Prime Minister early next year". '

There was a long silence. I don't think either of us trusted ourselves to say anything. We returned to Downing Street where crowds of onlookers, almost exclusively well wishers, cheered us as we drove in. There was a great crush of press and television cameras outside Number Ten and I had the strangest feelings of humility, alternating with pride, at being present while history was happening all around me. Denis got out of the car. 'Thank you, Paul, for a super lunch,' he said, 'See you soon,' and without a glance at the media he strode, for almost the last time, into 10 Downing Street. That story is certainly the most momentous event of these last few years. There were others of less importance to the world at large, but of significance to me and my family.

My retirement as Chairman of SAF and, fairly soon thereafter, my illness seemed strangely linked and together were another watershed in my life. I had awakened from my anaesthetic to find that I had been resigned from every one of my charity and sports committees by the ever-protective Helen. Very laudable and really quite sensible. It enabled me to concentrate my time and energy at my office and I did so with enthusiasm.

I quickly put into train an idea which I'd been playing around with for a few years. Simply, it was to demerge the two main-core businesses in the Group – Pools and Bingo. The Pools business had funded and nurtured the Bingo business from its inception . . . now Bingo was big enough to go it alone. So with the help, skill and advice of our two City professionals – Rothschilds and Wood MacKenzie – the task was put in hand and successfully concluded. The result left me as Chairman of two independent Public Limited Companies – Zetters Group PLC (Pools) and Zetters Enterprises PLC (Bingo). 'What,' you may ask, 'was the point?' Well, there existed an extraordinary restriction, imposed upon the Company by Littlewoods in the Spotting-the-Ball partnership agreement. The restrictive clause required Paul Zetter (and/or the immediate Zetter family) effectively 'to own over fifty per cent of the Pools business' in order to remain a member of the partnership. Their reasons were somewhat obscure and could, I suppose, be interpreted as being flattering. Nonetheless, it meant that as we, the family, collectively held around 52% of the Group shares, we were debarred from acquisitions or take-overs – where a diminution of shares in the Company were involved – if I wished the Group to remain a partner in Spotting-the-Ball . . . which I did. The key words in the clause were, of course, '*Pools* business'. If we separated . . . or demerged . . . the resultant Bingo company would not be so restricted. That's why I did it. The demerger still left me in control of about 50% of Bingo and I reckoned that I could safely seek to expand using up to – say – 25% of my Bingo stock. Together with a healthy cashflow, it was easy to envisage the possibility of real growth on the Bingo side by acquisition. All this was accomplished, leaving the shareholding in the now separated Pool business unaltered, with the Zetter family still holding over 50%. Thus, the restriction was satisfied and the STB partnership preserved.

The best laid schemes of Company Chairmen 'Gang aft a-gley' . . . but not on this occasion. Within a few months of the demerger, Corals, the

Bingo Division of the giant Bass Corporation, made a take-over offer I couldn't refuse . . . so I didn't! Our shareholders profited handsomely from the deal. My senior management, including David Isaacs, were not best pleased, but I treated them fairly. The family were made very wealthy and we were quite stupidly and erroneously quoted as 'one of the hundred richest families in Great Britain'. What nonsense! I remained, of course, Chairman of the Pools business, a circumstance I considered to be wholly satisfactory.

That brings me to 19 March 1991 when the Chancellor of the Exchequer introduced his Budget. Amongst less important things, he proposed a cut in Pools Betting Duty, on the understanding that the Pools Promoters allocate the revenue so saved to the benefit of a Foundation for Sport and the Arts. The proposal also required the Pools Promoters to contribute double that amount from their own turn-over, for the benefit of the Foundation. It was estimated that some £60M per annum would be available for distribution to worthy sporting and artistic causes, split two thirds and one third respectively. It was a deal. The scheme had been cobbled together secretly, between Littlewoods and the Government, to pull the rug from the vociferous lobbyists who were persistently seeking a National Lottery for good causes. Swallowing my outrage at learning that negotiations affecting my Company had been all but concluded without my knowledge, I went along with the concept. Firstly, I am in favour of helping sport and the arts and, with over £60M a year to spend, that will certainly be achieved. Secondly, I have been appointed Chairman of the Sports Sub-committee and am immensely flattered to have sporting celebrities like Chris Chataway and Clive Lloyd as fellow Trustees and members. Last, but not least, we might just succeed in keeping that damned National Lottery at bay.

(Since pencilling that last sentence but clearly, before going to press, the Conservatives have won a thrilling General Election on 9 April 1992). Delighted as I am at that outcome there is, as always, an ant in the honey. John Major has included in his manifesto his intention to introduce a National Lottery for good causes. Well, it's not here yet but I'm no longer taking bets!)

# Epilogue

That's up-to-date, but it would be wrong to finish without a little tidying up, and a few reflections. There is, it seems, a great deal of interest among close associates, about my retirement plans . . . 'and will either of my children succeed me and take over the running of the Company?' When I express doubt, the inevitable reaction is of regret and, indeed, an apparent sympathy for me. There is no need of it. I have not created a dynasty. Neither would I have wanted to do so.

My son Adam found himself a splendid wife, Joni, in Santa Barbara. Joni Zetter (née Dahlstrom), with Adam's help, has produced two gorgeous grandchildren for me and Helen. Isn't that nice of them! Alex (a girl) came first. She was actually conceived on one of their trips to England, so Helen sent her a T-shirt with 'MADE IN ENGLAND' emblazoned across the front. Alex is nearly four years old now and all joy. We love her, but regret that she lives 5,000 miles away. Their second child was Jake, my grandson, and he was born on 12 July this year. I haven't seen Jake yet, but we're going to spend two months with them in October and November, just to show Adam and Joni how to spoil him – and Alex – of course. Adam is very happy in his chosen environment. He must cleave to it.

Carrie, my beloved daughter, has just bought a home for herself in Surrey. She now has thirty acres of the best of England . . . stables . . . a lake . . . much woodland . . . two delightful cats called Peterboro' and Leicester and a mongrel, brimming with character, named Dakota. Dakota was an abandoned puppy rescued by the RSPCA and Carrie adopted him. Lucky dog! Carrie, you will have gathered, is still unbelievably single. Someone out there doesn't know how unlucky he is. She is a remarkable young woman who will achieve anything to which she sets her mind. I wonder what will next motivate her. I doubt if it will be Zetters Pools. I am so proud of both

198

my children and the fact that they have chosen their own style of life. I wouldn't have it otherwise. They have chosen their own destiny, which is more than I did. I joined my father's business after the war because he wanted me to do so. As to my retirement plans, I will know when the time is right. In the meantime, I'm having fun.

Helen is an enigma. Her qualities abound and she still drives me nuts, but what I owe her cannot be quantified. Actually, she went through a very rough time in the years after my recovery and I always suspected that the strain and anxiety of my illness may have been contributory factors. Anyway, she's fine now, too energetic by half, and enjoying life. She has a new hobby, dolls houses, which she has tackled with all her usual enthusiasm. She's brilliant at it, of course, and making quite a name for herself in the Dolls House World.

We still live and love living in our small but beautiful apartment just one minute from Sloane Square (and Peter Jones!). Our chores are minimal and we enjoy the very considerable benefit of the best caretakers in London. Bill and Sheila Harris look after the flats . . . and us. They epitomise the best Cockney qualities. I am proud to claim the same birthright and delighted that they are our friends. I am also fortunate to use a splendid Bentley, a luxury I much enjoy but even more my driver, Richard Tresadern. Richard is more than a driver, he is a kindly helpful man who adds significantly to the quality of life for Helen and me.

Jim Clarke is still around. Our relationship has been long and remarkable. As the years go by it becomes even more so. I shall always be in his debt, not least, I must say, for the help, corrections and advice he has given me with this book.

While I'm expressing gratitude I should mention Sylvia Bradley. Sylvia is my secretary. She took the job when Iris Ainsworth (née Hills), who had originally been my father's secretary, retired some years ago. Iris had been splendid, a tower of strength, thoroughly efficient but distinctly formidable. Although Iris was very loyal, because I'd inherited her from my father she tended rather to consider me as 'the boy'. Sylvia is different. Always smiling, a bit scatty, but always fun. She has suffered my idiosyncrasies with such good humour that I can forgive her almost everything. If she were a little slimmer, she'd be worth her weight in gold. I must be nice to her because she has typed (and re-typed and typed yet again) this whole manuscript.

That's about the end. I don't believe anyone reading this book will have learned much about my character, for that was never the aim. Neither is it intended to be wholly authoritative, rather what is now known as anecdotal.

I said right at the beginning that 'nostalgia was my favourite emotion', which is why I've enjoyed writing it. I do hope you've enjoyed reading it.